IMAGES
of America

Berkshire County's Industrial Heritage

ON THE COVER: Generations of workers stand alongside the machinery to make woolen cloth at the Taconic Mill in Pittsfield. Looking directly into the camera, they seem to want to share their stories—how they arrived at the mill, where they lived, the pride they felt in making something and mastering the equipment, their plans on spending their earnings, and the hope or fear they had for their future. Their faces speak for the thousands of people like them—men, women and children—across Berkshire County in the 19th century, in the paper and textile mills, in quarries and mines, and in glass factories and iron furnaces that dominated the landscape. (Courtesy of the Berkshire County Historical Society.)

IMAGES
of America

BERKSHIRE COUNTY'S INDUSTRIAL HERITAGE

John S. Dickson

ARCADIA
PUBLISHING

ISBN 978-1-4671-2533-8

Published by Arcadia Publishing
Charleston, South Carolina

Printed in the United States of America

Library of Congress Control Number: 2016958695

For all general information, please contact Arcadia Publishing:
Telephone 843-853-2070
Fax 843-853-0044
E-mail sales@arcadiapublishing.com
For customer service and orders:
Toll-Free 1-888-313-2665

Visit us on the Internet at www.arcadiapublishing.com

I dedicate this book to my family and in memory of those who went before and helped build our future.

CONTENTS

ACKNOWLEDGMENTS

This story of industrial development in this book is confined to the 19th century. Where there are images from the 20th century, they show the same industry as the paper, textile, iron, glass, shoe, and even rake businesses that endured into the contemporary era. The chronology ends before the launching of the next economic transformation of the region toward electrical manufacturing.

History is often approached through personal connections and interactions with the past. Living next to one of these mills in a house where its workers resided first prompted me to explore this past. Bonnie Parsons at the University of Massachusetts showed me the methods to research historic buildings. Outreach to Will Garrison and the Berkshire County Historical Society resulted in the suggestion to do this book. He opened up the archives of historical images at Herman Melville's Arrowhead for this research. All of the photographs, unless otherwise indicated, come from their extensive holdings. This project was a volunteer effort on behalf of the Berkshire County Historical Society, and all royalties go to that organization in its pursuit of preserving our past.

I am indebted to Will, Eileen Myers, Barbara Bell, Norma Purdy, and Maida Henriques at Arrowhead for their support. The Local History Section of the Berkshire Athenaeum in Pittsfield is a unique treasure in the whole region; Kathleen Reilly and Anne-Marie Harris went the extra mile too many times to find information and products. I also tapped into some of the many resources available in the county through the following experts and their organizations: Gene and Justine Carlson of the North Adams Historical Society, Peter Hopkins of the Crane Museum of Papermaking, Gary Leveille of Berkshire Archive, Steve Kolis from Crane Paper, Barry Emory from Cheshire, Sarah Currie at the Williamstown Historical Museum, and Joshua Hall from the Stockbridge Library Museum and Archives. The veritable encyclopedia that Bernard Drew compiled on the mills of the Housatonic River was an indispensable source of information. Finally, I want to acknowledge the support of my wife, Mary Boyle, who was my first reader, editor, and partner on this journey.

INTRODUCTION

The nation's development in the 19th century played out on the smaller stage of Berkshire County. A young nation, eager to protect and expand its manufacturing, supported a cast of entrepreneurs and inventors coming to this region in order to take advantage of its natural resources and make a living for themselves, for their neighbors, and for the county. The falling streams, the geological formation, and the forests and hillsides ripe for grazing all made the county an ideal place to start woolen, paper, iron, glass, and countless other mills.

Quick to adopt the new machinery to make their products, these mills were ideally situated between Boston and New York, capable of serving both markets. Access to the Hudson River and the ports of New York City meant that products made in Berkshire County found their way around the nation and also to places as far away as China.

Success breeds imitation, and mills sprang up throughout the county. More mills meant a demand for more workers, and owners and managers shifted their search for workers from rural farm families to immigrants from Canada, Ireland, Italy, Poland, Germany, and even China, mirroring the immigration waves that poured into the country looking for work.

The numbers reflect the importance of this county to the entire nation's growth and development. Berkshire County, on the eve of the Civil War, produced roughly half of the wool in the entire nation. The 1895 census of Pittsfield, for example, found 221 manufacturers hiring over 4,000 employees and producing over $6 million of goods a year. There were 40 iron blast furnaces along the Housatonic River. In Lee alone, by 1840, the town was producing one-fifth of the paper used in the country. A decade later, there were 25 paper mills, needing 14 million pounds of rags acquired from around the world to turn into paper.

The county also marks its industrial prowess in the 19th century as the site of the first region in the nation to manufacture cathedral glass and to roll flat glass, as well as the first to turn wood pulp into paper. The first company in Massachusetts to install a Fourdrinier machine was in Lee, and the first to produce airmail paper was in Dalton. Articles appeared in *Scientific American* extolling the virtues of paper and wool operations in the county. Products made here earned awards and prizes at national exhibitions and world's fairs.

The 19th century saw the rise of a powerful class of industrialists, and those owners and managers in Berkshire County tell the story of their counterparts around the country. In the days before government regulation, owners collaborated more than competed, such was the growing demand for their products. They often worked together to share water reservoirs and innovative methods and equipment. Their daughters married the sons of other mill owners, creating dynasties of Cranes, Pomeroys, Plunketts, Blackintons, and Smiths.

These industrialists branched out and invested their profits to launch services such as banking and rail transportation to aid their mills. They used their positions to run for and hold public office in Boston and in Washington, DC, and the line between laws they promulgated and their personal business interests blurred. Without other protections such as bankruptcy laws, they were vulnerable to the cycle of economic panics that hit the nation and the county routinely through the century, resulting in frequent closures and ownership changes. They also understood a civic responsibility to their communities, donating the funds to build churches, libraries, schools, and museums for their workers and families.

The story of industrial development in Berkshire County parallels the rise of photography, which came to the region in the 1840s and rapidly found a commercial hold. Etchings and drawings, maps, and insurance surveys make up the rest of the documents. They show vividly the scope of the mills, the complexity of their operations, the dangerous and unhealthy conditions people worked in, and the dependence on the natural resources the region offered to sustain the factories and mills.

Today, the mills that remain line our towns and cities, many adapted for other uses, while some closed and await their next chapter. Many of us who live here are descendants of the immigrants that made their way to the county looking for work, opportunity, and the freedoms that did not exist in their home countries. The images here tell the story of their toil and sacrifice that contributed to the growth of our towns and cities and the nation.

One

Berkshire Advantages

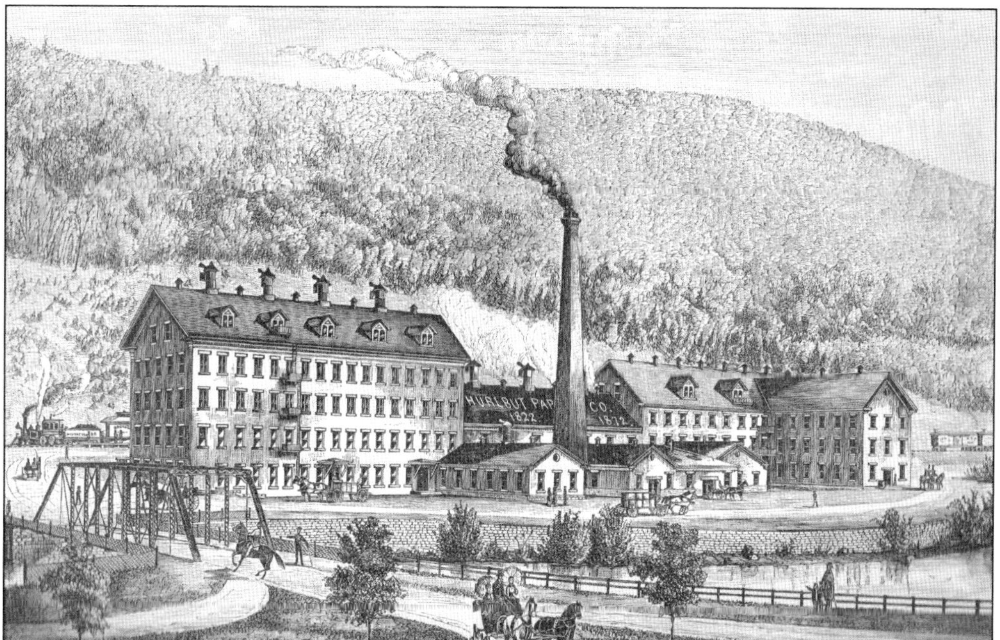

This 1876 Beers map drawing of Hurlbut Mill in Lee shows many of the advantages enjoyed by Berkshire industry. Two early entrepreneurs in Lee were Thomas Hurlbut and Charles Owen, who seized on the swiftly moving water for paper mills in three different locations. They bought out the sawmills and gristmills that had first harnessed the Housatonic River and its branches to run their machinery. Amidst the thick forest, mills took advantage of the abundant timber for construction, heat, and making the fiber for paper. Finally, adequate roads and then rail transport were key to providing access to markets east to Boston, but more importantly, west to the Hudson River, and from there, New York City.

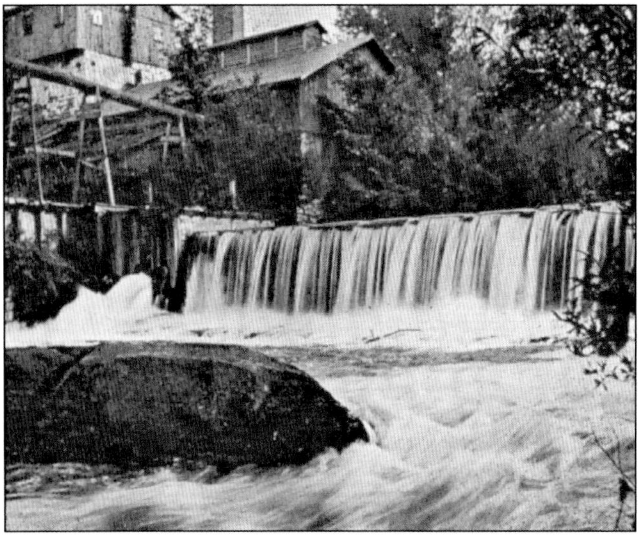

The rushing flow of water at the old furnace dam in the Van Deusenville section of Great Barrington demonstrates the power that emanated from this energy source. Originally built by John Williams in 1750, this dam powered his sawmill and gristmill for grinding wheat into flour. It was here in 1833 that two enterprising young men from Connecticut—John C. Coffing and Timothy Chittenden—chose to erect their Van Deusenville Iron Furnace for the manufacture of pig iron from the iron ore mined nearby.

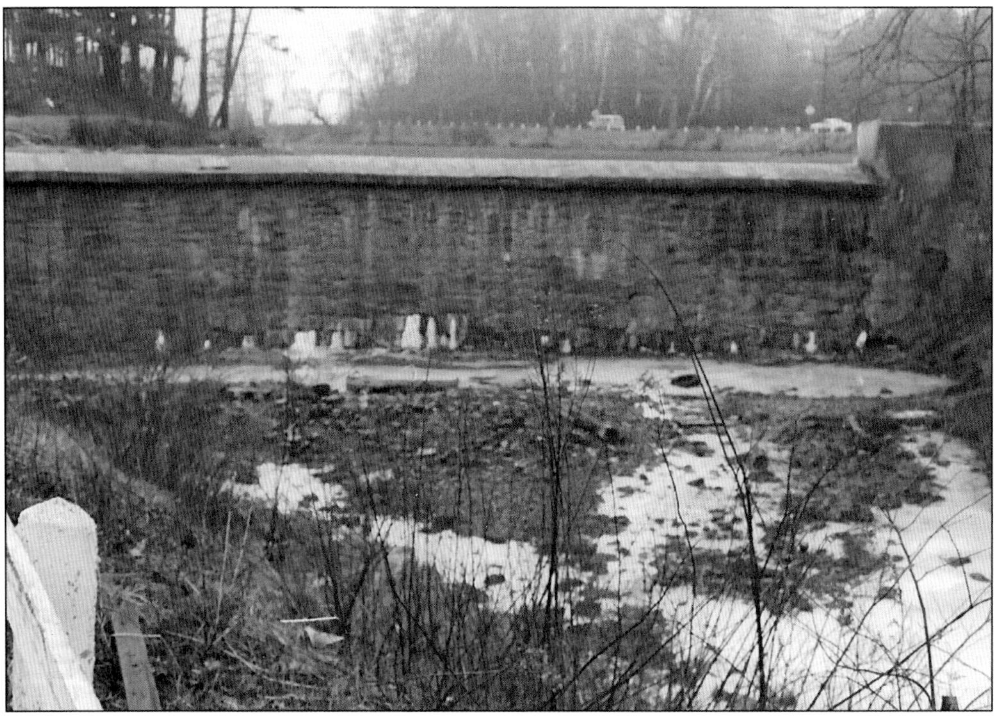

The different branches flowing into the Housatonic River in Pittsfield had elevation drops of water ranging from 148 feet to 40 feet, and the first dams were built at those sites where the drops were steepest. In 1762, Joseph Keeler built a dam on the southern tip of Pontoosuc Lake to power his sawmill and gristmill for grinding farmers' wheat into flour. By the time of this photograph in 1980, the dam had been raised several times in the 1800s to accommodate the increased power needs by the new, larger factories downstream.

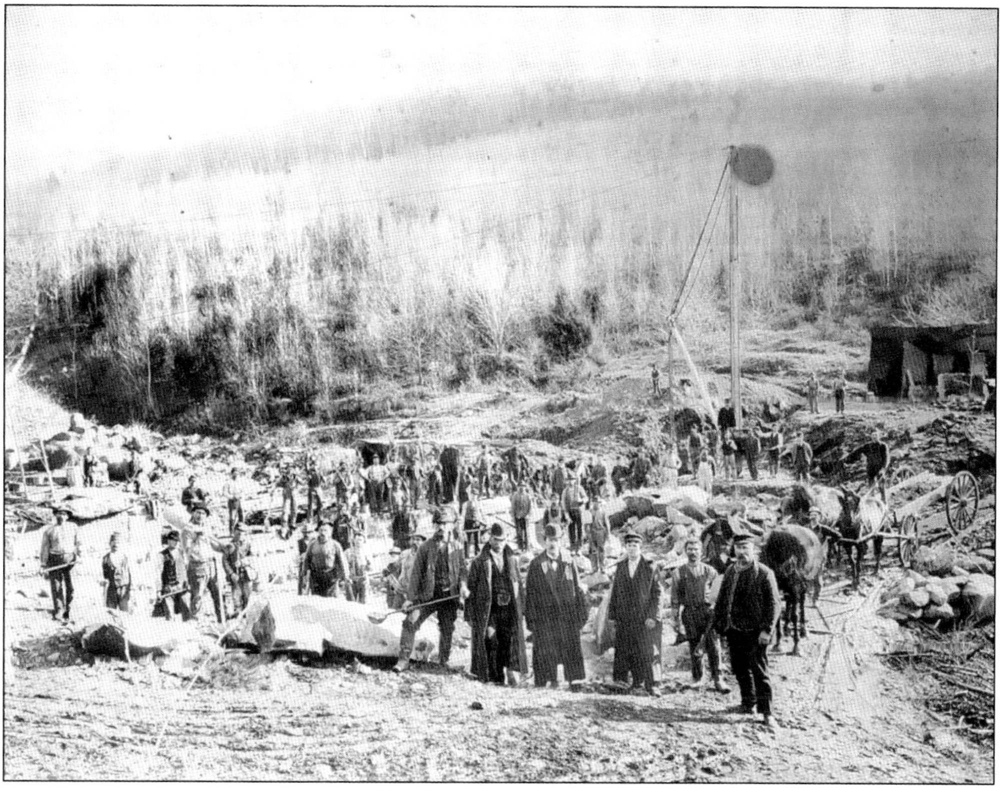

There were as many as 30 dams along the Housatonic River in Massachusetts, capturing the flow of water to power mills. Along the Hoosic River that flows north from Lanesborough and Cheshire, more dams were built for industries that made this region a manufacturing capital in the new nation. The increasing number of factories along the two rivers forced mill owners to join forces to build ever larger dams and reservoirs. In this photograph from 1910, a group of men work the teams of horses and pulleys for a new dam on Mill Brook in East Lee.

Well after the introduction of coal powered steam engines and electricity, water as an inexpensive source of energy continued in Berkshire factories not only to power the engines, but also to clean and dye the wool or to clean rags and dilute them into fibers for papermaking. This Associated Mutual Insurance Map from 1906 shows the vast complex of the Arnold Print Works in North Adams, situated to take full advantage of both the north and south branches of the Hoosic River.

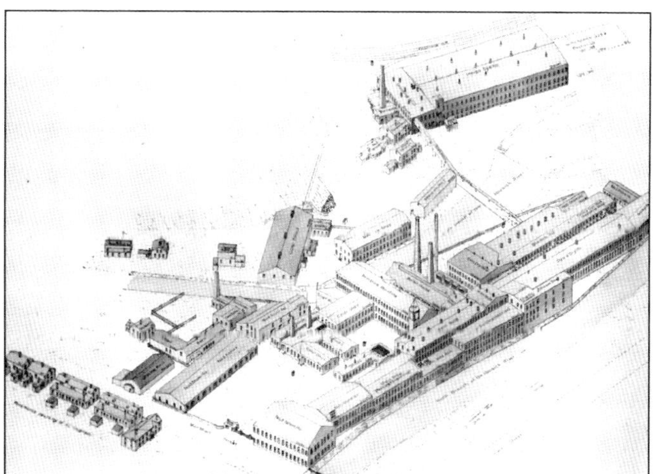

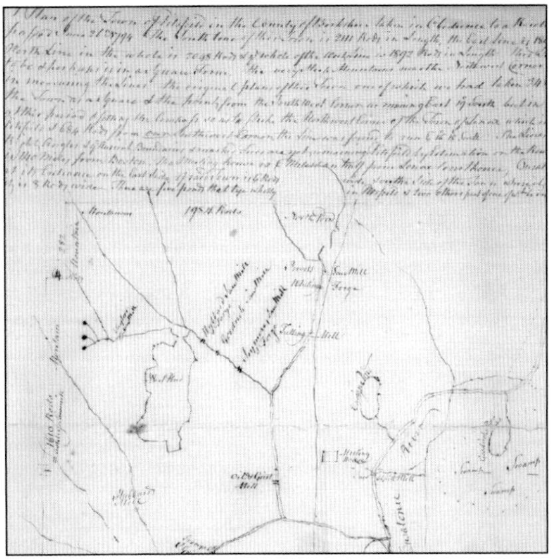

Large-scale 19th-century Berkshire industries were fortunate that early settlers had already built their shops by the streams and rivers. On this 1794 map of Pittsfield are sawmills, gristmills, fulling mills, and iron forges placed along dams that later became sites for larger textile industries. Pontoosuc Woolen Mill took over Jewett's Saw Mill; Pomeroy Muskets was placed near Whitney's forge; Colt's and then Crane's paper mill were located where the sawmill is in the upper far right; Peck and Russell Mills were built on the Goodrich and Hubbard sites near "West Pond"; and Barker and Stearns Mills occupied the site of the fulling mill in the lower right-hand corner. (Courtesy of the Berkshire Athenaeum.)

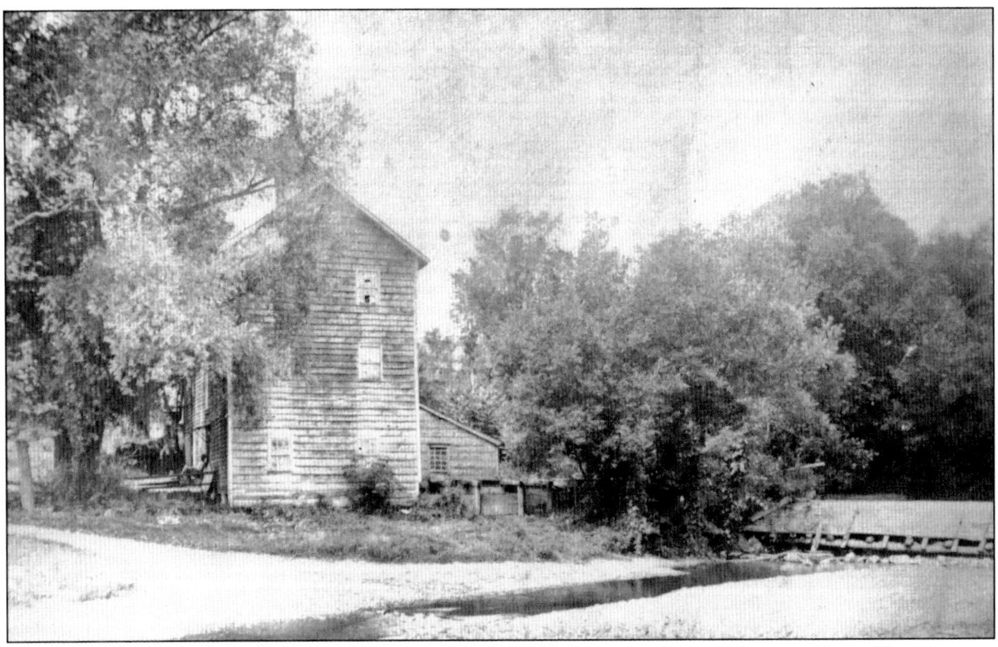

Built around 1760, the Kellogg Mill was one fulling mill along the Green River in Great Barrington. Local residents who sheared their sheep, carded the wool, and wove cloth in their homes brought the raw material to these fulling mills for finishing before it could be used in clothing and linens. The cloth was cleaned and then beaten until soft, using large hammers powered by water. Maj. John Kellogg purchased the land, buildings, and water privilege that had been operating since 1760.

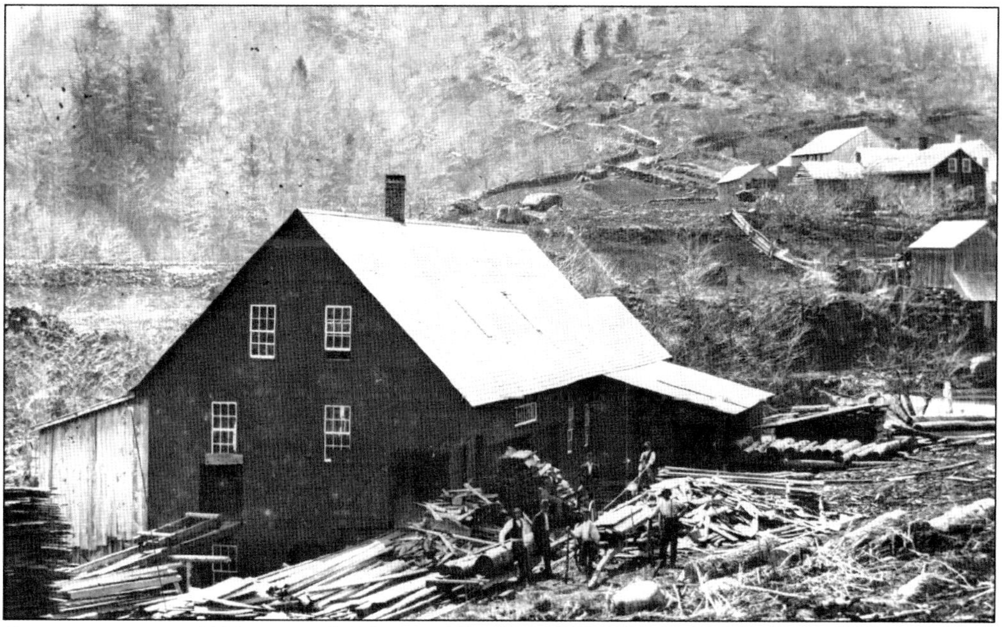

One inventory in 1828 counted 185 sawmills throughout the county. When larger textile and paper industries formed, they would often buy out the water privilege and land where the earlier industries had developed. This photograph of a North Adams sawmill shows the extent of cutting in the vicinity as well as the logs entering the sawmill on the right-hand side of the mill and exiting on the left as finished planks. (Courtesy of the North Adams Historical Society.)

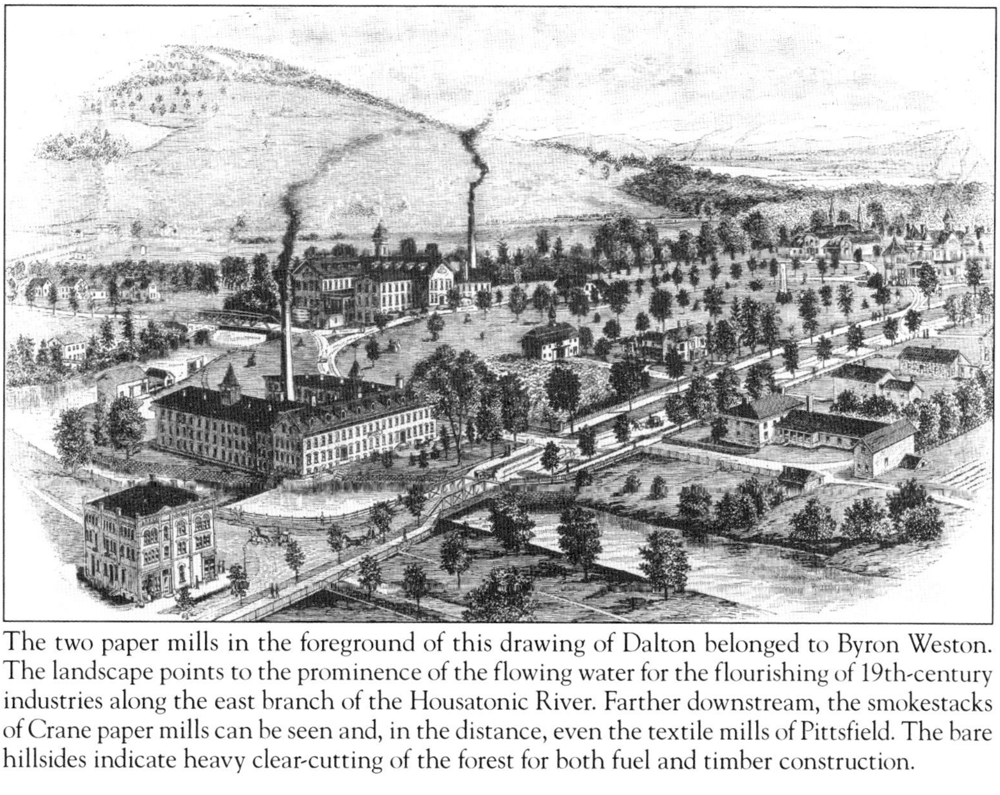

The two paper mills in the foreground of this drawing of Dalton belonged to Byron Weston. The landscape points to the prominence of the flowing water for the flourishing of 19th-century industries along the east branch of the Housatonic River. Farther downstream, the smokestacks of Crane paper mills can be seen and, in the distance, even the textile mills of Pittsfield. The bare hillsides indicate heavy clear-cutting of the forest for both fuel and timber construction.

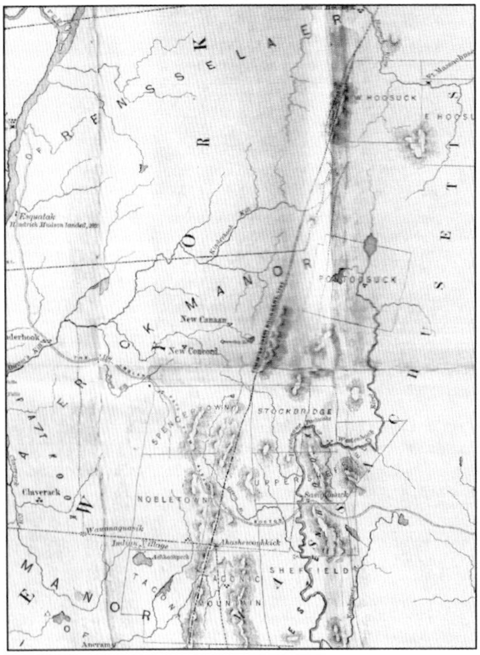

Enterprising engineers and craftsmen came to the Berkshires eager to replicate the success of the mills across eastern New England. They needed to move their products to larger markets beyond the region. The first main road crossed southern Berkshire County from Springfield to Sheffield and then onward to Albany, as seen in this map drawn by Franklin Leonard Pope. This road opened access to the Hudson River, and the region became a principal source of manufactured products for New York City. (Courtesy of the Berkshire Athenaeum.)

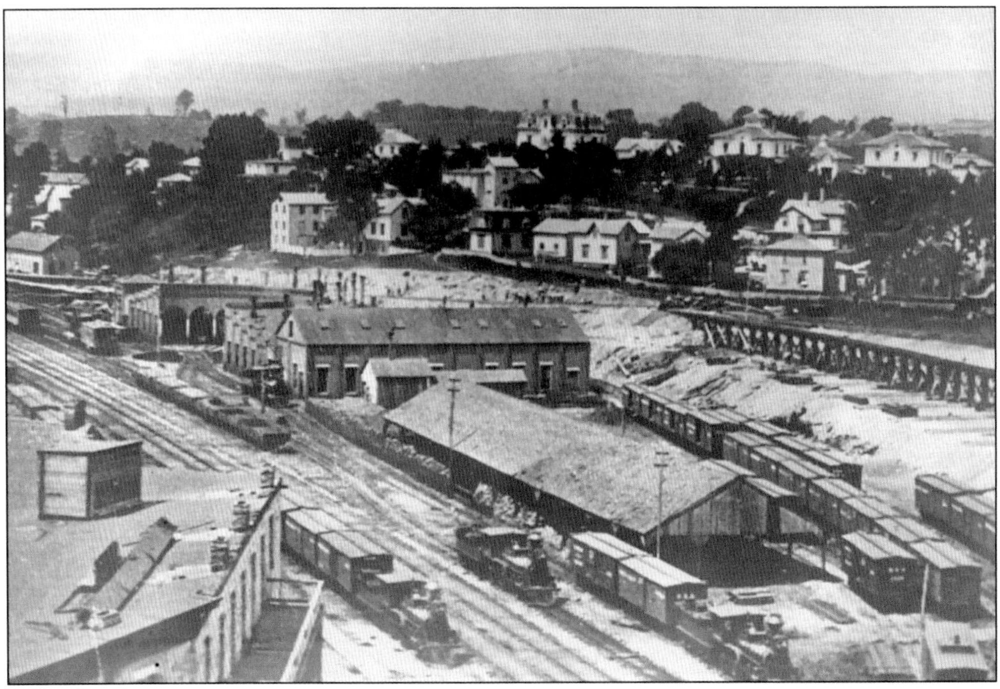

It was still a rough haul over mountains, even when new roads were built from Pittsfield and North Adams. The first rail line opened in 1838 linking West Stockbridge on the Hudson and Berkshire Railroad. Mill owners pushed hard for the expansion of rail transport, investing in the Boston & Albany Railroad. The leg from Albany to Pittsfield opened on May 4, 1841, and by October, the company completed the line all the way to Boston. A north-south line to New York opened in 1849, and, by the 1870s, when this photograph was taken, Pittsfield had become a busy terminus for both railways.

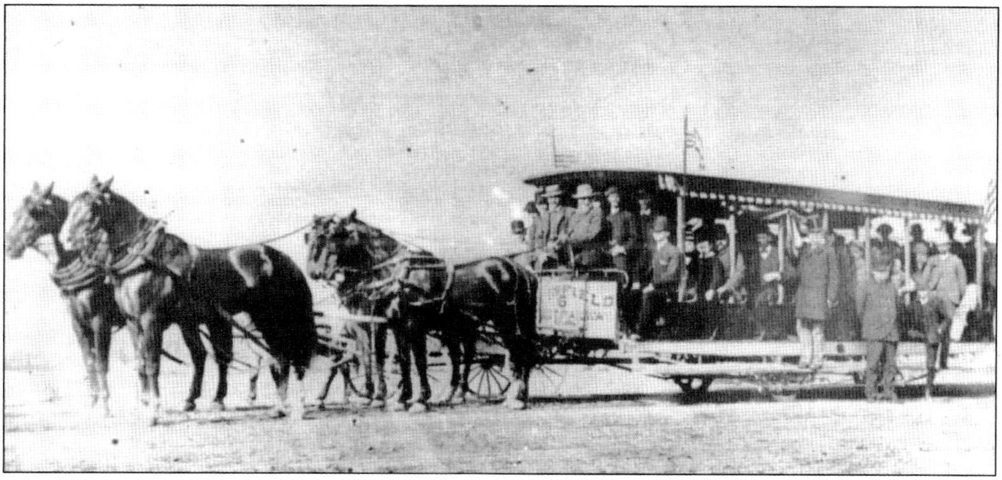

In the early 1800s, workers lived within walking distance of the mills, often built away from town centers. Owners and managers also liked to live nearby their operations, as men like Zenas Crane, who made paper, worked side by side with their employees. Clusters of houses, stores, and churches grew up in small villages on the outskirts of the towns. By mid-century, however, owners and workers began to move away. Thaddeus Clapp, from Pontoosuc Woolen Mill in Pittsfield, also served as one of the original directors of the first street railway corporation, which opened in 1886 with a horse-drawn line that ran just past the mill.

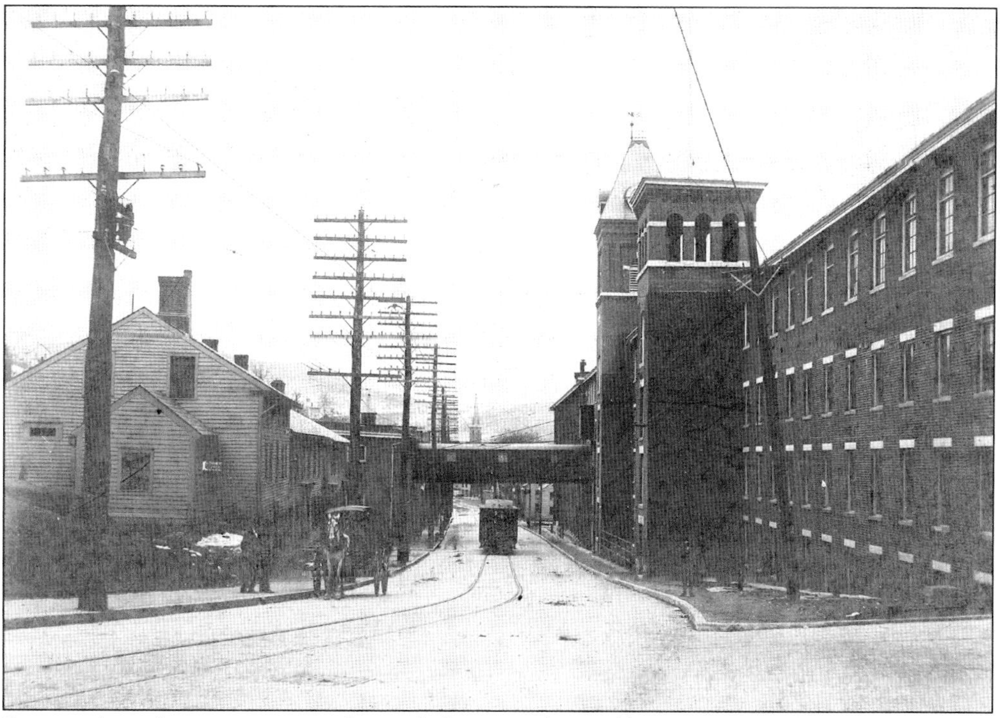

Street railway directors continued to push for expanding public transport so that workers did not have to live right near the mill, since turnover was high and workers changed employment often. By 1891, the first electrically powered trolley opened in the Berkshires, connecting the mills to the town centers and residential areas. In this photograph, the trolley runs right between the buildings that make up the Eclipse Mill in North Adams.

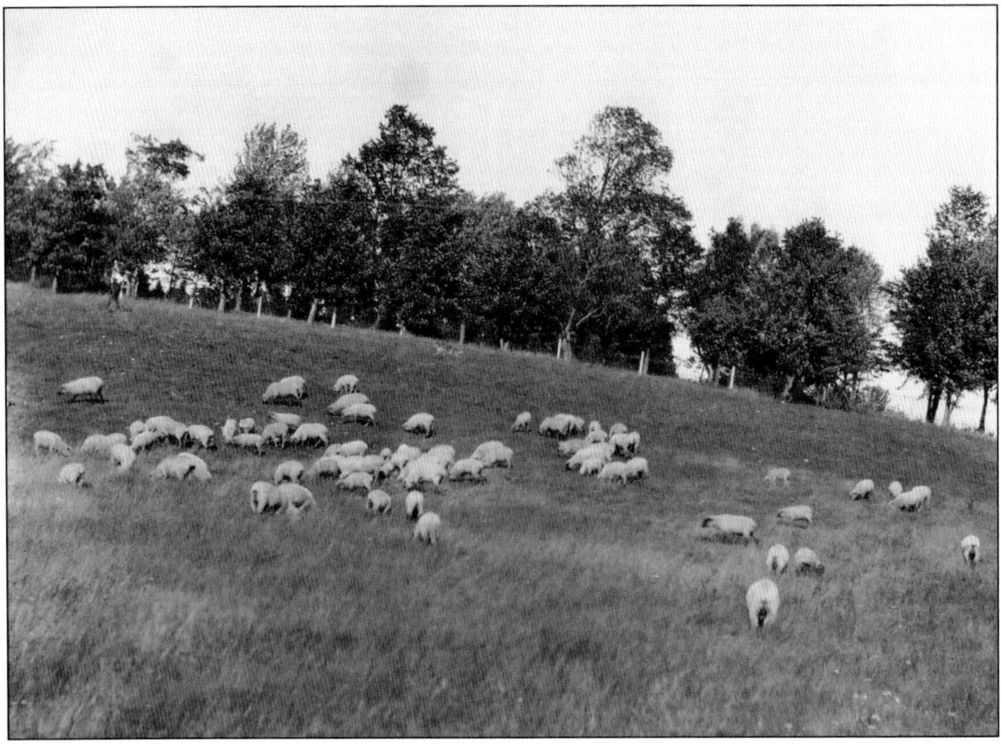

The Berkshires could not compete with textile mills farther east because of their proximity to sea shipping that brought cotton from southern plantations. Thus, the early mills here focused on wool and flax. The Berkshire mills got a boost when Elkanah Watson, who had worked in Rhode Island's cotton mills, decided to move to Pittsfield in 1807. He brought with him merino sheep he had imported from Spain that produced a high-quality wool. Its rocky, hilly terrain made the region ideal for large herds of sheep, including the one here at High Lawn Farm in Lee, started by Elizur Smith, who owned both paper and textile mills.

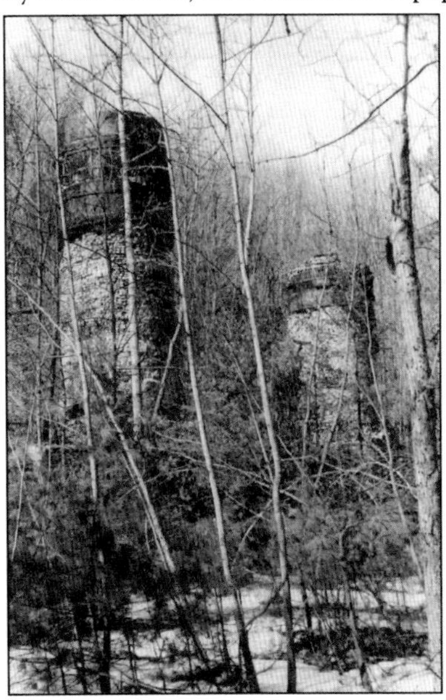

The Berkshires sits on top of a geologic formation rich in minerals necessary for the construction of the mills and in the raw materials needed to produce paper and textiles. Lime helped break down and bleach the rags for papermaking. Large lime deposits were exploited from Sheffield to Adams. In this 1978 photograph, only two chimneys remain from the lime kiln in Sheffield where limestone that was quarried nearby was processed.

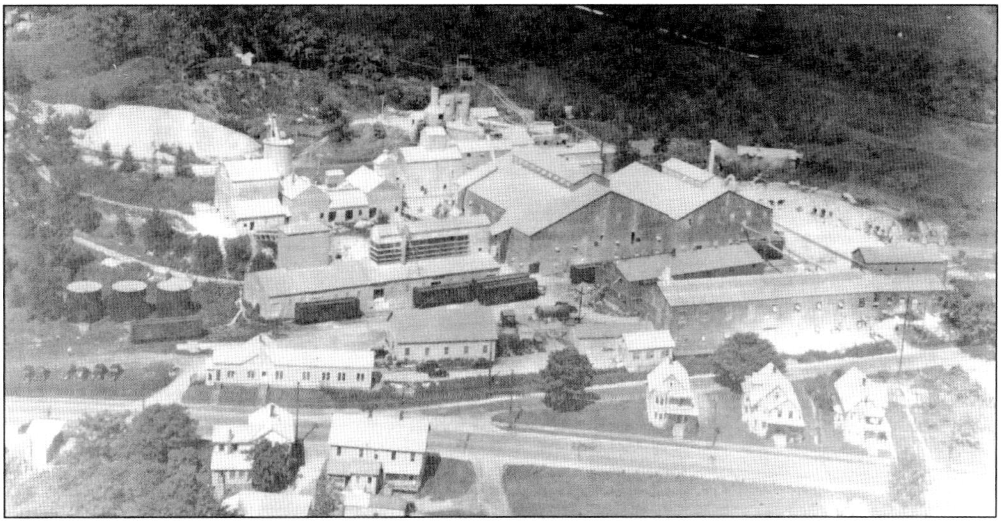

One of the largest lime quarries in the region was situated in Adams, and it is still in operation today. Limestone was blasted out of the mountain, where it was removed in large pieces and taken to the furnaces for heating at high temperatures to produce the lime. It was the arrival of rail transport that opened up this site to excavation in 1848, making it easier to ship the lime to the many paper manufacturers in southern Berkshire County. This photograph, taken in the 1930s, shows six railroad cars on a spur leading right up to the warehouses in the large complex.

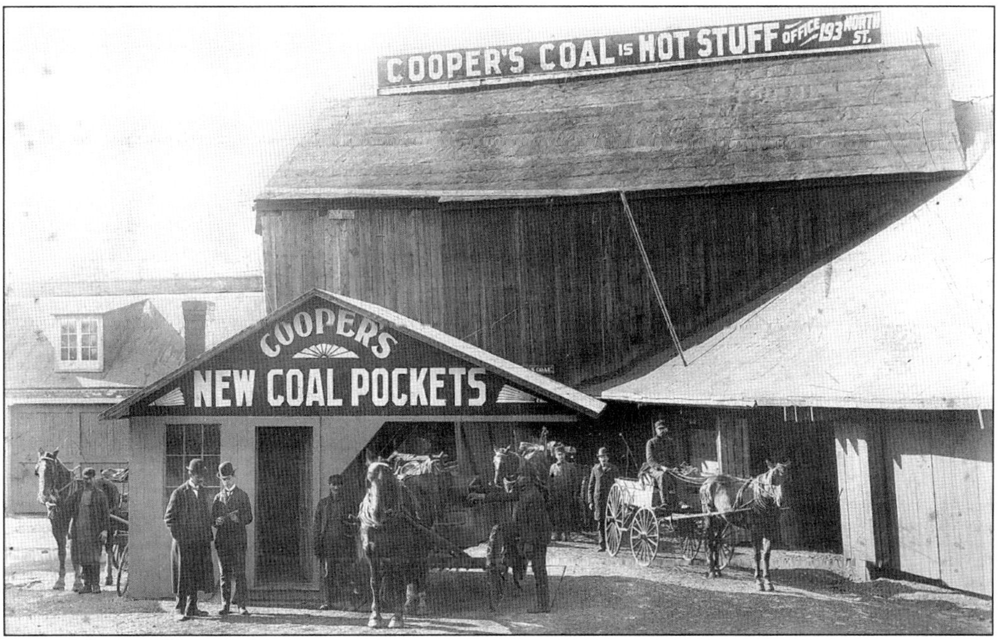

Steam engines powered by coal arrived late in Berkshire County because of inexpensive and available waterpower. Transporting coal from as far away as Pennsylvania was costly. However, with new rail lines opening across the country, delivery costs came down at the same time that fewer water privileges along the county's waterways were available. Six years after the railroad came to Pittsfield, the first coal shipment arrived. By the 1870s, four businesses in Pittsfield delivered over 24,000 tons of coal per year to manufacturing firms, including one owned by George H. Cooper near the train station.

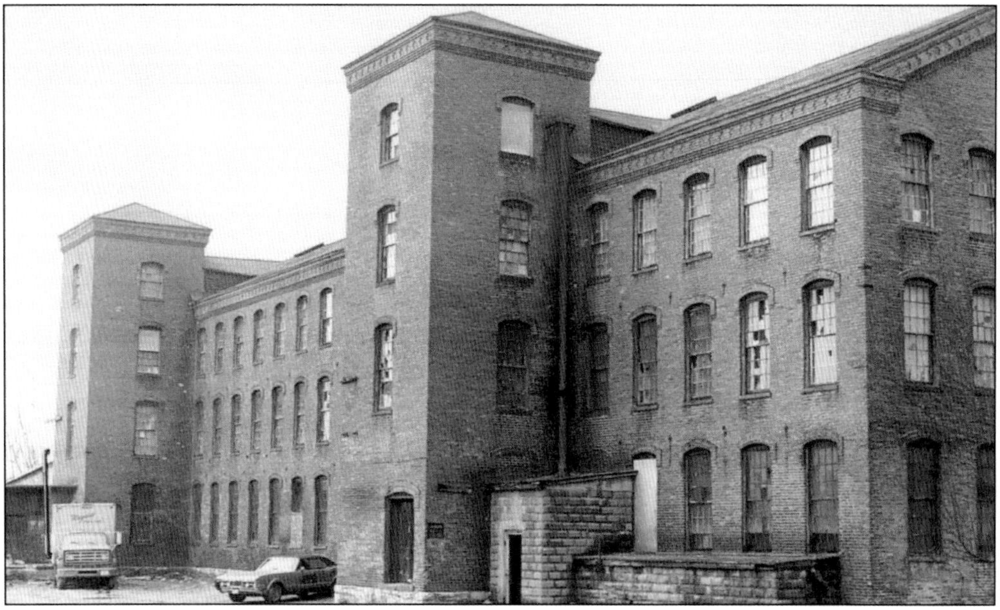

In Pittsfield, Ensign Kellogg, a businessman connected with local banks and the Pontoosuc Woolen Mill, established the Kellogg Steam Power Company, which leased space to small businesses that needed power, in 1872. Kellogg placed his new building not near any water, but close to the rail line going through the town for easy off-loading of coal. With the facility acting as a 19th-century incubator, entrepreneurs started their small firms here, drawing on the steam power available This picture from the 1980s shows a neglected building, abandoned after it housed silk, woolen, clock, and tack companies.

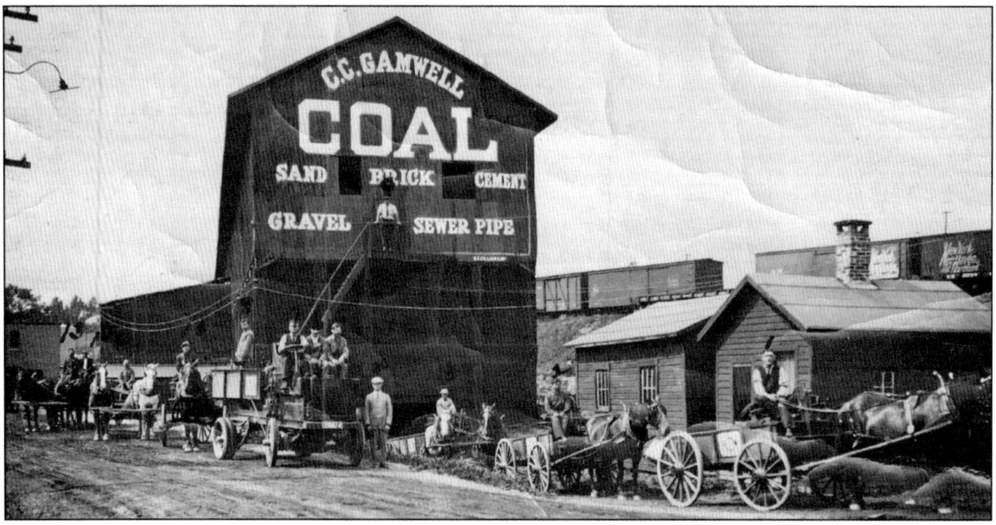

Cecil Gamwell, a young Pittsfield boy who worked in Kellogg's shoe company, bought himself a horse and wagon to deliver coal. He set up his business in 1877 on the other side of the railroad tracks from Cooper's Coal and quickly expanded his operation into deliveries of other materials for Berkshire businesses. Here, a line of horse-drawn carts await their loads. Listed on the back of the photographs are the names Angelo, Jimmie, Tom, "Spaniard," Sand-Bank John, Dominick, two brothers Joe and Tony Russetta, Sandy, and Clyde Woodruff. The man in the tie is listed as "CLG," perhaps Clarence L. Gamwell, the founder's first son.

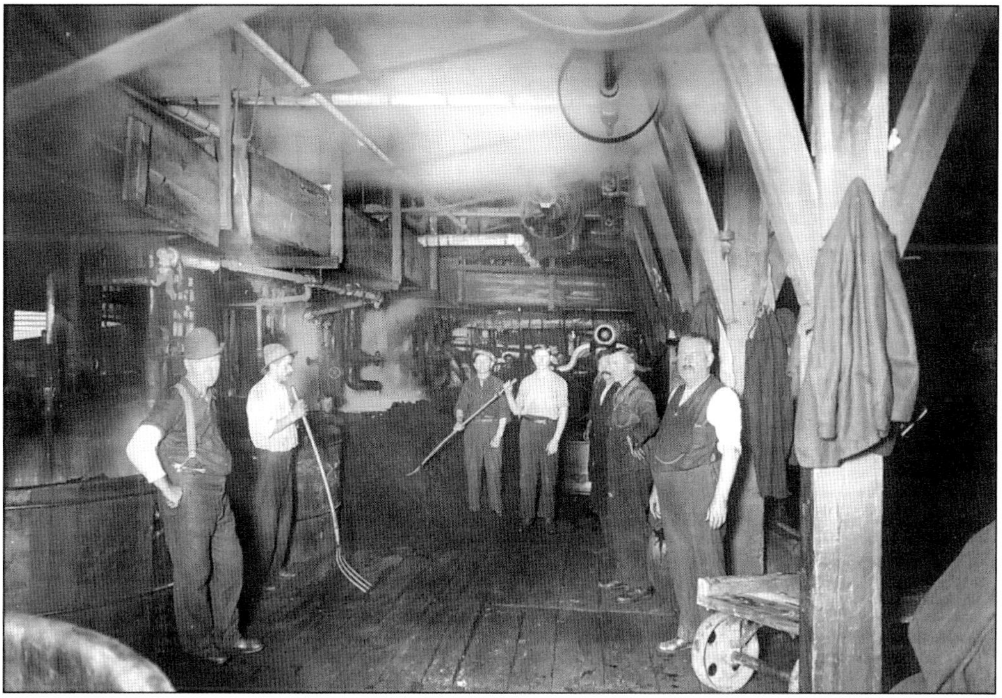

Textile mills were early adopters in Berkshire County of coal and steam power. By the late 1860s, they began to shift away from a dependence on water as the source for their power. By contrast, it took the paper mills until 1919 to generate more power from steam than by the streams near their factories. This picture of the Taconic Mill coal room in the early 1900s shows the large pile of coal behind the men and steam escaping into the room. Still in use is the system of belts and shafts—now turned by steam, not falling water.

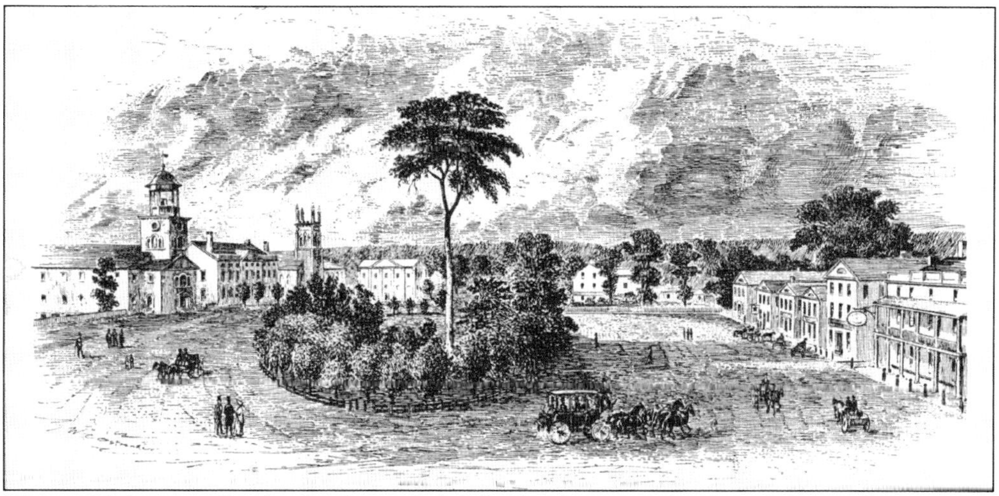

The establishment of banks closely paralleled the development of early Berkshire mills, as owners and managers served as officers in banks as well. The earliest bank in Pittsfield was the Berkshire Bank, chartered in 1806, with offices on Park Square. It failed just four years later, with its officers landing in jail. It took another eight years for businessmen to start another bank, but, in 1818, First Agricultural Bank opened its doors in the same building as its predecessors, one of the four small wood-frame buildings on the right in this drawing.

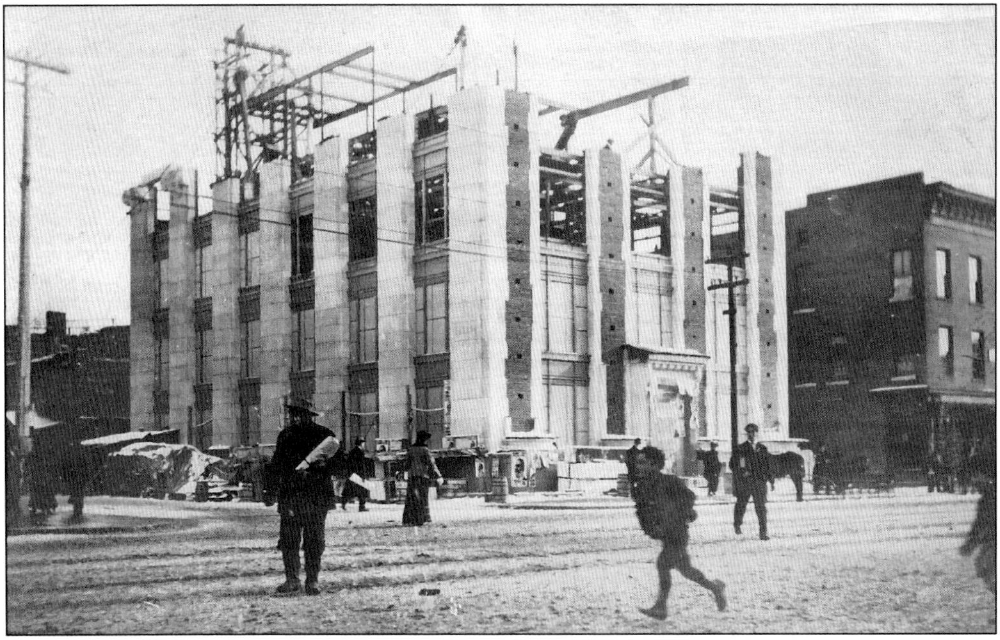

The First Agricultural Bank underscored the heavy influence of farming in the early 19th-century economy. Its success, though, lay in its ability to support the investment into early manufacturing in Pittsfield and the surrounding areas. Officers of the bank continued to be drawn from the ranks of the mills and factories throughout the century. The First Agricultural Bank moved four times before settling into these offices on North Street, built in 1908.

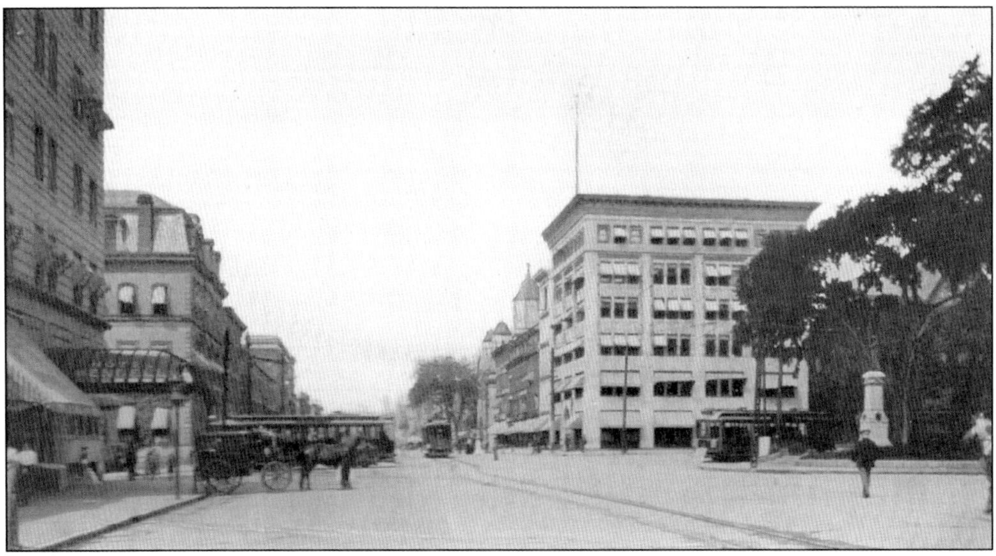

When the Berkshire County Savings Bank was chartered in 1846, its list of officers read like a who's who of the business world in the county. Owners of the Pontoosuc Woolen Mill, Peck's Mill, Russell Woolen Mills, and the Pittsfield Woolen and Cotton Mill were board members. The bank drew in leading names such as Zenas Crane from the paper mills in Dalton, as well as Sanford Blackinton from North Adams and Charles Owen from Great Barrington, who started textile and paper mills. In 1896, the bank moved into its new headquarters in the six-floor building on the corner of Park Square in Pittsfield.

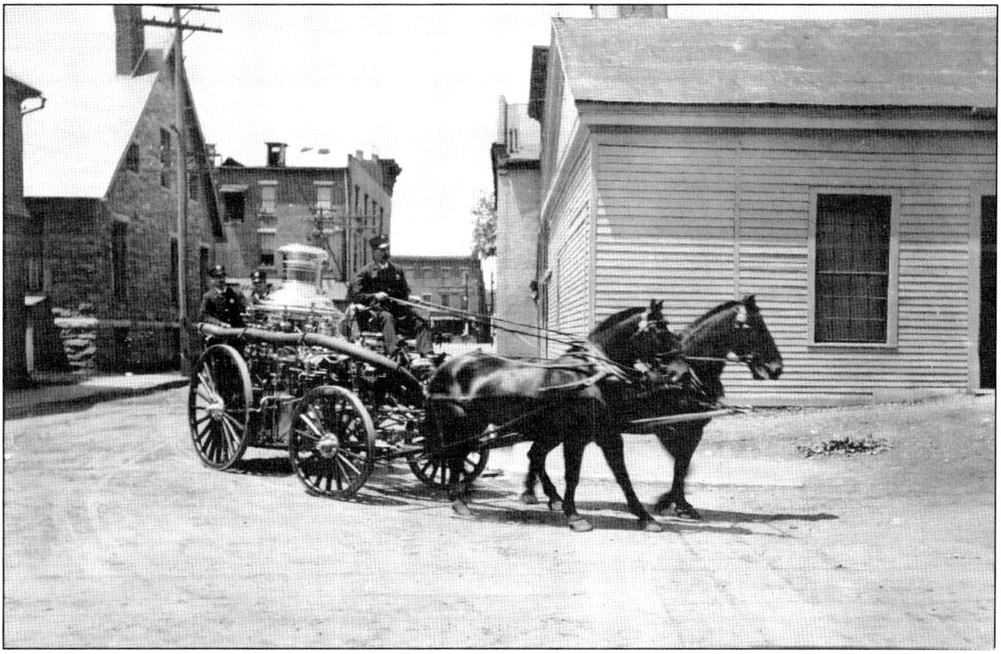

Fires took their toll on the 19th-century mills and factories. Metal machinery that produced sparks and oil lamps near the highly flammable cotton, wool, and paper resulted in many fires that shut down businesses repeatedly. As early as 1814 in Pittsfield, Maj. Thomas Melville (Herman's uncle) led the effort to purchase a fire engine for an all-volunteer company. It was not until 1844 when damage caused by fires to the mills pushed the town to establish the Housatonic Engine Company. This photograph, taken towards the end of the 19th century, shows a fire engine in downtown Pittsfield.

BERKSHIRE MUTUAL

Fire Insurance Co.,

PITTSFIELD, MASS.

INCORPORATED 1835.

DIRECTORS.

JOHN C. WEST, Pittsfield, ZENAS CRANE, Dalton.
J. V. BARKER, Pittsfield, S. W. BRAYTON, North Adams.
O. W. ROBBINS, Pittsfield, HASCAL DODGE, Pittsfield.
R. W. ADAM, Pittsfield. SIDNEY BARNES, Becket.
J. L. PECK, Pittsfield. CHARLES S. COLE, Williamstown.
T. G. RAMSDELL, Housatonic. F. W. HINSDALE, Pittsfield.
P. A. RUSSELL, Gt. Barrington. J. B. DEAN, Cheshire.
H. R. PEIRSON, Pittsfield. S. N. RUSSELL, Pittsfield.
W. B. PLUNKETT, Adams. W. D. CURTIS, Lenox.
D. M. COLLINS, Pittsfield. DEWITT S. SMITH, Lee.

Assets, $100,778.00. Liabilities, $48,557.00.

Surplus, $52,220.00.

Dividends Paid, 40, 50 and 70 per cent.

OFFICE IN WEST'S BLOCK.

To reduce risk, insurance companies sprang up, also led by owners of the mills. In 1835, the Berkshire Mutual Fire Insurance Company opened its doors, offering policies to reduce the risks of fire. By the 1870s, it had 4,150 policies on its books. The fire insurer had links not only to the mills and factories but also to the banks, as the company shared officers and offices with the Berkshire County Savings Bank and then the First Agricultural Bank. This advertisement for fire insurance appears in the *1893 Pittsfield City Directory* showing names of Berkshire mill owners.

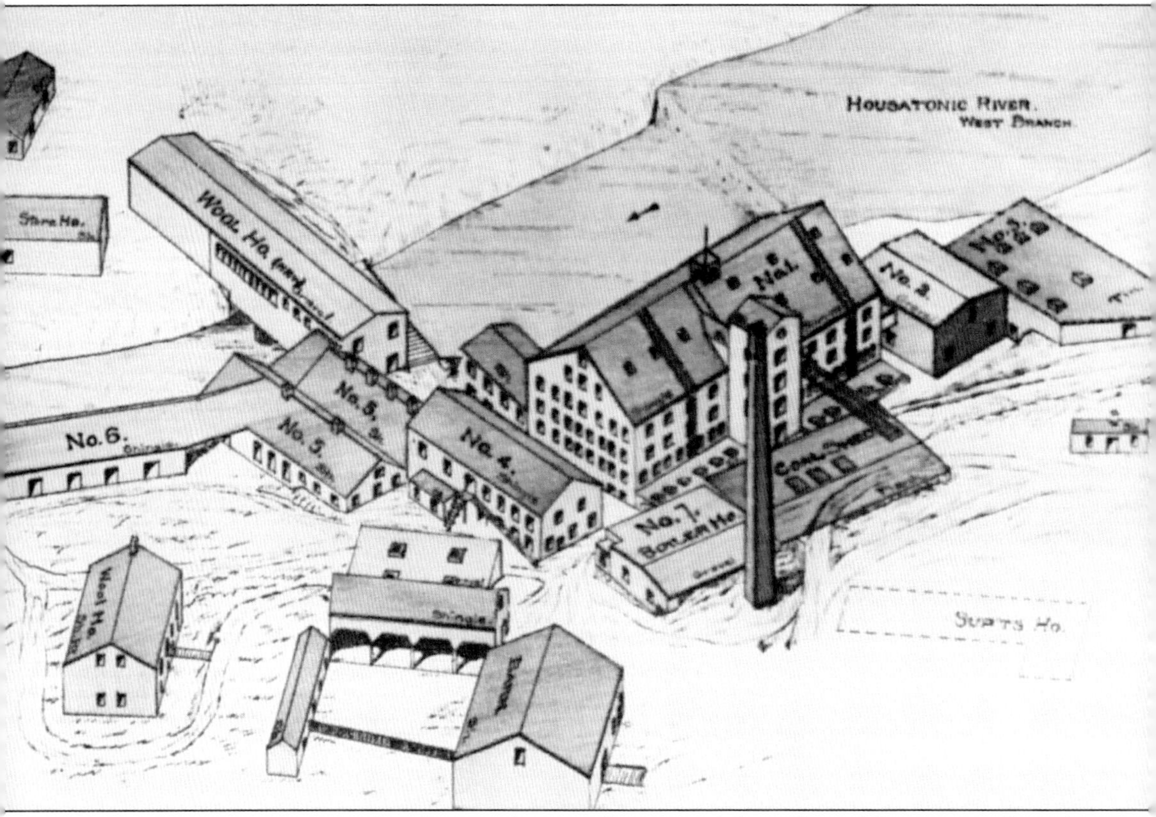

Insurance companies produced comprehensive drawings of the mills and factories, such as this one of Tillotson-Collins Woolen Mill in Pittsfield. The designs were used to calculate prices of the policies and to track the extent of any damage caused by fire. Today, these maps and drawings by Associated Mutual Insurance and Sanborns, among others, are a principal source for the understanding of the mills and factories and their expansions through the years. They indicate what the operations were in each building and on each floor, including details such as composition of the walls and numbers of fire doors and sprinklers.

Two

TEXTILES

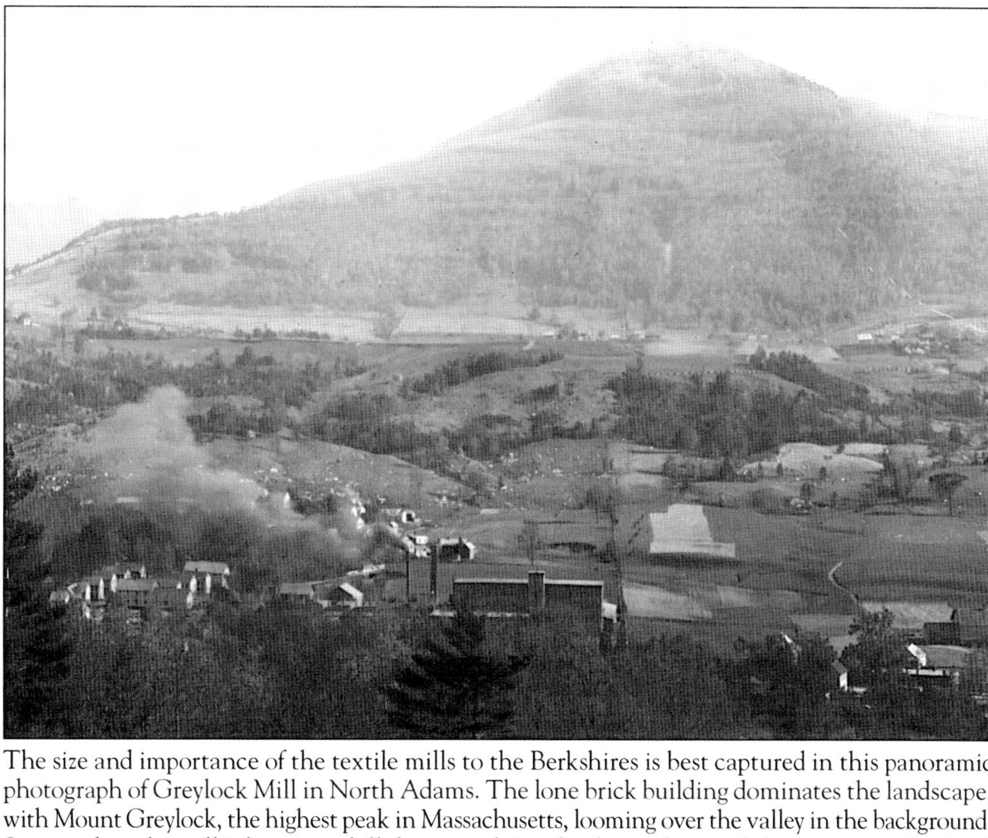

The size and importance of the textile mills to the Berkshires is best captured in this panoramic photograph of Greylock Mill in North Adams. The lone brick building dominates the landscape, with Mount Greylock, the highest peak in Massachusetts, looming over the valley in the background. Surrounding the mill is housing of all shapes and sizes for the workers and the managers who lived close enough to the factory to walk, but never to escape its dominance in their lives.

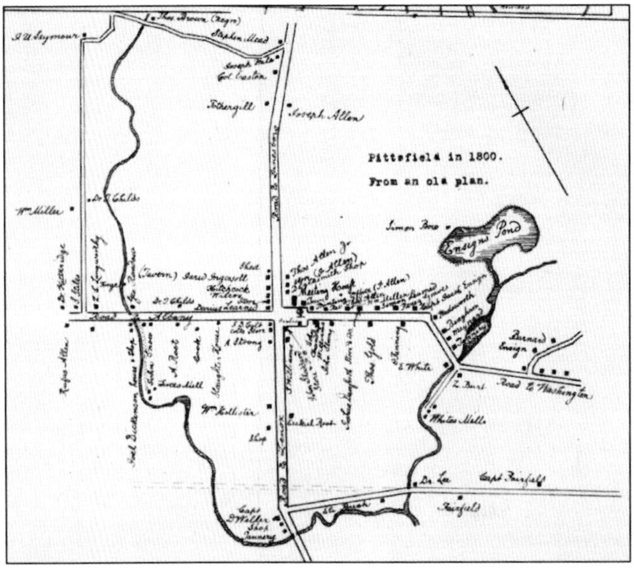

When Arthur Scholfield arrived in Pittsfield in 1799 at the age of 42, this was the town he found. After years of working in mills, first in England and then in New England, Scholfield had memorized the mechanics to build machines to process textiles. He was drawn here by the confluence of rapidly falling streams that could power the machinery he had in mind to build. White's Mill on the east branch of the Housatonic and Luce's Mill on the west branch would be sites of the earliest forays into the new textile industry. (Courtesy of the Berkshire Athenaeum.)

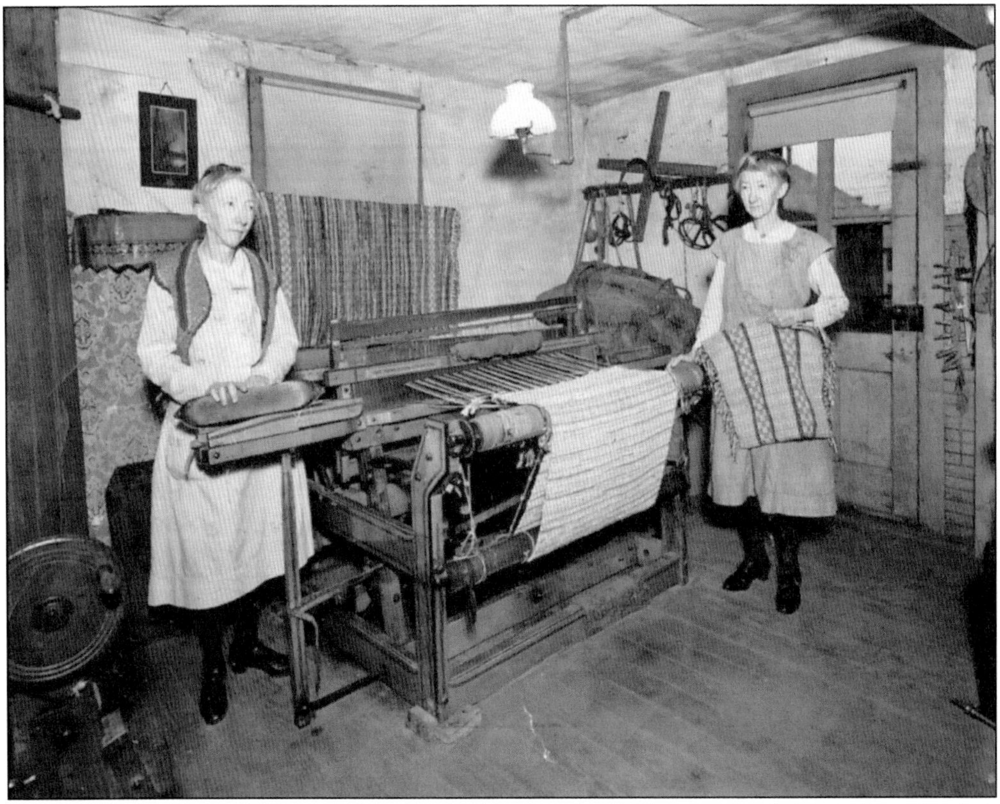

Before Scholfield built his first carding machine, women made the cloth and the clothing for their own use as part of the daily household chores. The carding, spinning, and weaving were all done in the household, and women developed their own cottage industries making the cloth for resale. They still needed fulling mills that would clean the cloth and prepare it for the hand sewing of clothing. This tradition of working at home continued into the 1900s, as Carrie Dorman and her twin sister, Renie, wove up to 1,000 rag carpets a year on their hand loom.

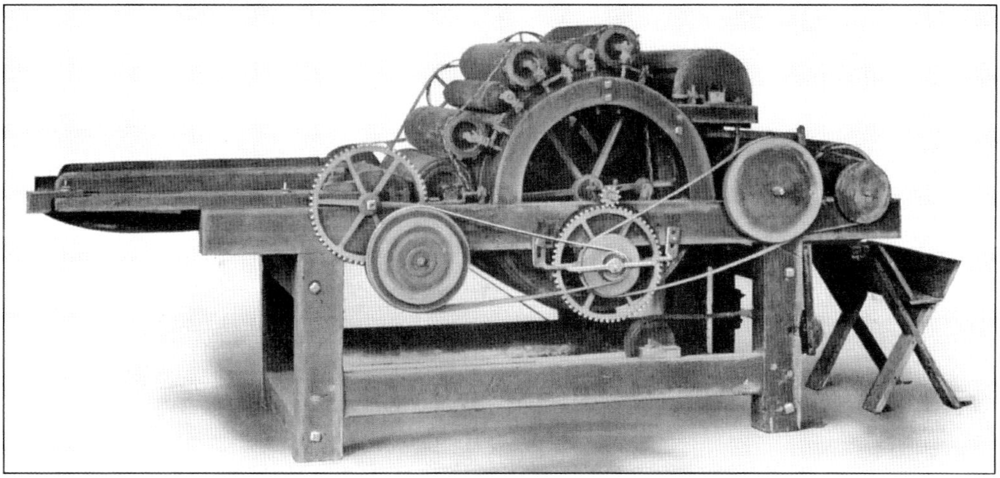

Scholfield initially set up a fulling mill in west Pittsfield. There, he built from memory the machines he and his father had used in England and then in Newburyport, Massachusetts. He set out to relieve women of the laborious carding function of working the raw wool into strands lying in the same direction. His first carding machine, featured in this drawing, was ready for use by November 1, 1801, when an announcement appeared in the *Pittsfield Sun*: "Arthur Scholfield respectfully informs the inhabitants of Pittsfield and the neighboring towns, that he has a carding-machine half a mile west of the meeting-house." (Courtesy of the Berkshire Athenaeum.)

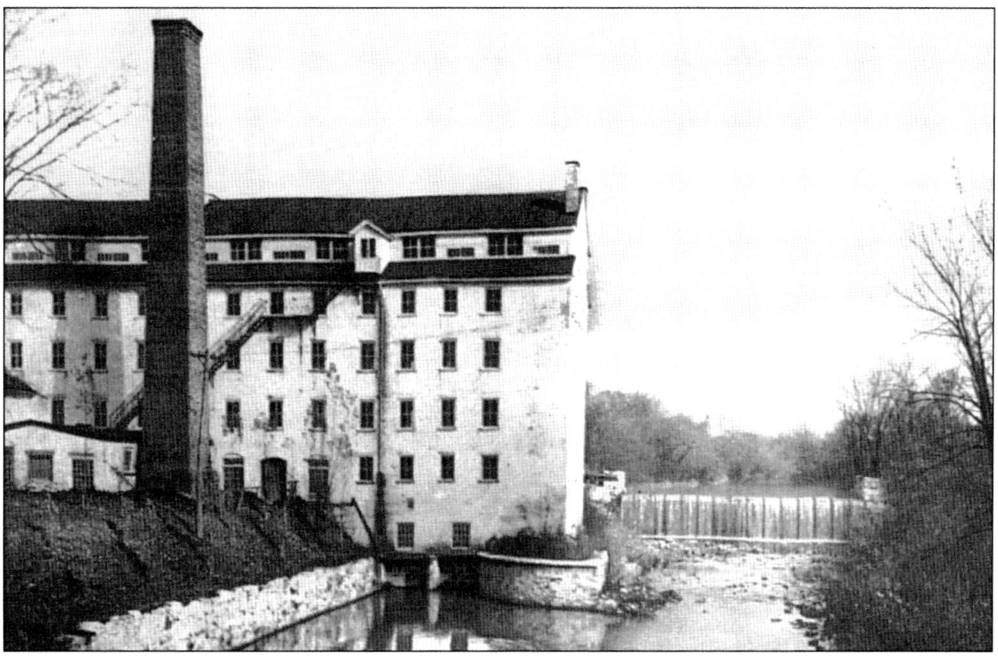

Within a few years, Scholfield focused his attention on just building the machines for textiles. He set up shop with James Strandring near Pontoosuc Lake, and the two men began selling machines to textile mills. By the time the first mill in Berkshire County was built in 1810, a total of 54 textile mills operated in other parts of the state. The first mill, the Housatonic Woolen Mill, stood on the east branch of the river near Elm Street. It eventually became the Van Sickler Mill, named after its owner, who employed 90 people in the late 1880s, and produced 30,000 yards of cotton cloth per week.

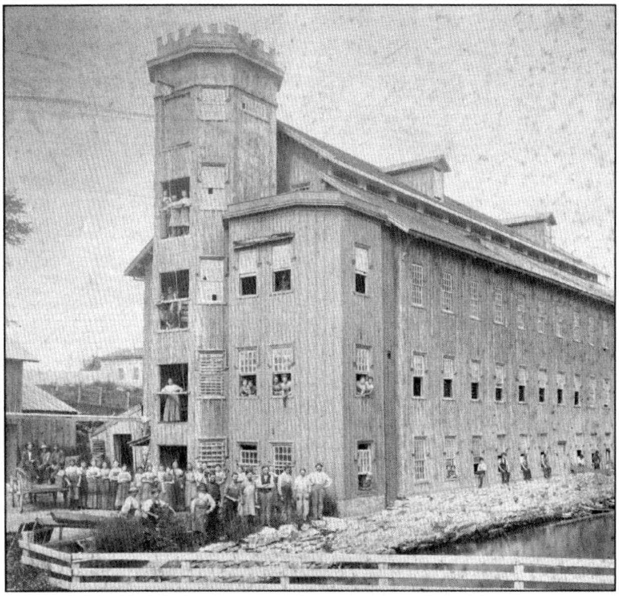

Scholfield lent his name and his money to another new factory that sprang up on the west branch of the Housatonic, under the leadership of Lemuel Pomeroy, the owner of a profitable gun factory north of the town center. It was originally called the Pittsfield Woolen and Cotton Company, but Pomeroy changed the name in 1839 after he brought his sons into the business, calling it L. Pomeroy & Sons. Just upstream from their factory lay the old Luce mill that they purchased and converted into a woolen mill producing satinet. Pictured here is the Upper Pomeroy Mill that stayed in operation until 1912.

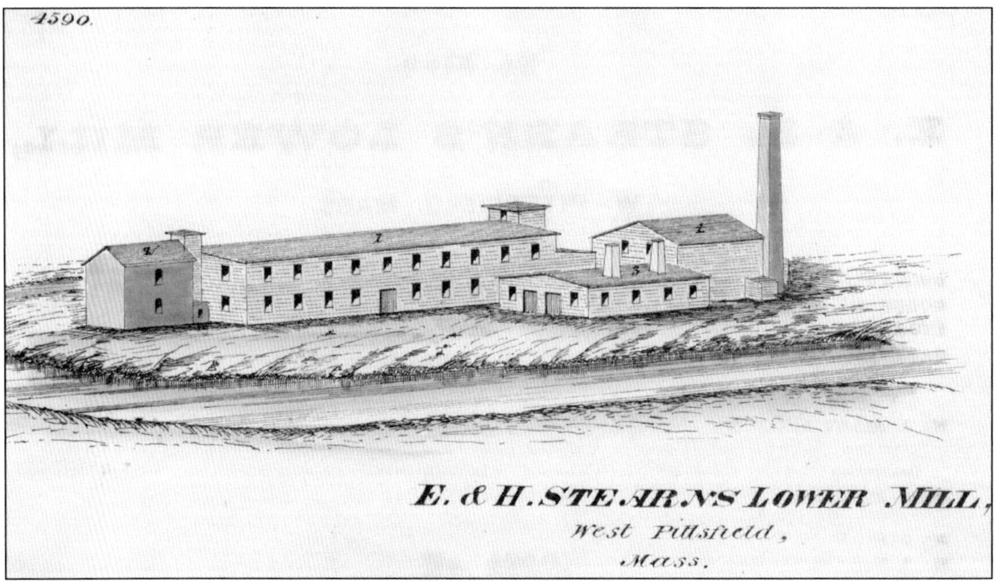

In 1801, Daniel Stearns took over a mill farther upstream from Pomeroy's site, where women brought the wool they carded in their homes for dressing, fulling (cleaning), and dyeing. Stearns purchased a spinning jenny from Scholfield, and in his "New Woolen Factory," he placed this equipment as well as one of Scholfield's first carding machines. By the time of the Civil War, Stearns's sons ran the company that commanded five different factories along the southwest branch of the Housatonic, 30 dwellings for its workers on 45 acres of land, and even a small church. (Courtesy of the American Textile History Museum, Lowell, Massachusetts.)

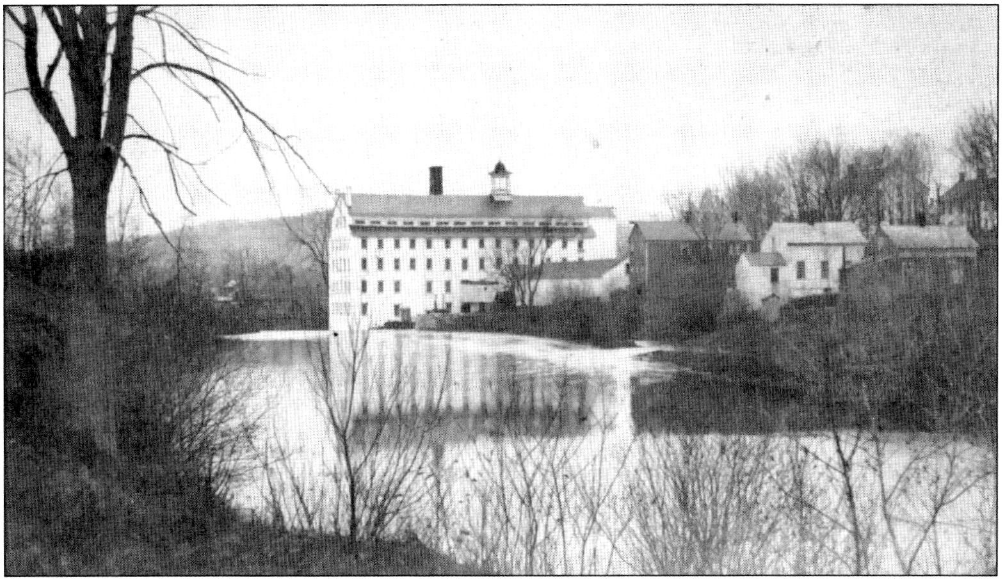

An employee at Stearns Mill, John V. Barker, went into business with his brothers Charles and Otis and bought the original, vacant Stearns Mill in 1832. A testimony to the determination that would see their wool business become the largest in Pittsfield, the Barkers first had to lift the old building to prevent the recurring floods from the rushing streams. As business increased, they kept adding extensions on to the original wooden structure, and by 1870, they had constructed one of the largest mills in the county. (Courtesy of the Berkshire Athenaeum.)

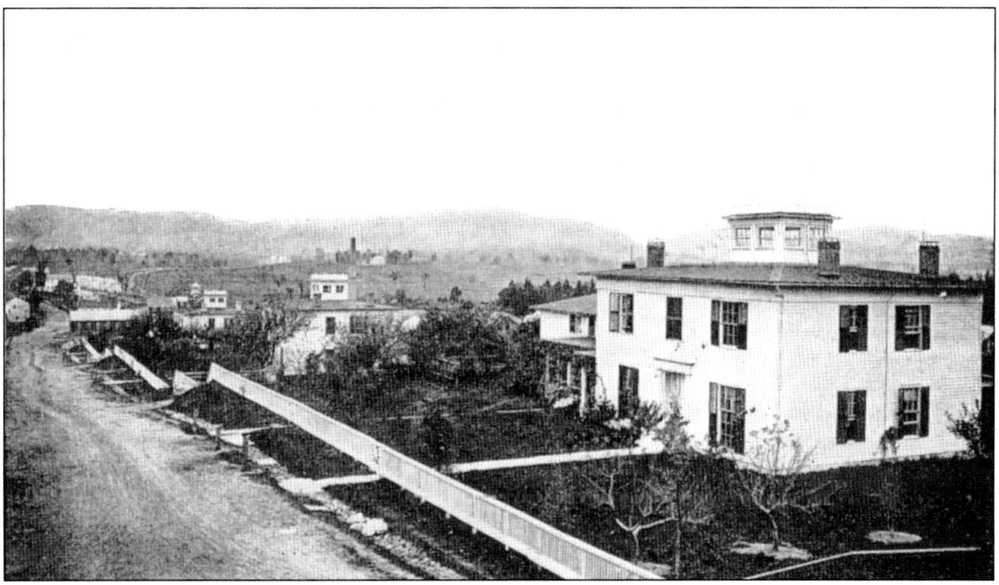

The Barker brothers lived in three duplicate, neighboring Italianate villas within walking distance of their mills, seen in the background of this photograph. In 1865, they bought out most of the Stearns buildings downstream, renaming these newly acquired mills Lower Barkerville, while their original complex became known as Upper Barkerville. There, in 1879, a fire broke out on an early January morning and burned down several of the Upper Barkerville buildings, including the main factory. They never fully recovered, and one by one, buildings were dismantled so that by 1890, the company went out of business, leaving only the villas that survive today.

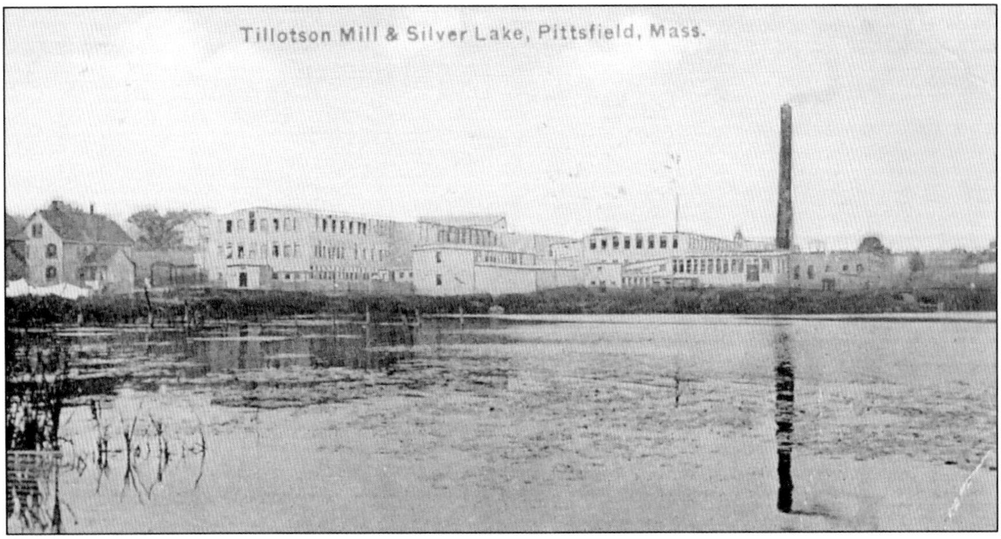

Downstream from the Barker and Stearns Mills, Tillotson-Collins Mill stood on a dam that originally powered a sawmill, a gristmill, and even a plaster-of-Paris mill. In 1867, a local grocer named Otis Tillotson bought the property and went into business with Dwight Collins, gaining a foothold in the competitive woolen industry. After Otis died, he left his share of the business to his brothers, one of whom, William, oversaw an expansion that turned it into the second-largest employer in Pittsfield. In 1889, William launched a second textile factory near Silver Lake, pictured here. (Courtesy of the Berkshire Athenaeum.)

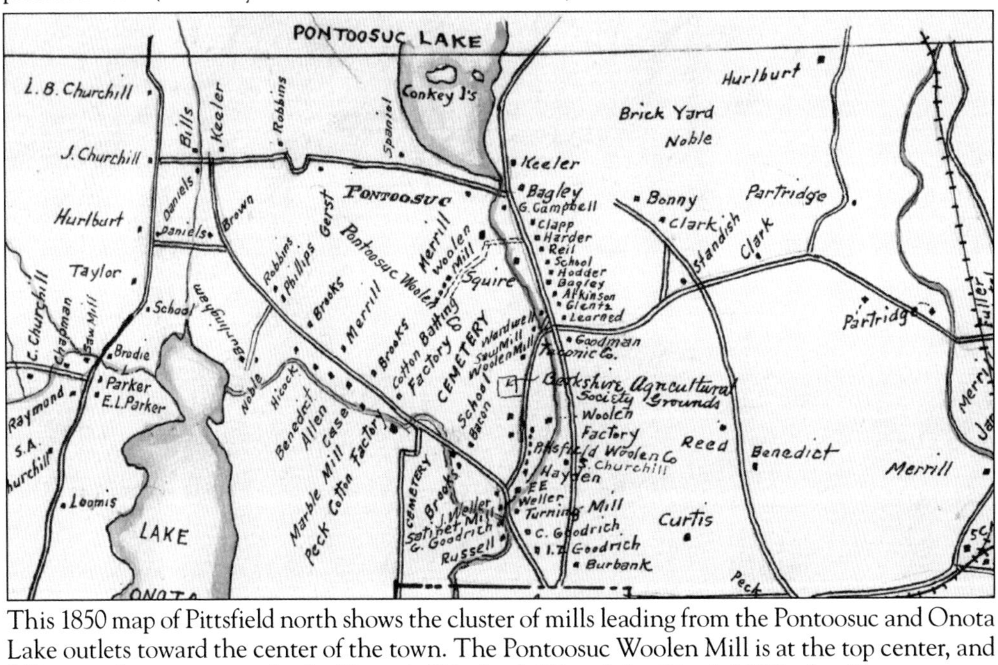

This 1850 map of Pittsfield north shows the cluster of mills leading from the Pontoosuc and Onota Lake outlets toward the center of the town. The Pontoosuc Woolen Mill is at the top center, and following the stream south, the Taconic Woolen Mill and the Pittsfield Woolen Company can be seen. On Onota Brook are the Peck brothers' original cotton batting mill and, on the other side, their new cotton mill. At the juncture of the two streams, a satinet mill that was the first textile venture of the Russell brothers before they built their woolen mill upstream can be seen. (Courtesy of Berkshire Middle Registry of Deeds.)

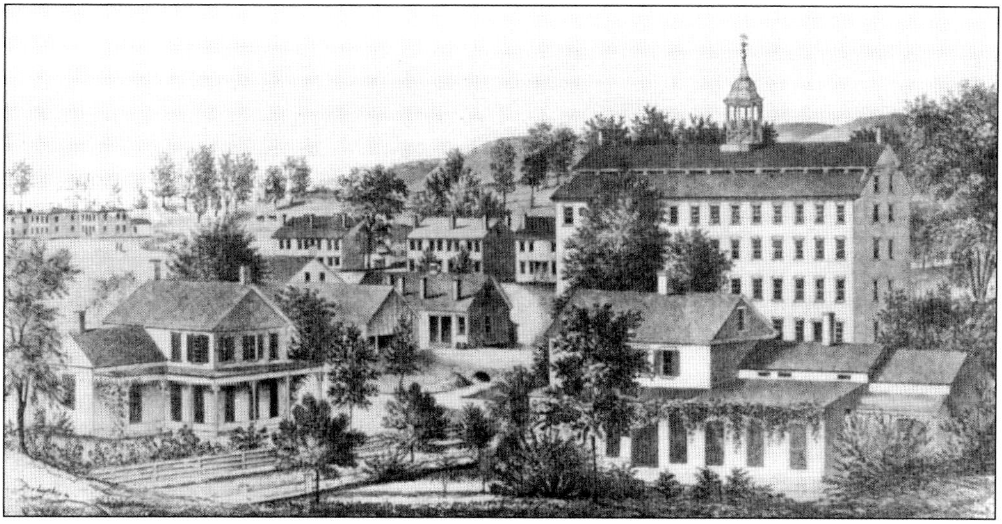

In 1825, a group of investors, led by Henry Shaw, a congressman from Lanesborough, purchased land south of Pontoosuc Lake in Pittsfield to build a woolen mill. Shaw safeguarded his investment when he voted in favor a tariff to protect American manufacturing from British imports, as part of the "America system" promoted by Shaw's friend, Henry Clay. Ground was broken, and Pontoosuc Woolen Mills began operating in 1827 in a large four-story brick structure measuring 145 by 50 feet, with surrounding housing for workers and managers and a store. (Courtesy of the Berkshire Athenaeum.)

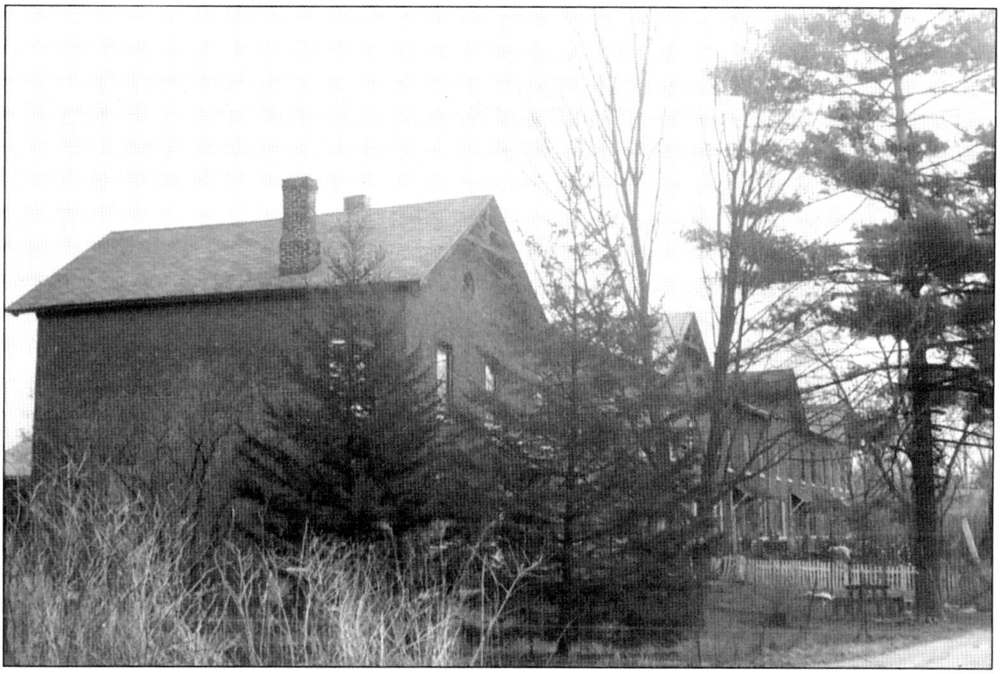

Workers and their families employed at Pontoosuc Woolen Mill crowded into these row houses within walking distance of the mill, still standing in 1980 when this photograph was taken. Securing water privileges meant that mills were often placed at the outskirts of towns, too far to travel each day from the town center. So, owners created villages around the mills, including housing for managers and workers as well as stores, taverns, inns, and even a church at one mill.

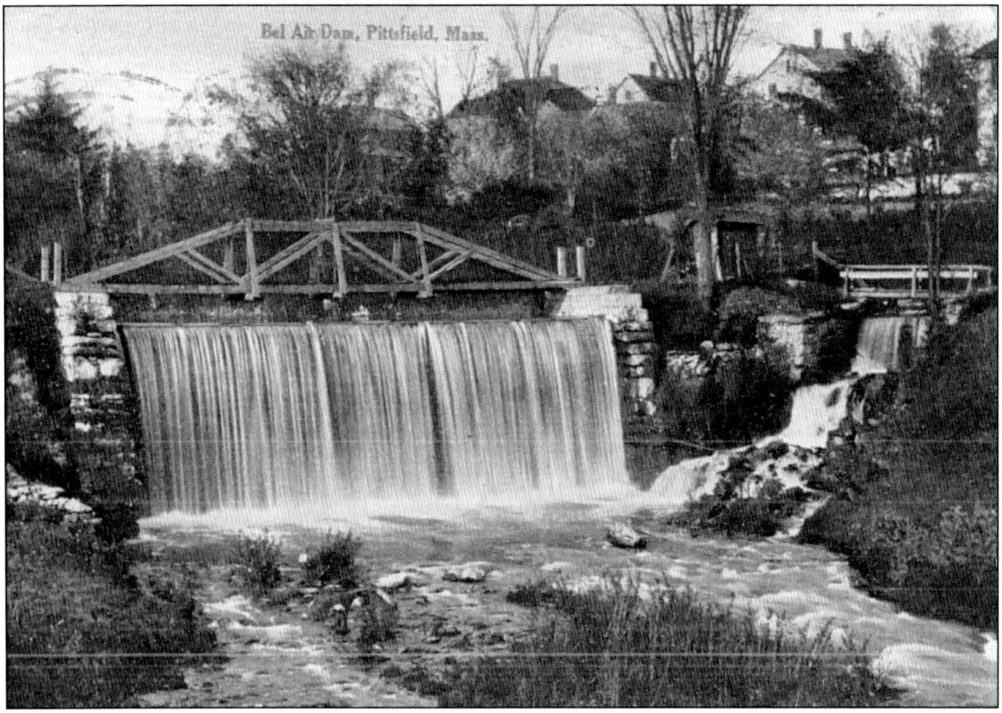

Not all investors venturing into the textile business were successful. Just a few years after the Pontoosuc Woolen Mill was launched, another entrepreneur, E.M. Bissell, bought the water privilege downstream to start his woolen business. In 1832, he contracted out the construction of the Bel Air dam on the western branch of the Housatonic and then built a four-story brick factory. However, a dispute arose over water with the owners of a privilege upstream. Bissell was unable to produce one yard of cloth and eventually sold his empty building in 1852.

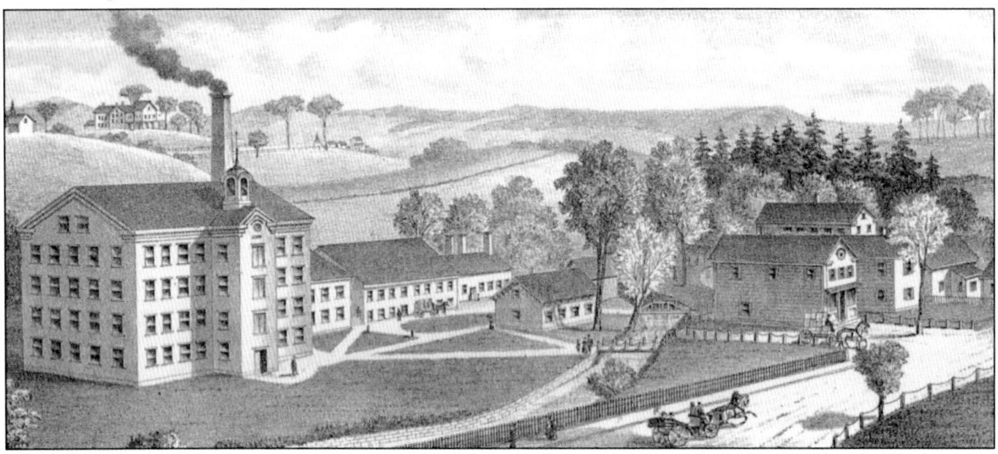

The original name of the new textile mill on the Bel Air dam was Pittsfield Woolen Company, whose specialty was a fine "cassimere" cloth, similar to cashmere. A fire on the top floors of the mill was put out by members of the 10th Massachusetts Regiment training in Pittsfield for the Civil War. With demand for woolen textiles high, the factory was quickly rebuilt. Renamed the Bel Air Manufacturing Company in 1873, the main building housed on different floors the functions of carding, weaving, spinning, and dyeing. Outbuildings pictured in this 1876 Beers Map drawing were for storage, an office, and workers' housing.

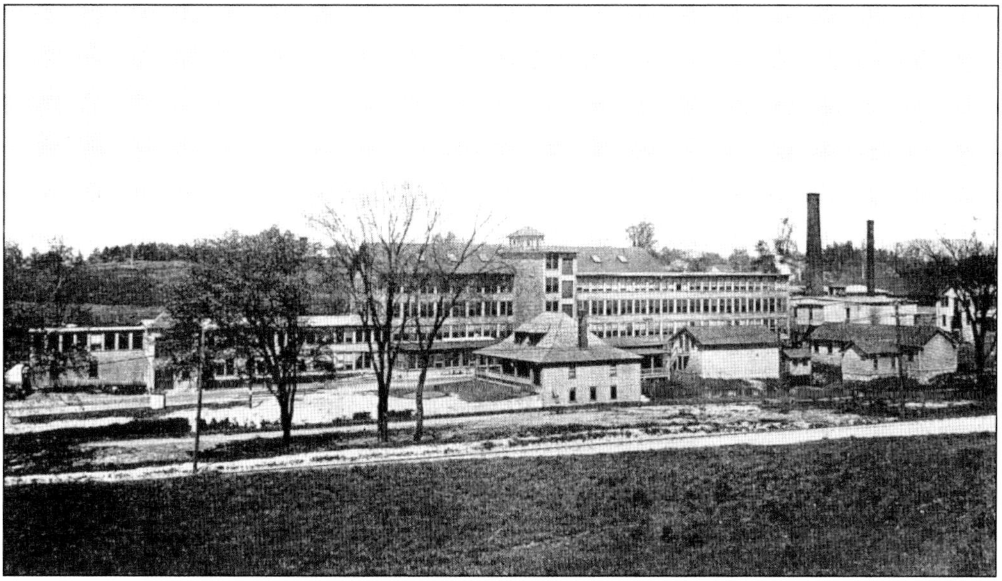

Between the Pontoosuc Woolen Mill and the Pittsfield Woolen Mill lay the successful Pomeroy armory that had started producing guns as early as 1808. A blacksmith, Lemuel Pomeroy quickly obtained government contracts to furnish 2,000 muskets a year, but he closed the business in 1846 when new percussion-style muskets required equipment changes. Pomeroy had since established a highly successful cotton mill and, nearing the end of his life, turned the business over to his sons. In 1856, on the site of Pomeroy's armory, Edward and George Learned launched their woolen mill, which they called the Taconic Mill, shown here in this 1911 photograph.

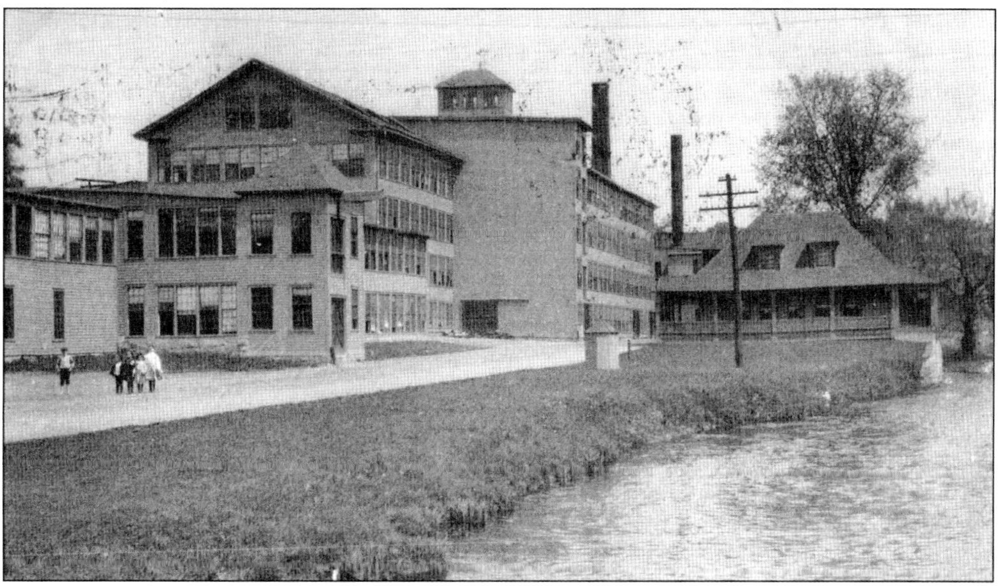

In this postcard, a group of small children stands to the side of the original Taconic Mill building, unique in that it was a large wooden structure measuring 150 feet by 50 feet and four stories high. The company ran a brisk business through the Civil War, employing over 150 workers to produce 450,000 yards of woolen cassimere each year. The economic Panic of 1873 forced the company out of business. The buildings were later leased and then purchased by James Wilson, who expanded the complex to include this unique office building on the right.

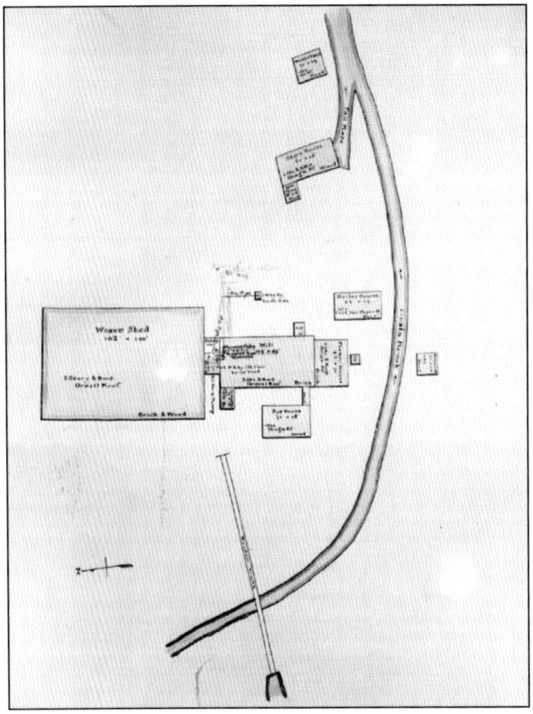

Just below the Pittsfield Woolen Mill, water from Onota Brook feeds into the same branch of the Housatonic. Like the other streams, the rapidly flowing water initially powered the small industry in the county, and on Onota was an iron forge owned by John Seymour. Two brothers, Elijah and Jabez Peck, owned a tin manufacturing company but, upon seeing the prospects for textile manufacturing, decided to branch out. They bought the water privilege from Seymour in 1844 and, three years later, had built a large wooden mill for producing cotton warp.

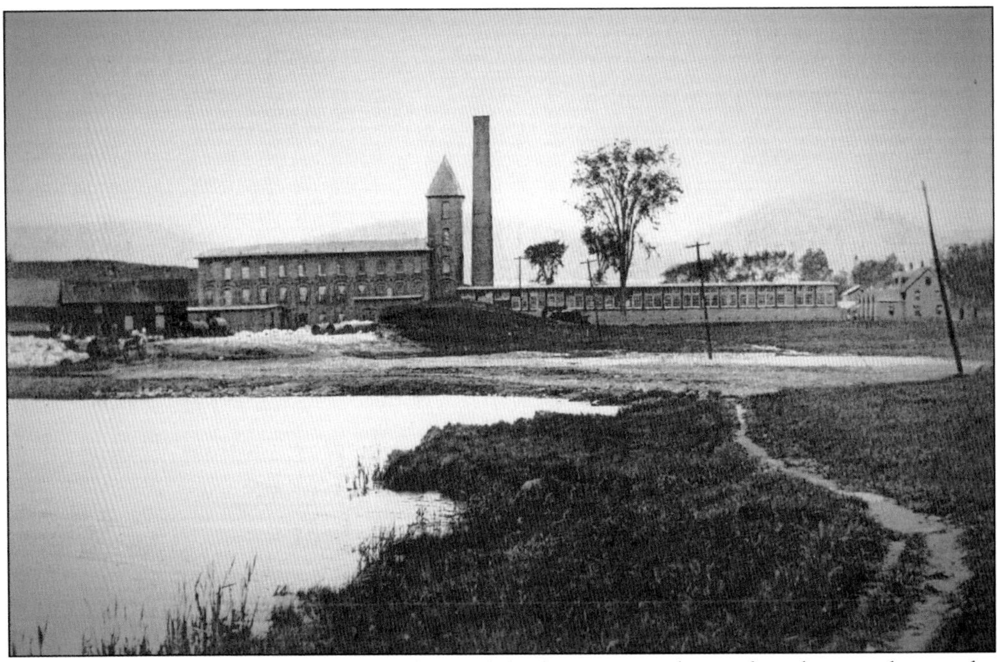

In 1853, the two Peck brothers wanted out of the business, and transferred ownership to the next generation, changing the name of the company to J.L. Peck. In the middle of the Civil War, Jabez bought another water privilege just upstream from his cotton mill to build a factory for producing wool. At its height, the two mills employed over 300 men, women, and children who operated carding machines, narrow and broad looms, and thousands of spindles to wind the thread produced.

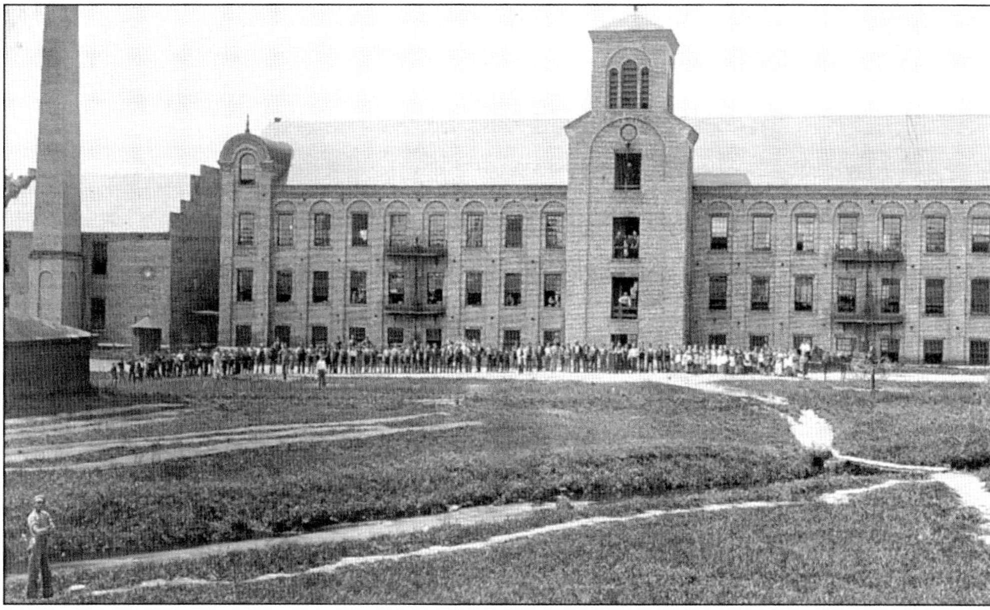

Workers at the newly established S.N. & C. Russell Mill congregate for a group photograph. The Russell brothers—Charles, Hezekiah, and Solomon N.—moved to Pittsfield as young boys, and, in 1845, they bought a small factory for carpenters' tools that stood on the site of what was once an iron forge on Onota Brook. Increased demand for wool products during the Civil War fueled their decision to open a woolen mill on the site that employed 100 people in its first year. It is now the home for Pine Cone Outlet.

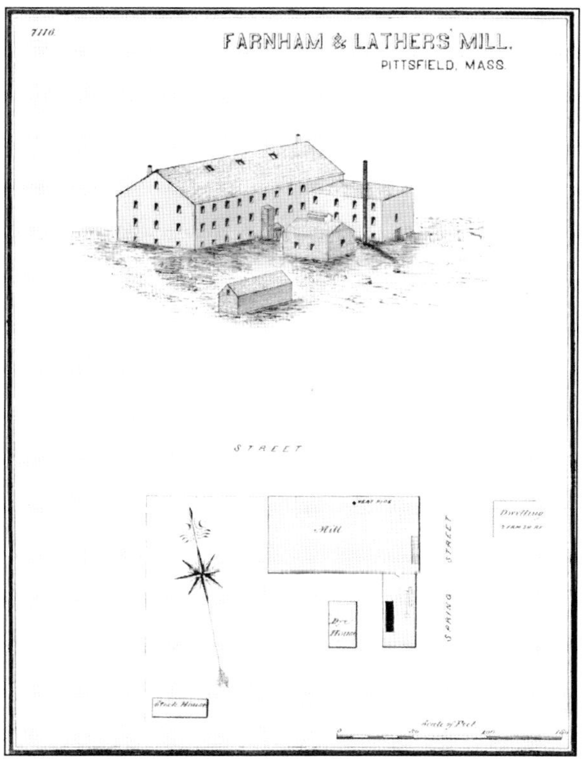

With the introduction of steam power, mill owners no longer needed to site their factories next to streams. In 1876, a former woolen mill employee of both the Taconic and Osceola Mills, E. Farnham, decided to go into the business for himself. He persuaded wealthy investor and former Union army officer Richard Lathers to construct a new mill on Burbank Street, closer to the rail line than to water. Facing an established competition and uncertain economy following the Panic of 1873, the firm went out of business just eight years later. (Courtesy of the American Textile History Museum, Lowell, Massachusetts.)

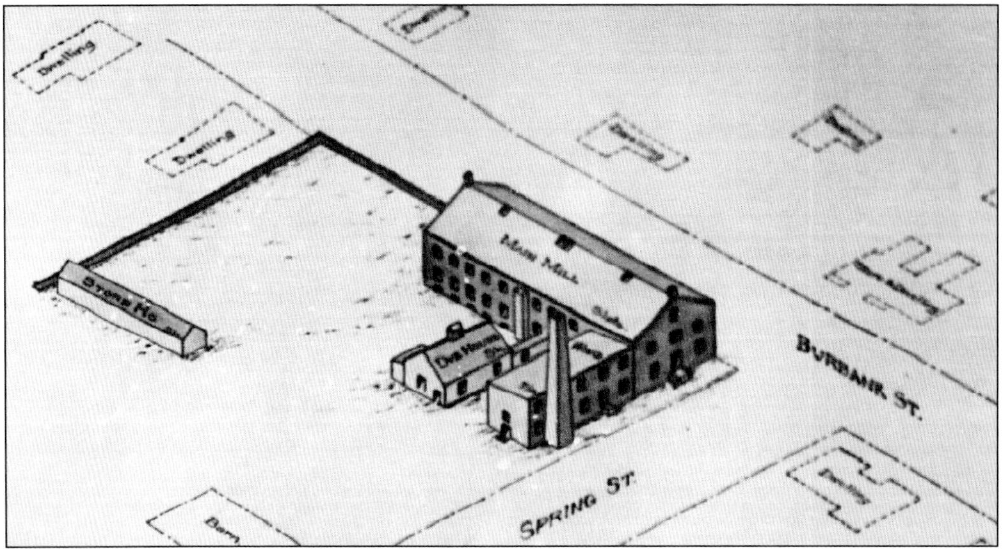

The Farnham and Lathers building stayed vacant until 1886, when William Rice and his son Arthur converted the mill for their prosperous silk factory. The company grew fast, expanding from 125 employees in the 1890s to 250 in 1915. For years, its famous silk braid was turned into uniforms—government and commercial—worldwide. Finally, in 2006, the company closed its doors and moved to South Carolina, and the brick structures were converted to apartments. It was the last remaining textile factory in Pittsfield. Here is an insurance drawing of the mill in 1890 from Associated Mutual Insurance.

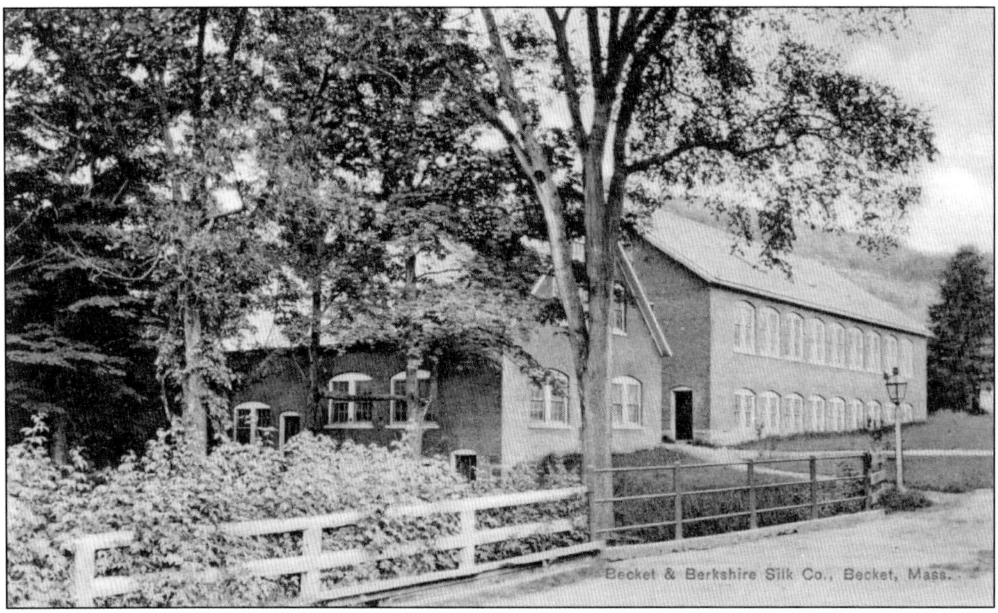

The Rices had learned the business working under a foreman named Samuel Smith for the Saunders Silk Company, located in the Kellogg Steam building. Smith took his textile expertise to the hill town of Becket where he launched his own silk thread company. Smith built his first mill in 1885, but within a decade, he had moved to a new location with a larger brick structure, pictured here. Located on the Yokum Brook, south of the village center, the Berkshire and Becket Silk Company initially had a workforce of 80 people, including three of Smith's children.

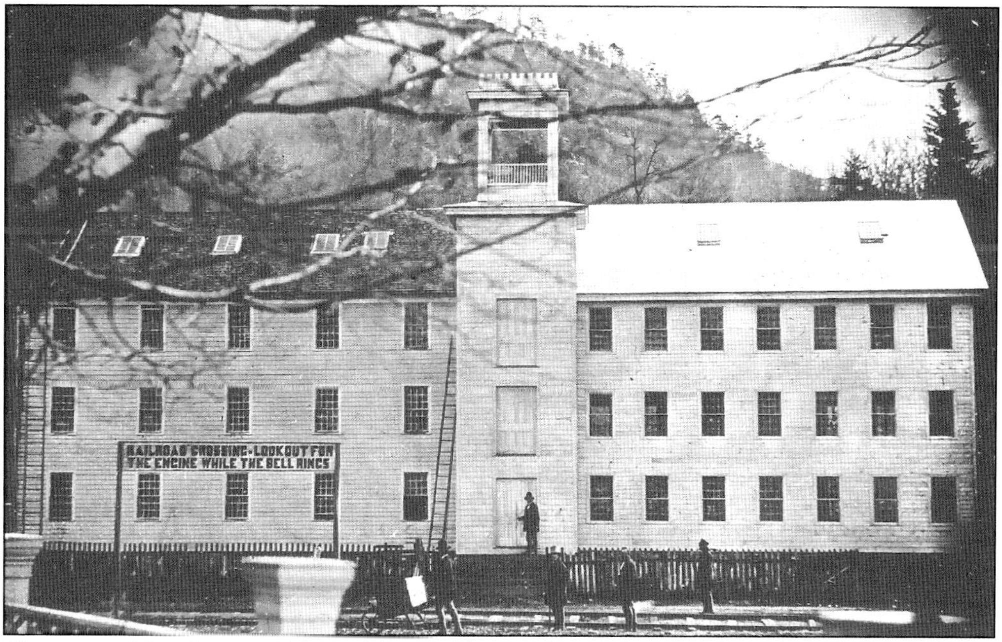

The new rail line between Lee and Pittsfield opened in 1850 and passed through the village of Housatonic, giving new life to a cotton manufacturing operation that later became one of Berkshire County's largest mill complexes. The first building was erected in 1825 on the Housatonic River in the northern part of Great Barrington. The original mill was absorbed in 1835 under the name Housatonic Manufacturing Company, which produced cotton twine and print cloths. It failed in 1848, just two years before the rail line opened up. New investors, John and Asa Russell and John H. Coffing, bought the property, giving it the new name Monument Mills.

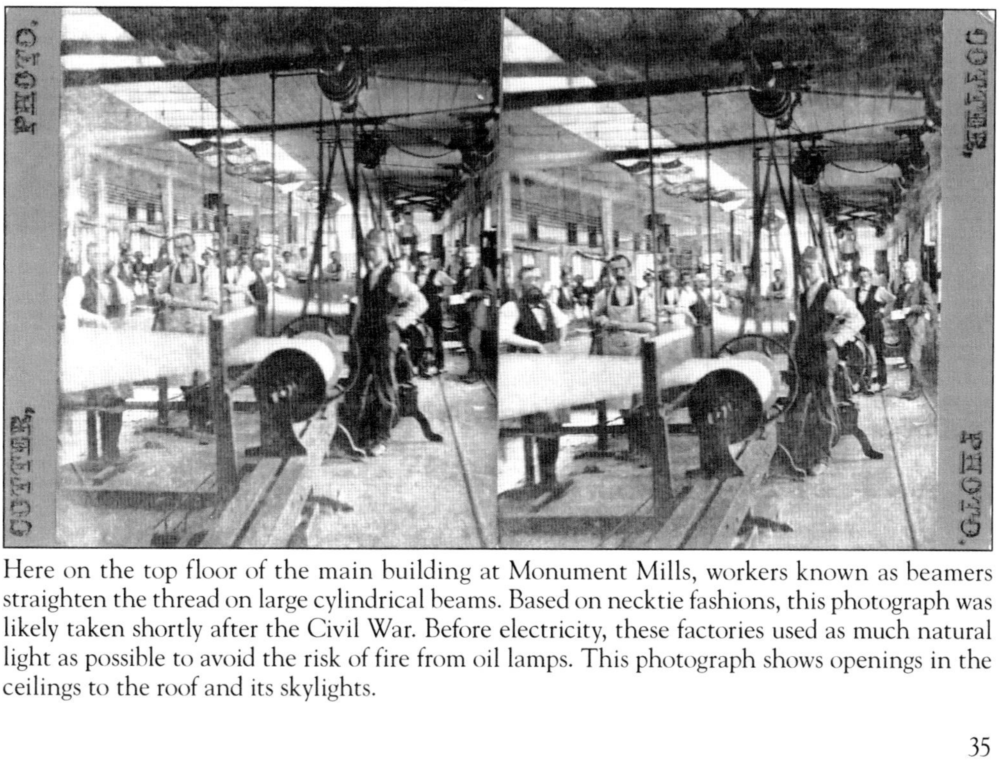

Here on the top floor of the main building at Monument Mills, workers known as beamers straighten the thread on large cylindrical beams. Based on necktie fashions, this photograph was likely taken shortly after the Civil War. Before electricity, these factories used as much natural light as possible to avoid the risk of fire from oil lamps. This photograph shows openings in the ceilings to the roof and its skylights.

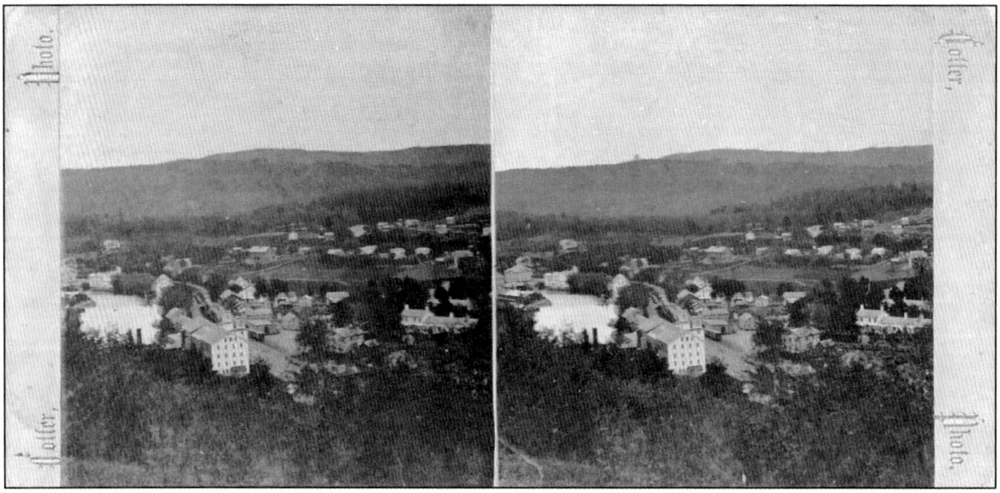

This stereoscopic view shows the growth of Monument Mills into the 1870s, with an expanded original building that now has two bell towers. Worker housing has grown up around the complex for the 350 people who were employed in 1878. Working the 1,800 spindles, they produced close to 3 million pounds of cotton warp per year. The success led the mill agent John Seeley to set out on his own, but not too far from his former employer. With partners Henry Adams and Joseph Fuller, he purchased the water privilege just south of Monument Mills after the end of the Civil War.

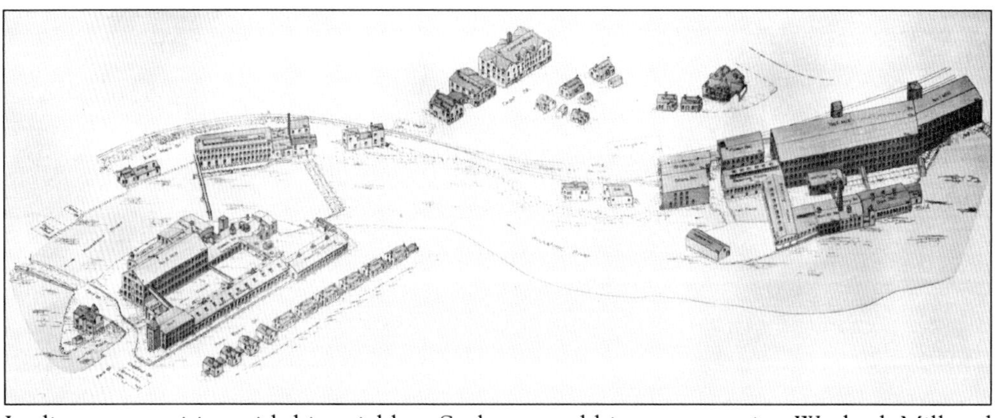

In direct competition with his neighbor, Seeley named his new operation Waubeek Mill and produced cotton warp. The rival mill only lasted a few years before Monument Mills bought it in 1871. By 1892, Monument Mills had grown to include multiple buildings on both the original site and the southern Waubeek site. This fire insurance map from 1892 shows the extent of the complex of both mills. The original building at the left still shows the bell tower. Next to it are new worker houses to accommodate the growing number of employees.

Isiah Weston came to textile production by way of the church as an ordained Unitarian minister in Fairhaven, Massachusetts. Relocated to Dalton before the War of 1812, he recruited British prisoners of war housed in Pittsfield to come to Dalton to dig out the canal for his mill. Weston built a wooden mill for the production of wool that continued until his death at the age of 48 in 1821. By the time this three-story brick building was constructed in 1873, ownership had changed several times. The mill continued to operate under different ownership until the 1940s, and today, it is an apartment complex.

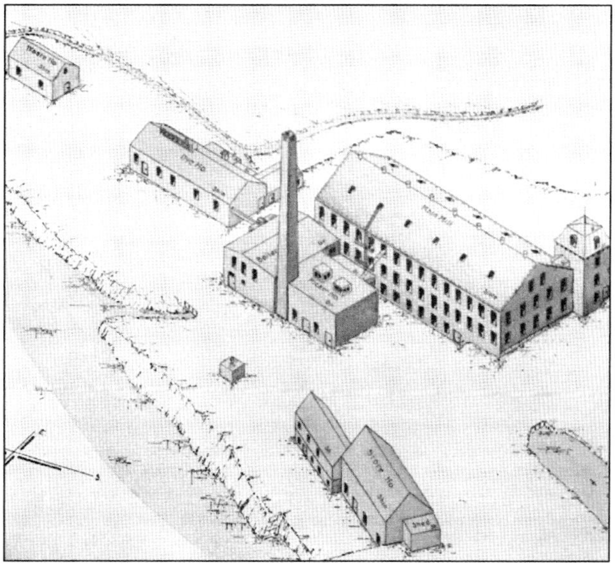

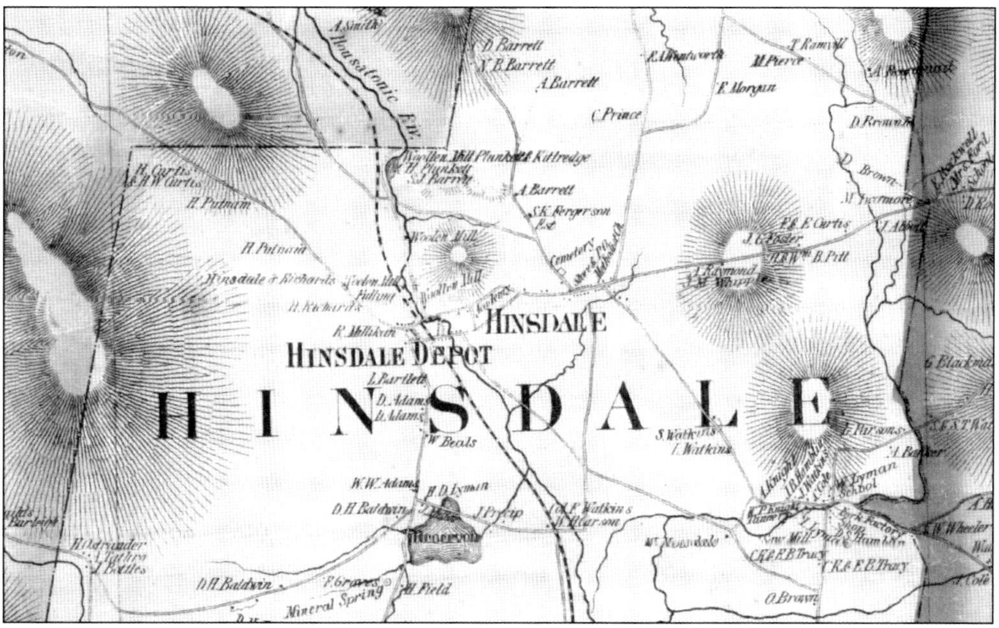

Upstream from the paper manufacturers in Dalton, two textile mill companies competed and then later merged in the small village of Hinsdale. One fell under the leadership of the Plunkett family, a name well known in textile mills across the county. In 1830, Charles H. Plunkett followed the model his older brother established in Adams to start his own woolen mill in Hinsdale. Within a few years, he had brought his sons Thomas and George into the business. Eventually, the company expanded to three different sites along the eastern branch of the Housatonic River, labeled in this 1858 Walling map.

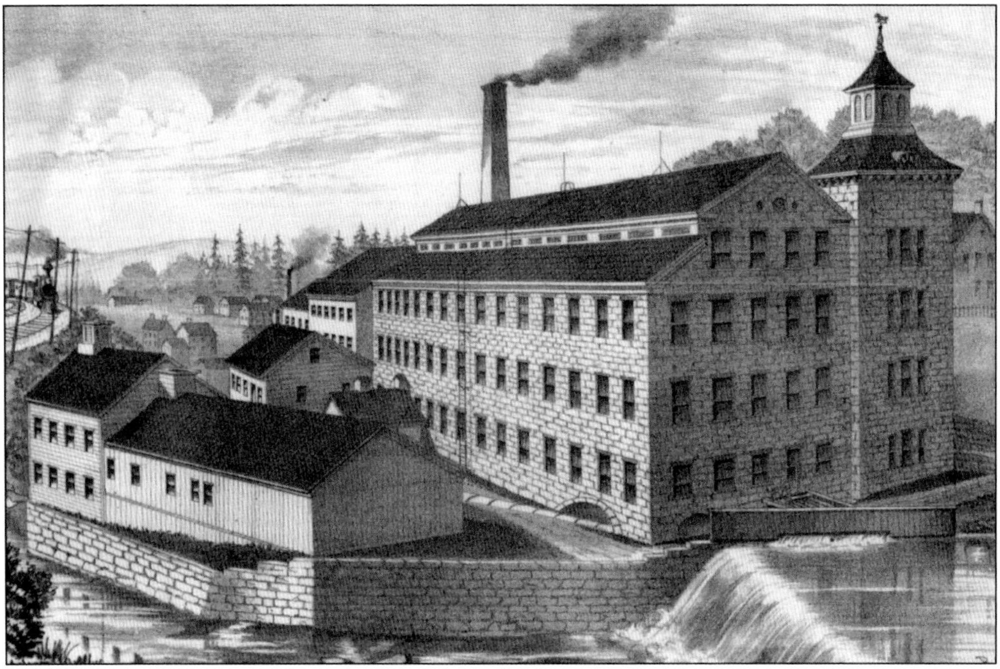

The second mill complex in Hinsdale belonged to two generations of descendants of Rev. Theodore Hinsdale, who was the founder of the Congregational church there. In 1804, in his honor, the village took his name. In 1836, his sons launched the Hinsdale Manufacturing Company, which became the center of village life for the rest of the 19th century. This engraving from F.W. Beers in 1876 depicts one common feature of most mills: the prominent outside stairway and bell tower whose ringing ordered the daily lives of the 400 men, women, and children who worked in the mill at its peak.

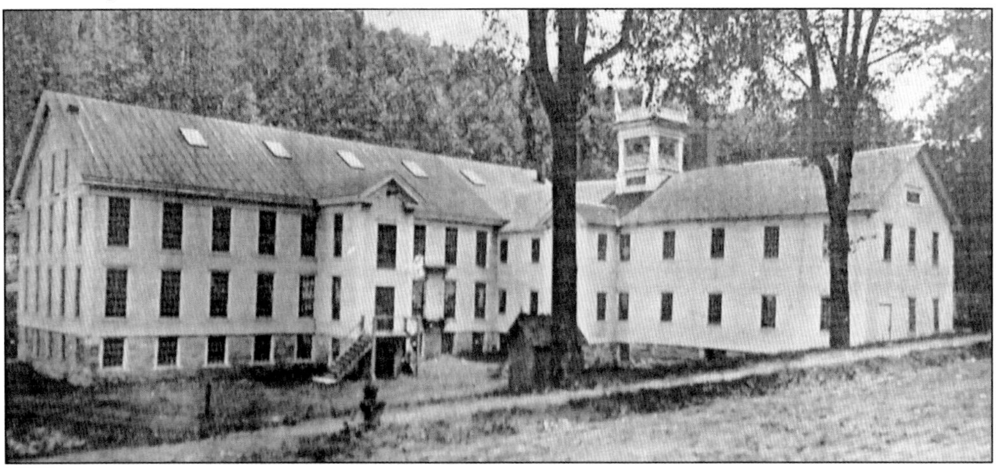

The headwaters of the Hoosic River in Cheshire powered early small industries such as sawmills and blacksmiths. Alden Potter, the son of a blacksmith, traveled to Rhode Island to work at the new Slater Mill. When Potter returned home, he built the first machines for cotton production in the region. A small cotton mill established at Cheshire Harbor in the 1820s under the ownership of Elisha Jenks grew to the point where he needed a new factory building, shown here. Built in 1843, the Harbor Mill stayed in operation beyond Jenks's death in 1871 with a workforce of over 40 employees producing 5,500 pounds of cotton warp each week.

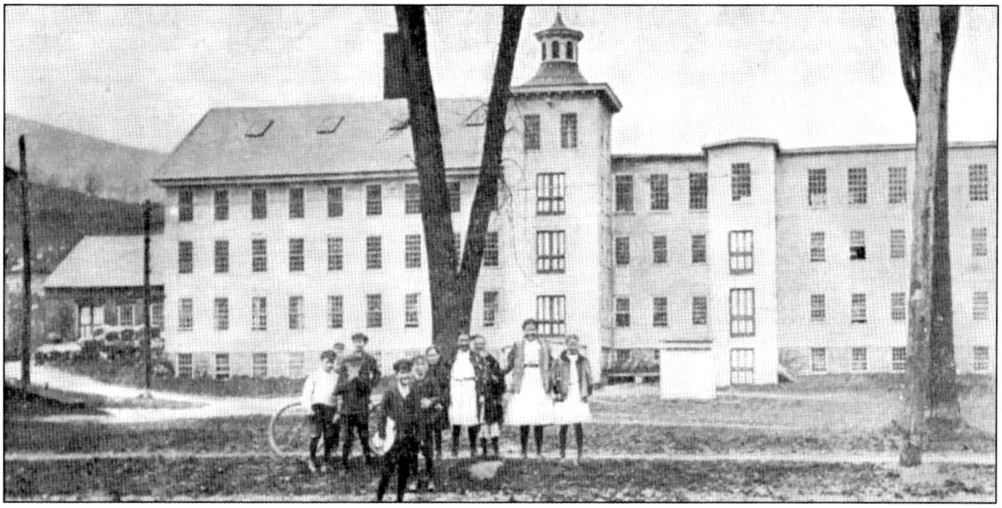

Children stand outside the Adams Brothers Grove Mill, just downstream on the Hoosic River from Cheshire. Are they workers or just walking past? The clapboard structure was opened in 1846 as a factory producing cotton warp. The patriotism of the owners was evident in their names: Washington Adams (and John Seeley) started the company, and Adams passed ownership along to his two sons George Washington Adams and John Seeley Adams. In the 1880s, approximately 125 people produced warp, operating over 4,000 spindles. The Adams Brothers Grove Mill stayed in business until the late 1930s when the building became a warehouse.

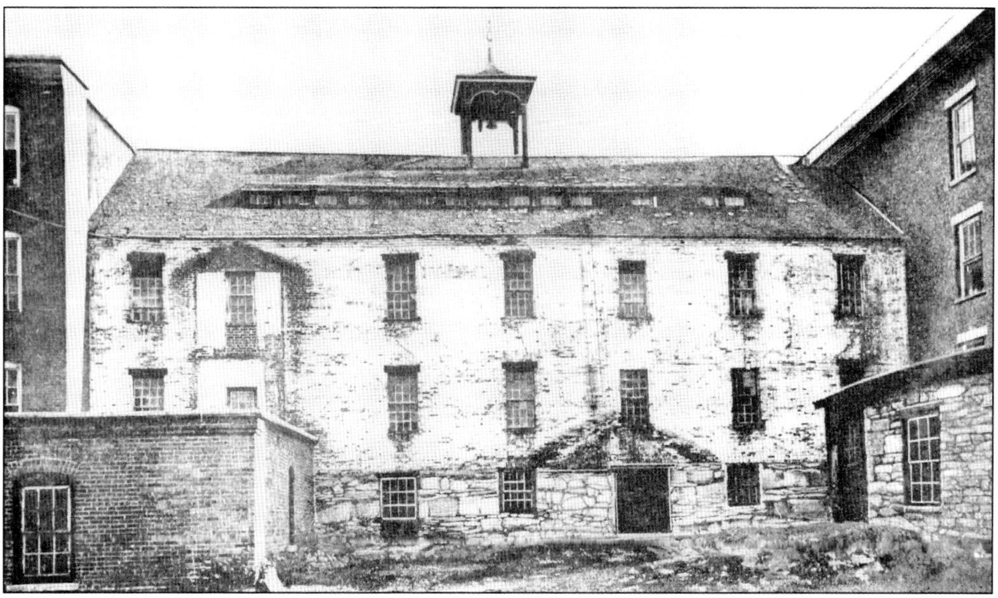

The earliest textile mill in Adams lay farther downstream, closer to the city center, and was built as the Adams South Village Cotton and Woolen Manufacturing Company in 1814. Demand for their cotton warp allowed owners William C. Plunkett and Russell Brown to double the size of this mill and build their "Stone Mill" farther downstream. High cotton prices during the Civil War allowed the partners to embark on a building spree adding a dyehouse, warehouse, and an engine room. Plunkett turned the entire operation over to his sons, who oversaw the complex of 11 buildings and expanded their holdings in other mills in Adams, North Adams, Hinsdale, and Pittsfield.

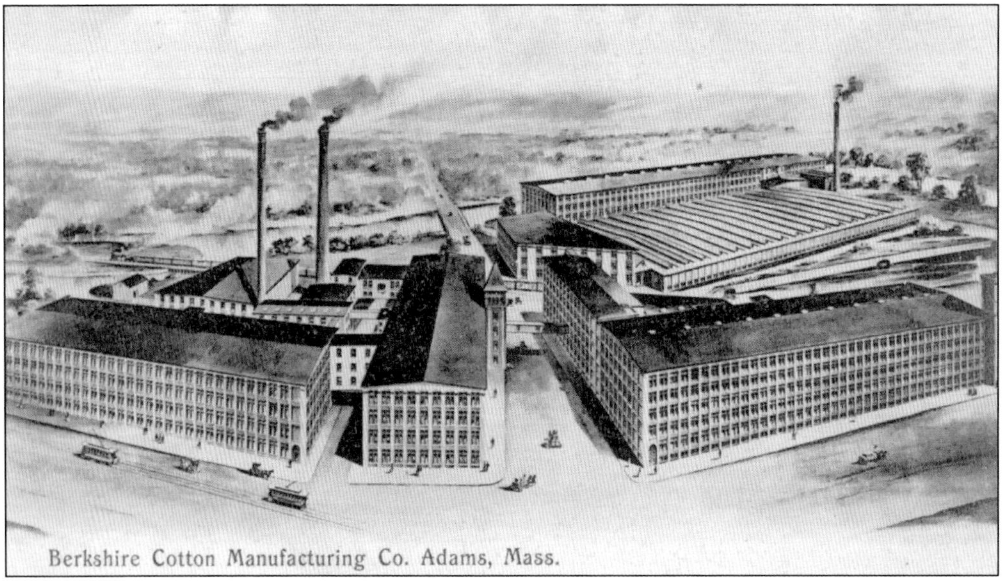

Growing demand for their consumer skirts and blankets meant the Plunketts were forced to look for more space, so in 1878, they leased an abandoned building that belonged to the defunct Adams Paper Company north of the town center. When that building burned in 1886, they bought the site and erected a new complex, starting a whole new company two years later that they named the Berkshire Cotton Manufacturing Company. Bought out by the Hathaway company, the factory eventually attracted the 20th-century investor Warren Buffet, who continued to use the name Berkshire Hathaway for his investment firm.

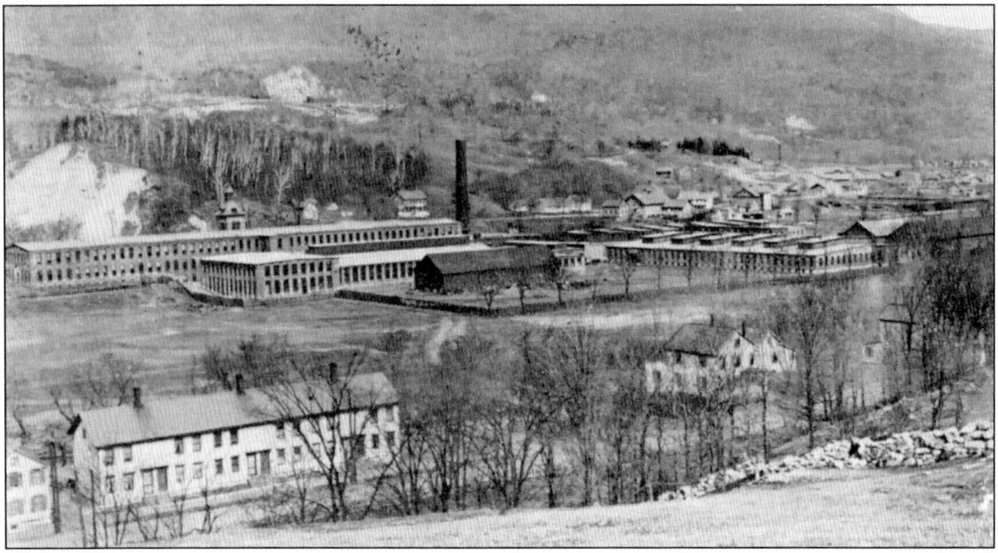

Competition in textiles was fierce in Adams, with over 20 textile mills by mid-century. Still, high prices for cotton in the Civil War motivated new entrants. In 1867, a group of investors led by the paper company owner in Adams, Levy Brown, bought farmland that was owned by Susan B. Anthony's uncle on the northern outskirts of Adams. They called their new cotton company Renfrew Manufacturing, after James Renfrew, one of the founders who was from Renfrew, Scotland. This mill, referred to as Mill No. 2, dominated the landscape north of Adams and included many worker tenements within walking distance.

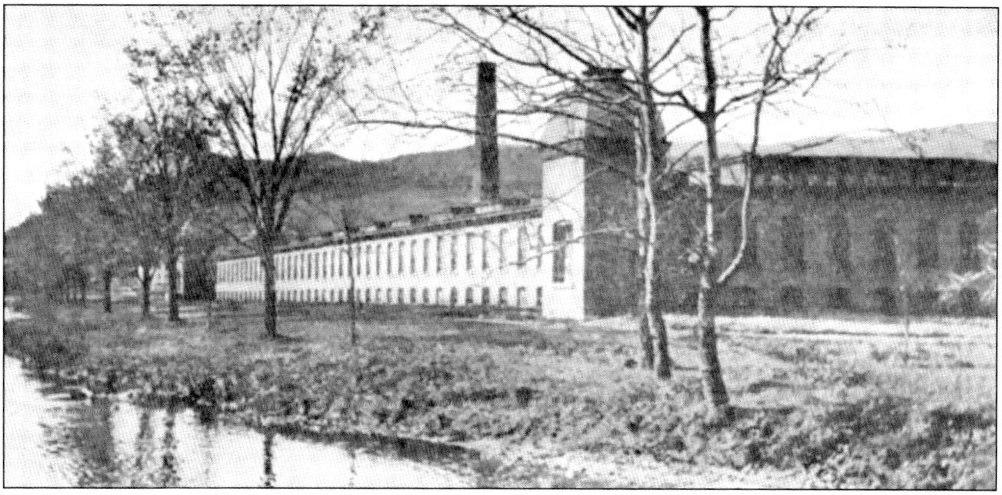

By the end of the 19th century, Renfrew Manufacturing owned six different mills, buying factories in Adams and Dalton. In 1892, the company found a water privilege squeezed into the heavily industrialized center of Adams and built a one-story building longer than a football field that served as an extended weave shed for the production of colored damasks made on a Jacquard loom. Appropriately, this complex was named Jacquard Mill.

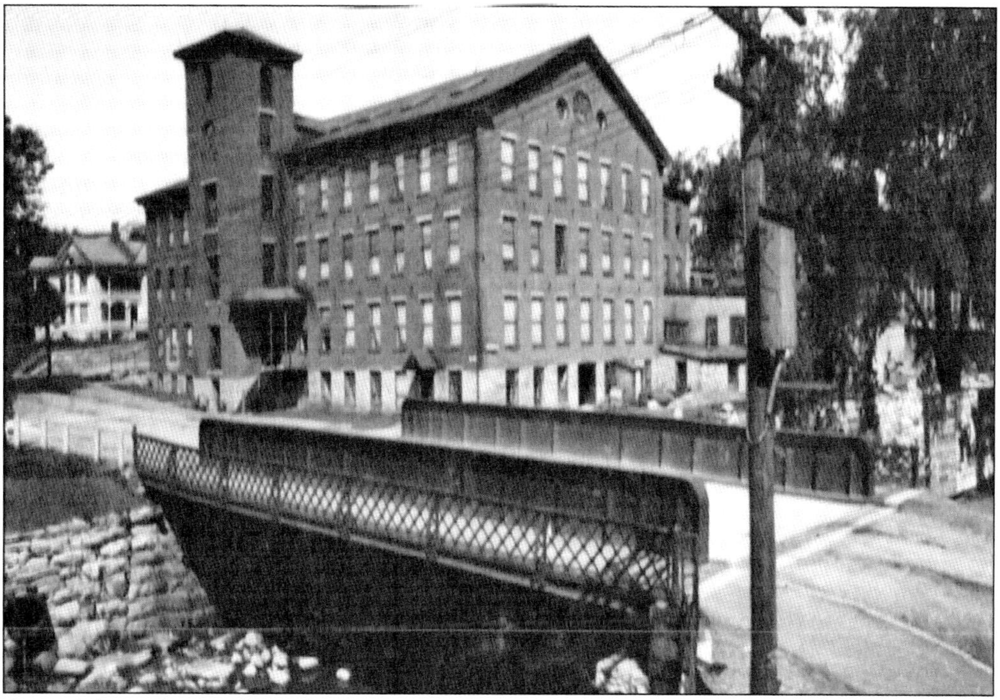

One of the earliest mills in the country to produce printed textiles was built in North Adams in 1828 by Caleb Turner on the site of an old iron furnace on the North Branch of the Hoosic River. After a fire in 1830 and an economic downturn in 1837, the firm failed and the buildings lay empty for another seven years. First under the name Freeman Manufacturing and eventually Windsor Print Works, the original Turner complex grew to incorporate the Eagle, Estes, and Stone Mills and many tenements to house the 600 to 800 workers employed in the final decades of the 19th century.

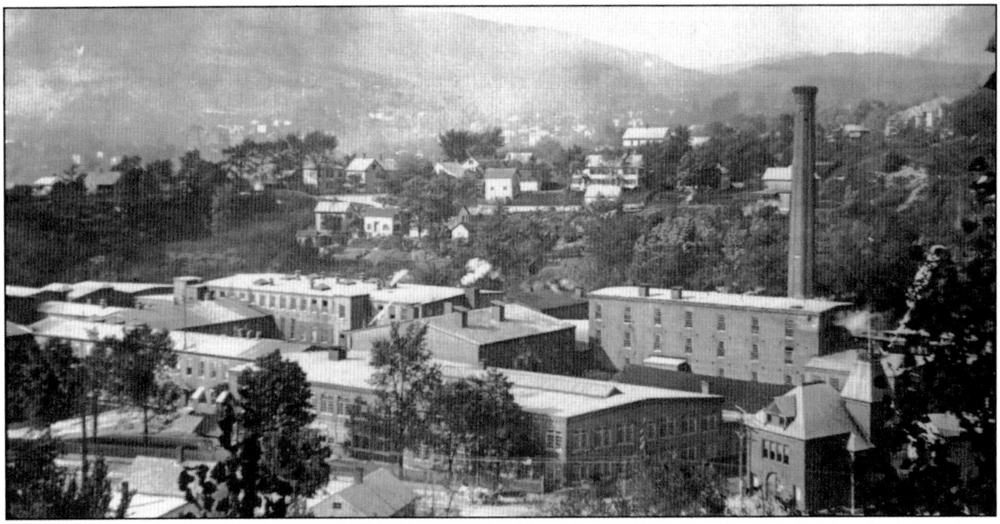

About the time that Arthur Scholfield was introducing carding machines in Pittsfield mills, a machinist named Giles Tinker arrived in the northern district of Adams. His interest was in power looms, so he traveled to Rhode Island and purchased first a wool satinet loom for a small factory and then a cotton loom for the Eagle Mill, pictured here at the turn of the 19th century. One of the oldest mills in the county, the Eagle Mill had been built in 1813 by Tinker and his partner William Brayton. (Courtesy of the North Adams Historical Society.)

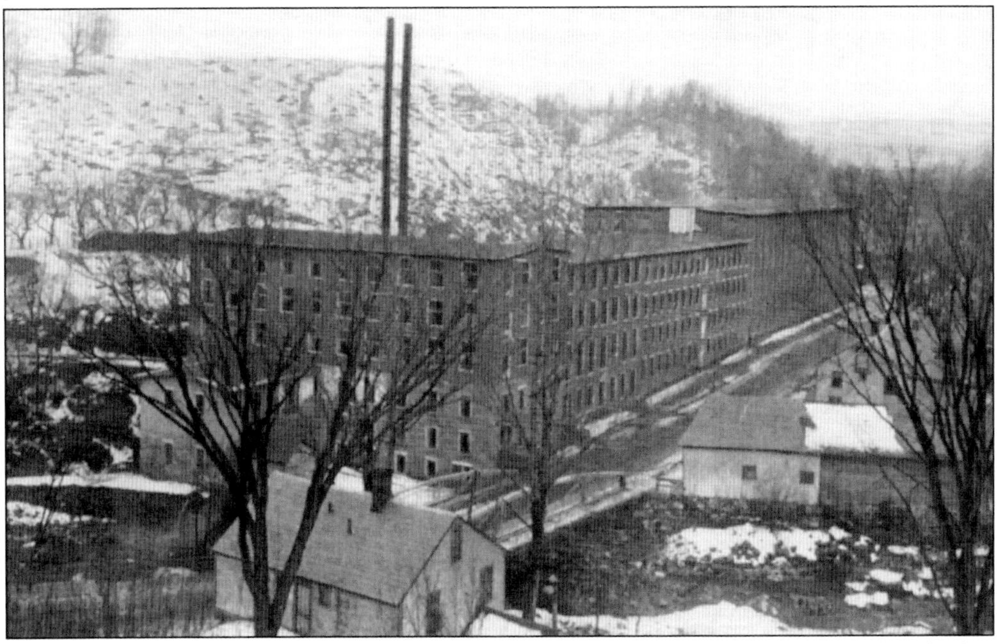

The Beaver Mill, situated on the eastern edge of the town, was named after a beaver dam farther east on this branch of the Hoosic River. Lorenzo Rice and George Bly erected the first building and then persuaded the town leadership to finance a road that passed in front of it, on the way to Clarksburg. Initially home to just 20 looms, Beaver Mill grew, survived fires, and passed through several owners before it landed in the 1880s in the capable hands of Albert C. Houghton and William A. Gallup. They oversaw an operation that employed 150 men, women, and children, with 210 looms that weekly produced 1,500 pieces of print cloth.

In 1810, Artemas Crittenden, a young clothier, moved to North Adams from Conway, Massachusetts. After helping to build several textile ventures, he was ready to start his own mill. In 1826, he purchased land known as the Gory lot, after an African American mill worker who resided there. Crittenden built the Union Mill, but sold out early when it passed through several different owners, including Samuel Ingalls and Sanford Blackinton. The mill operated until 1869, when it lay dormant for years. In 1882, mayor and mill owner Albert Houghton persuaded the town to buy the building for a new school. (Courtesy of the North Adams Historical Society.)

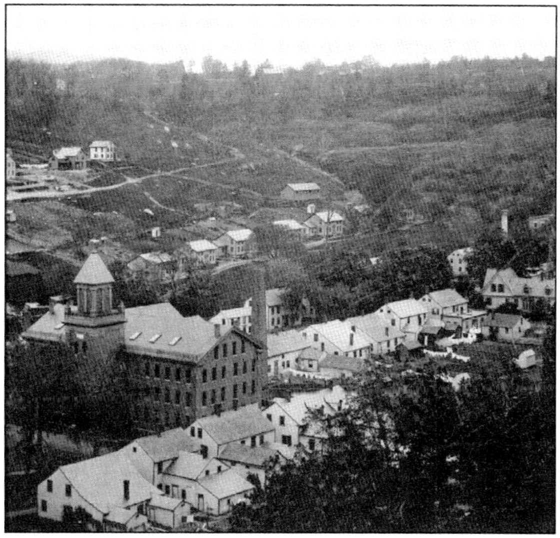

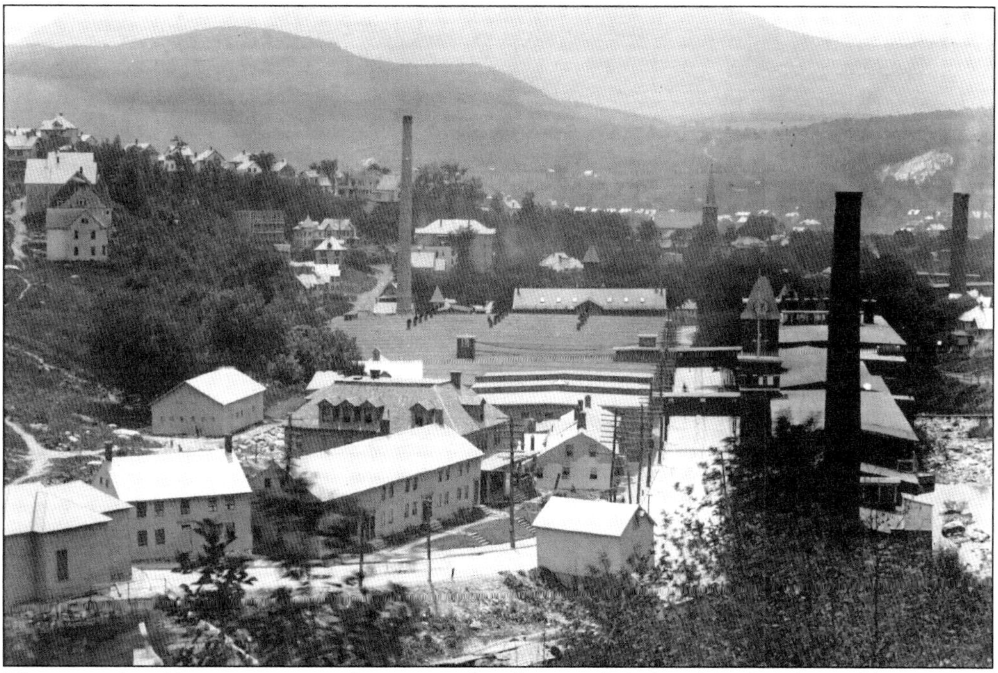

The name *Arnold* is most commonly associated with printed cloth in North Adams. Oliver Arnold moved to the town with his family in 1830 and went to work in a company that made machinery for textile production. Over the next 30 years, he and his younger brother Harvey bought up a series of failing mills and water privileges. One purchase in 1832 led to the construction of a stone mill that later became part of the Eclipse Mill in the Union section of the town. During the Civil War, the firm received lucrative contracts for the cloth used to make uniforms for the Union army. (Courtesy of the North Adams Historical Society.)

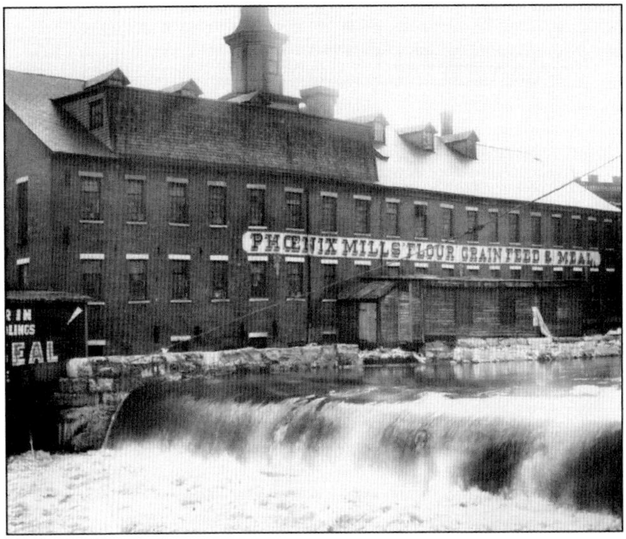

The lettering on the side of the Phoenix Mill in downtown North Adams indicates this is a flour and grain mill. While many textile and paper mills were built on the sites of gristmills, this building started in 1856 as a textile mill owned by Oliver Arnold and Willard Ray, who had invested in a large plot of land on the South Branch of the Hoosic River. Arnold built the Phoenix factory that would house 100 looms that produced textiles until 1873, when they sold this building to M.D. and A.W. Hodge, who reconfigured it as a flour mill.

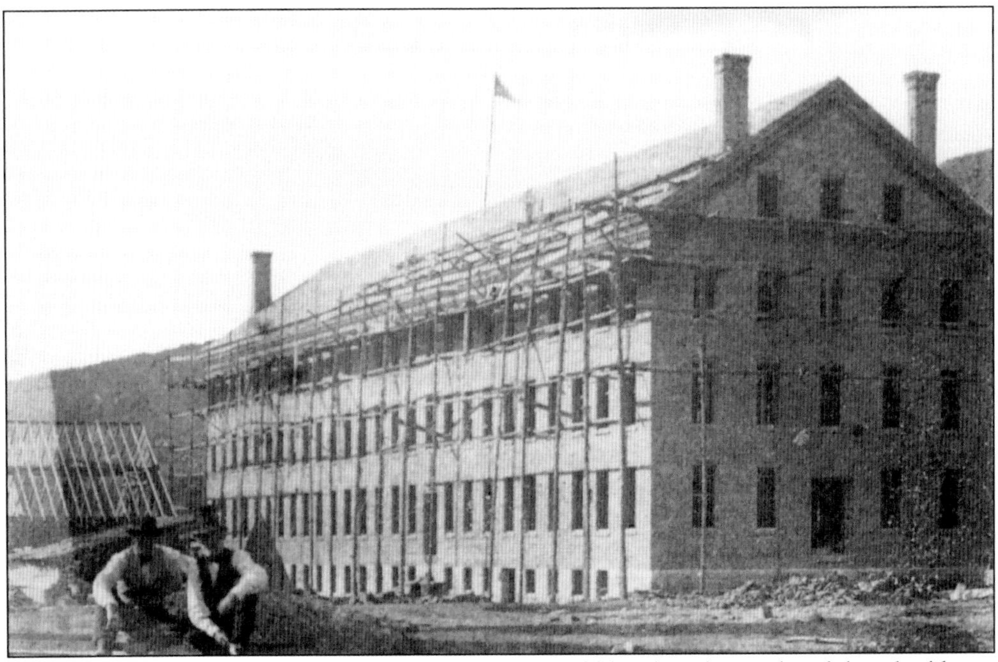

On December 27, 1871, in a tremendous fire, the Arnold brothers lost eight of their buildings. With cotton prices low and the demand for cloth high, they quickly set out to rebuild. They selected a site closer to the city center, located on the peninsula where the two branches of the Hoosic River meet. Boom turned to panic, and in 1876, the brothers sold their interest in the company to Albert Houghton and William Gallup, who were beginning to take control of much of the textiles in North Adams. This photograph shows the construction of Arnold Print Works at the new site. (Courtesy of the North Adams Historical Society.)

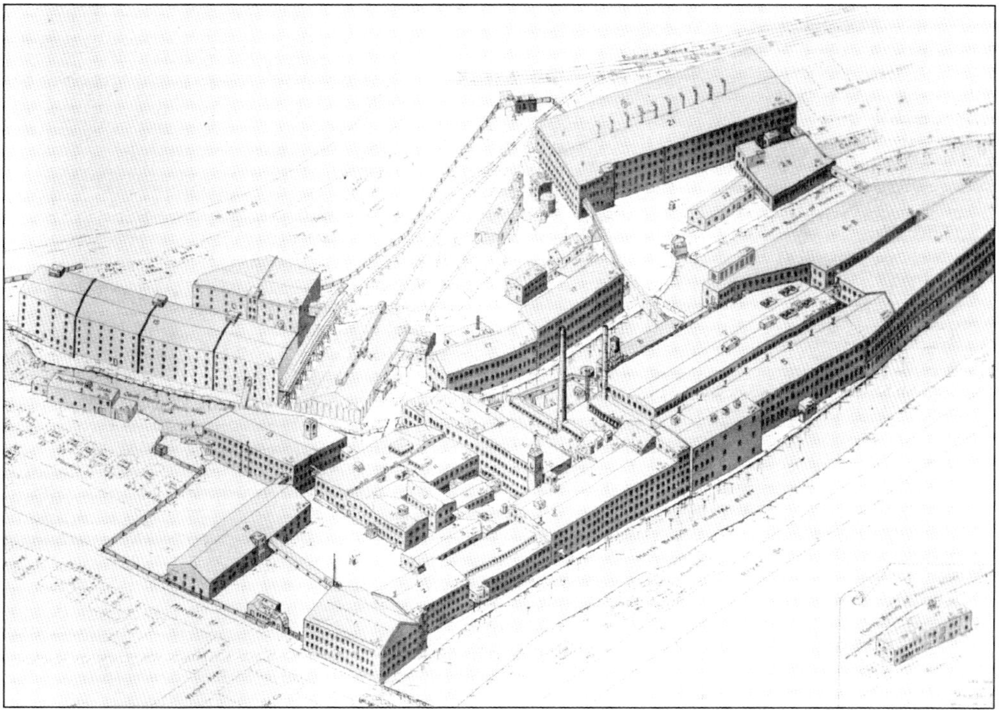

The new owners continued to invest heavily in the company, renamed as the Arnold Print Works. Across a site that spanned 24 acres in the center of North Adams, they erected a complex that consisted of eight buildings. By the turn of the 20th century, the company was the largest employer in the town, overtaking shoe manufacturing as the principal industry. With over 20 buildings now squeezed into the site and offices in New York and Paris, the company's global reach made it one of the largest printed cloth manufacturers in the world. More than 3,000 workers produced 330 miles of textiles cloth each week.

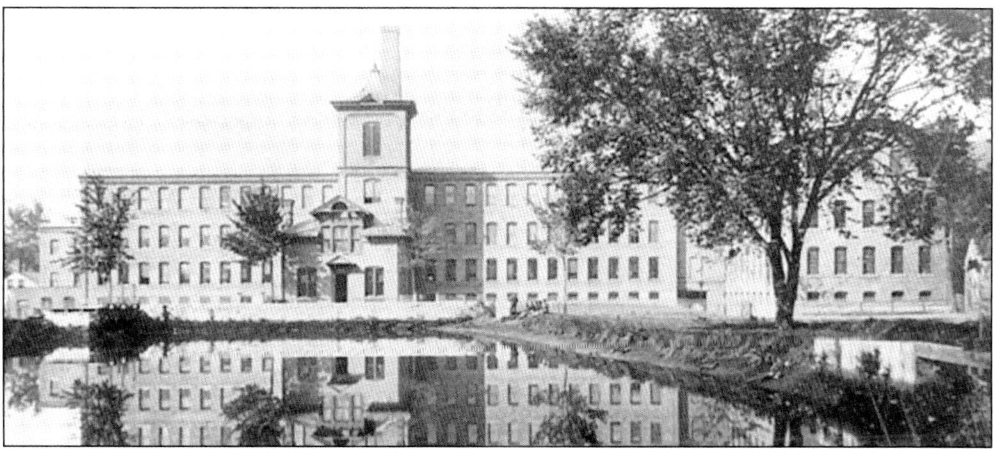

Just beyond where the two branches of the Hoosic River meet seemed an ideal site to capture the waterpower from both streams. There, a group of investors led by Sylvander Johnson in 1850 bought an unoccupied cotton mill that had been built in 1831 to print cloth. Johnson equipped the mill with looms and spindles to produce cotton warp. Fire destroyed the mill in 1871, but it was quickly rebuilt. Johnson ran the company until his death in 1882, when ownership was transferred to his son. (Courtesy of the North Adams Historical Society.)

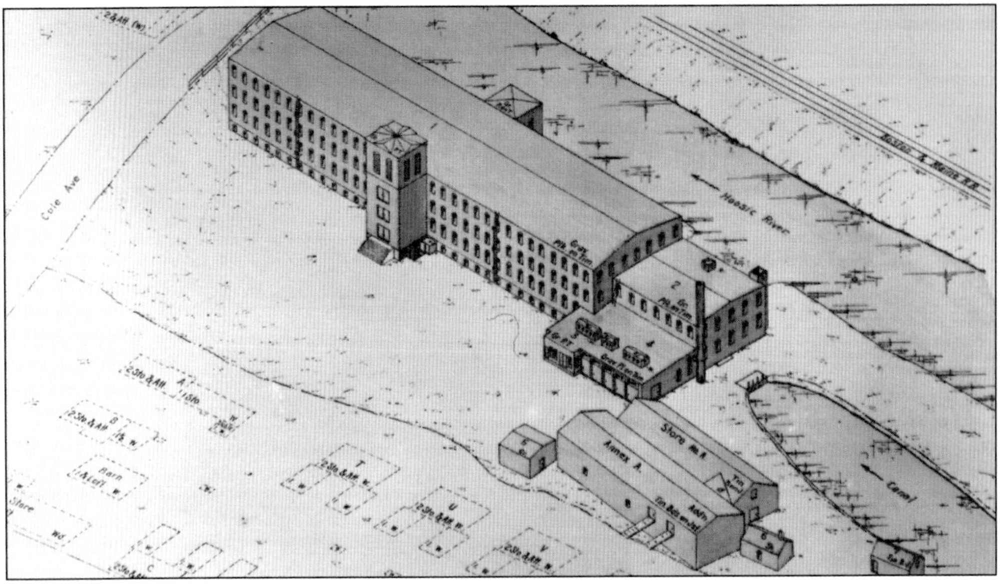

Greylock Mills managed to bring together ownership from three of the county's most well-known manufacturing names: Pomeroy, Plunkett, and Smith. Originally built in 1846 in the western part of North Adams, this cotton mill passed through several owners until 1880, when Theodore Pomeroy, who owned two mills in Pittsfield, bought this recently rebuilt brick factory. Two years later, William Plunkett, whose family had produced textiles in Adams since the 1820s, became president of the company. New worker housing helped draw the 325 people who ran the looms, which produced 250,000 yards of cotton cloth a month. Leadership eventually passed to Wellington Smith, whose family dominated paper manufacturing in Lee.

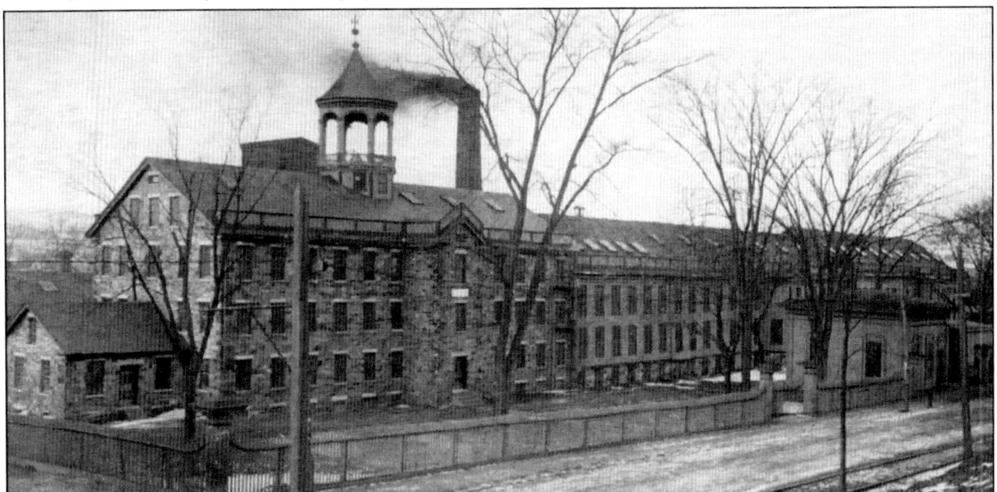

This end-of-the-19th-century photograph of the Blackinton Mill shows the old stone mill built in 1842 and a subsequent addition that extended the building to 500 feet in length. It was 25-year-old Sanford Blackinton who first introduced machine equipment in North Adams to produce wool. Given the ages of his partners, the original mill was nicknamed the "boys mill," and after the new complex was built, it continued to serve as a storage facility. Close to the town line with Williamstown, the business flourished, and a small village bearing the Blackinton family name grew up around the mill buildings.

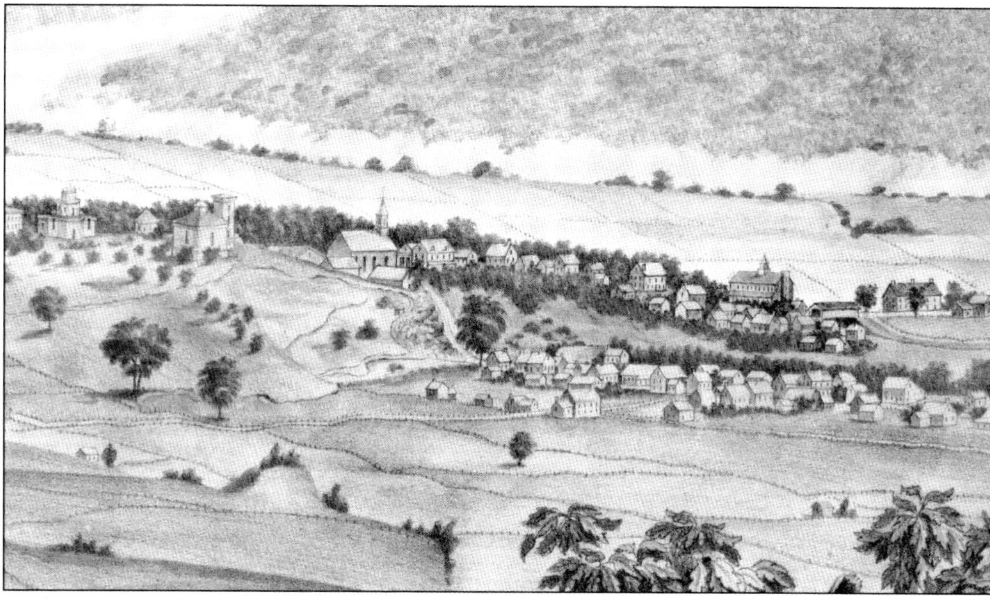

Farther west, before the waters of the Green River reach the Hoosic, early settlers of Williamstown harnessed the waterpower for a sawmill and a gristmill. Here, the town's first factory, a cotton mill, was built in 1826 by Caleb Turner. The mill employed 41 people working 1,000 spindles. Stephen Walley bought the operation and added looms and other machinery to produce print cloth. He successfully ran the company through the Civil War, before the Panic of 1873 drove him to sell to the president of Williams College, Paul Chadbourne. This close-up of George Yeoman's print from 1856 shows the Walley Mill with the covered bridge crossing the Green River. (Courtesy of the New York Public Library.)

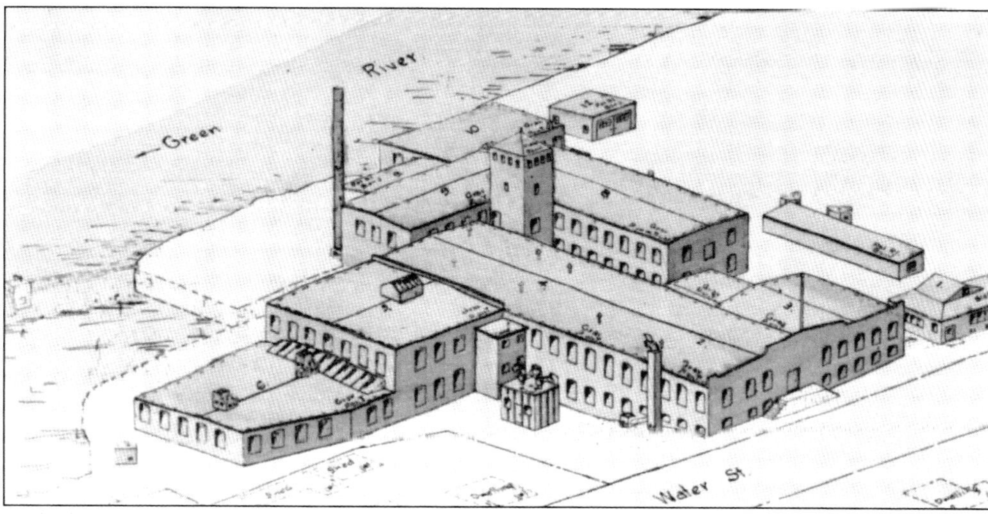

Unlucky timing doomed a new twine manufacturing company, farther upstream on the Green River in Williamstown, under the name of Loop, Hopkins & Company. Started at the time of the Panic of 1873, the firm struggled for 10 years, with a workforce coming from just three immigrant families—two from Quebec and one from Ireland. The buildings lay vacant from 1883 until 1892, when Boston Finishing Works bought the mill and added new buildings to house new looms and bleaching and dye operations. With mills moving south, the company folded in 1906 and later became Cable Mills; the building is now an apartment complex by that name.

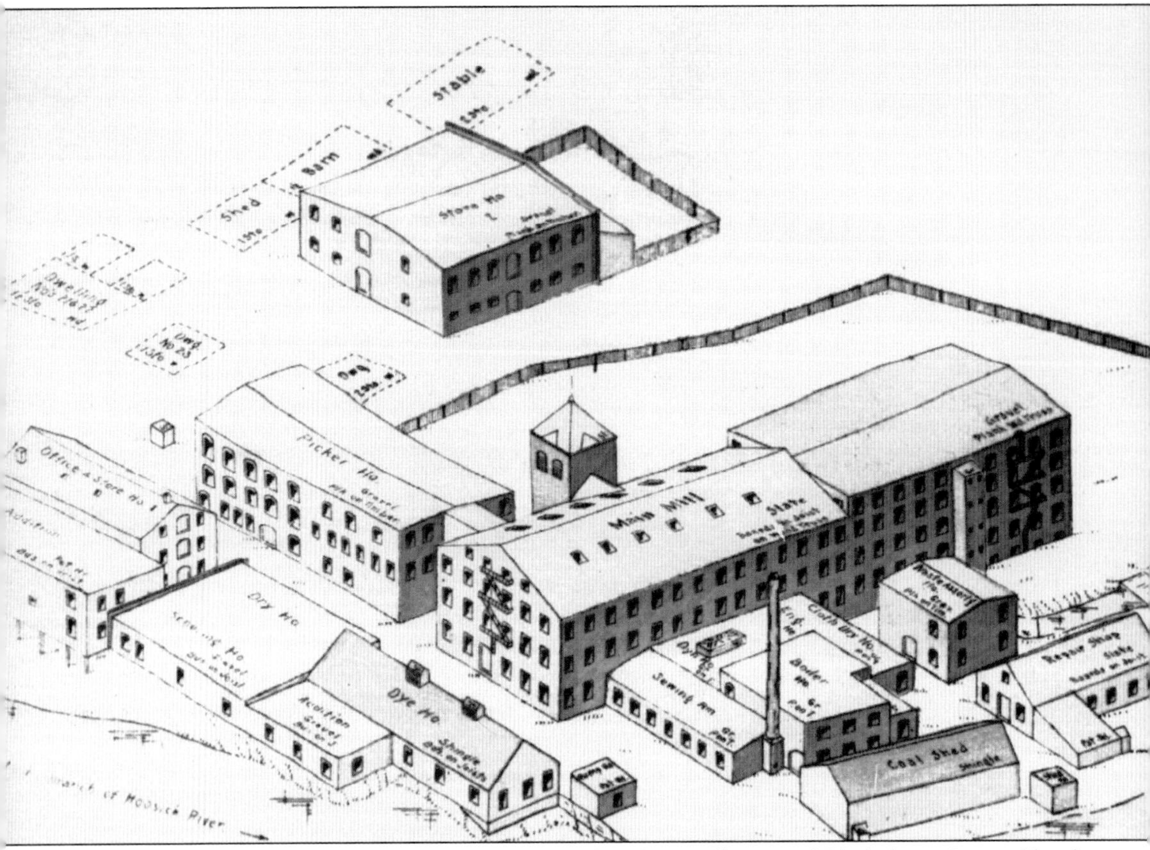

The textile activity of North Adams also spread to the small town of Clarksburg. Spurred by the demand for textiles in the Civil War, C.W. and Henry Briggs built their first mill alongside the North Branch of the Hoosic River. With a new, large brick building, they called their concern the Briggs Brothers Mill. Housing for workers turned the small settlement into Briggsville. The company made union cassimeres and melton, a fabric used for overcoats. The company lasted until 1883, when it was bought out by Stephen Linwood of Troy, New York. He in turn sold the premises in 1898 to Richard Hewat and Richard Strong who converted production to high-quality custom designed cloth.

Three

Paper

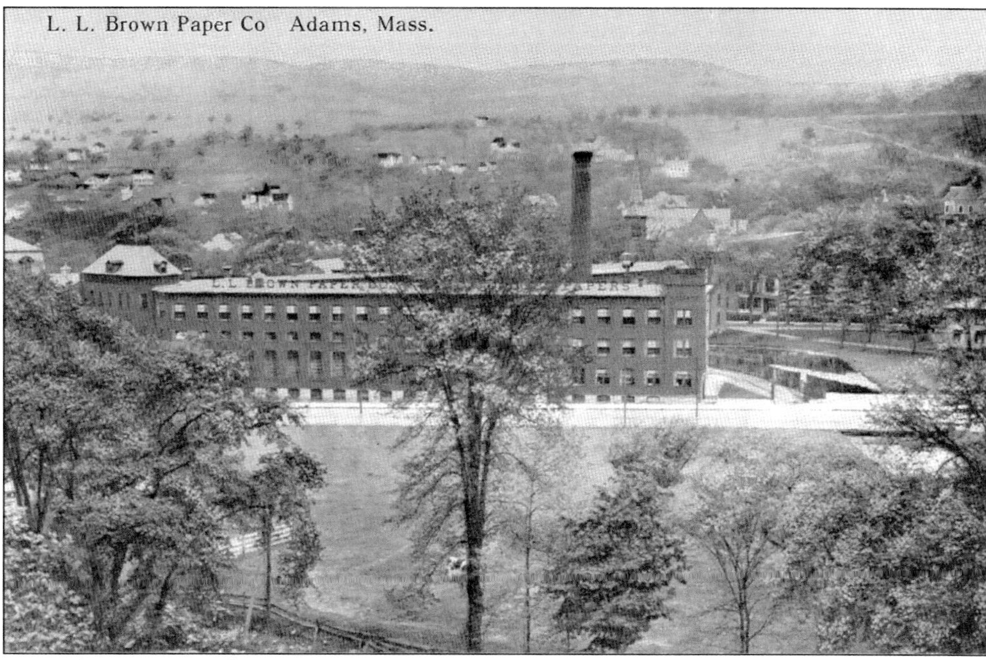

For its dominance in the nation, papermaking in Berkshire County stands apart. Mills sprang up first in Dalton, then quickly moved south to Lee, but the contagion also spread to other towns throughout the area. The L.L. Brown mill in Adams, pictured in this postcard, shows the stark contrast between an idyllic landscape nestled into the Berkshire Hills and an imposing brick structure. Paper brought prosperity and a livelihood to the region, the owners and the workers. The large smokestack hints that this growth came at a cost, certainly to the surroundings and the health of the workers.

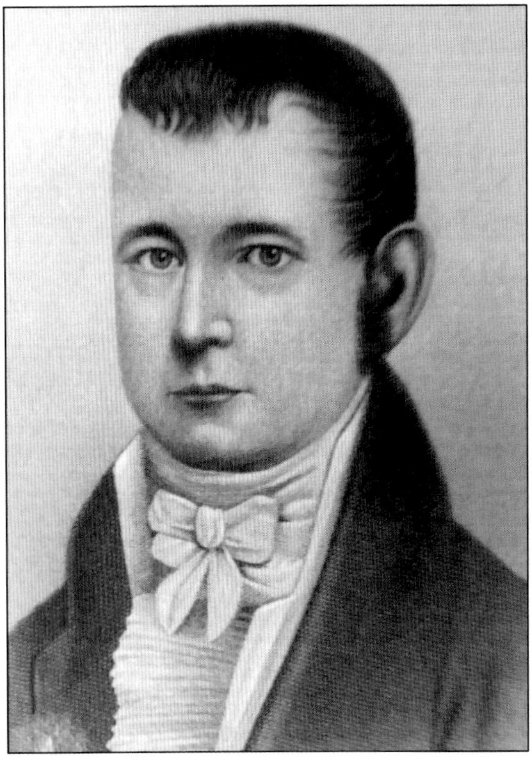

The story of the paper industry in the Berkshires begins with the arrival in 1799 of a young Zenas Crane, who had worked in a paper company in Worcester, Massachusetts. Anxious to start out on his own, he pushed west and, after scouting around, found all the necessary elements he would need to start his own paper concern in Dalton. Most importantly, he found not only the fast-flowing water but also water that was spring fed and of such pure quality that his paper would be free of the imperfections from water with too many minerals in it. (Courtesy of Crane Museum of Papermaking.)

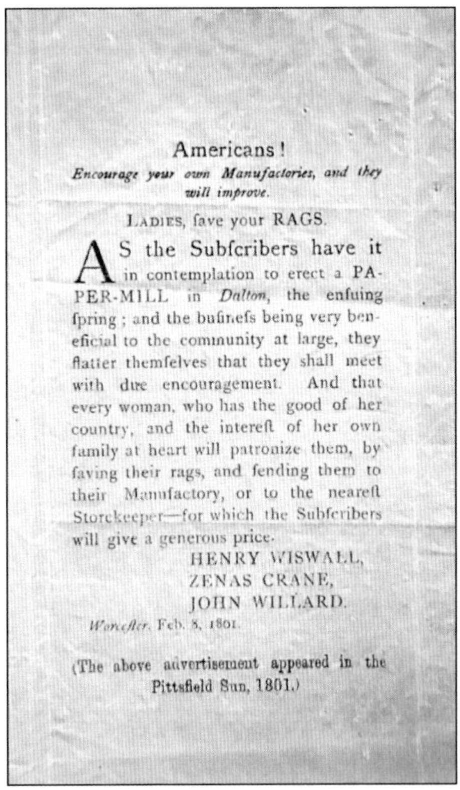

Americans!

Encourage your own Manufactories, and they will improve.

LADIES, fave your RAGS.

AS the Subfcribers have it in contemplation to erect a PAPER-MILL in *Dalton*, the enfuing fpring; and the bufinefs being very beneficial to the community at large, they flatter themfelves that they shall meet with due encouragement. And that every woman, who has the good of her country, and the intereft of her own family at heart will patronize them, by faving their rags, and fending them to their Manufactory, or to the neareft Storekeeper—for which the Subfcribers will give a generous price.

HENRY WISWALL,
ZENAS CRANE,
JOHN WILLARD.

Worcefter, Feb. 8, 1801.

(The above advertisement appeared in the Pittsfield Sun, 1801.)

The young Crane learned of nearby lime deposits that he would need for bleaching his paper products. He had no competition in locally collecting the rags needed to produce the pulp, and he was pleased that Berkshire residents used the flax they grew to make their clothing from linen. Linen rags produced a higher-quality paper. So, his first ad in the *Pittsfield Sun* encouraged women to "save your rags . . . for which the Subscriber will give a generous price." (Courtesy of Crane Museum of Papermaking.)

Crane purchased 14 acres of land from local Dalton farmer Martin Chamberlin for $194. With investors Daniel Gilbert and Henry Wiswell, Crane built his first mill, which came to be known as the Old Berkshire Mill. In the 1840s, Crane's large-sized "foolscap" paper bore this logo on its wrapper. It displays a drawing of the original wood-frame mill, two stories high, on the eastern branch of the Housatonic. Note the patriotic appeal with the federal eagles and the official motto of Massachusetts, translated to read, "By the sword we seek peace, but peace only under liberty."

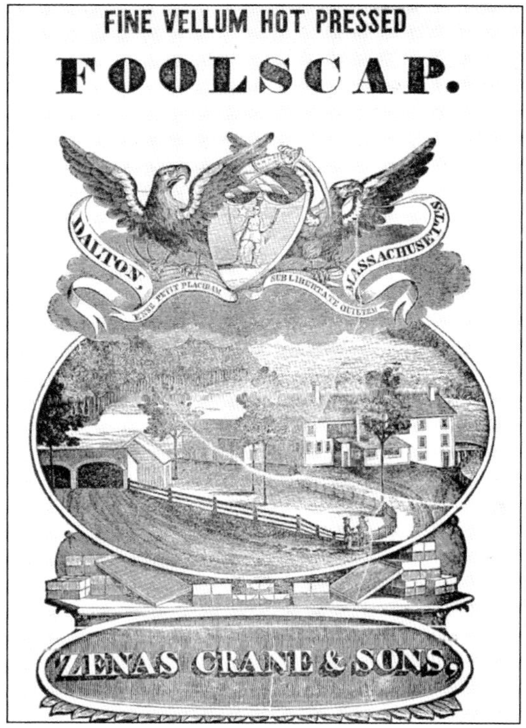

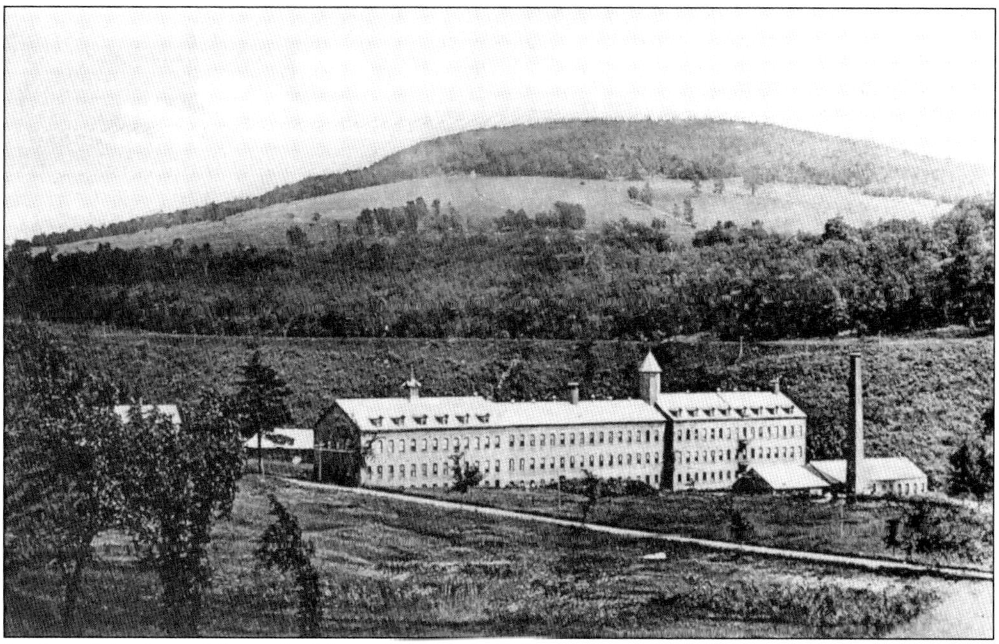

In the original wood-frame building, Crane hired a handful of men and women, eventually taking on his own sons and nephews to learn the papermaking trade. Within just a few years, Crane sold the mill to Henry Wiswell, his remaining partner. Crane reemerged as an owner just two years later and eventually sold out to a group led by David Carson. He and, later, his sons continued to operate the Old Berkshire Mill well into the 20th century, dominating the Dalton landscape, as this postcard shows.

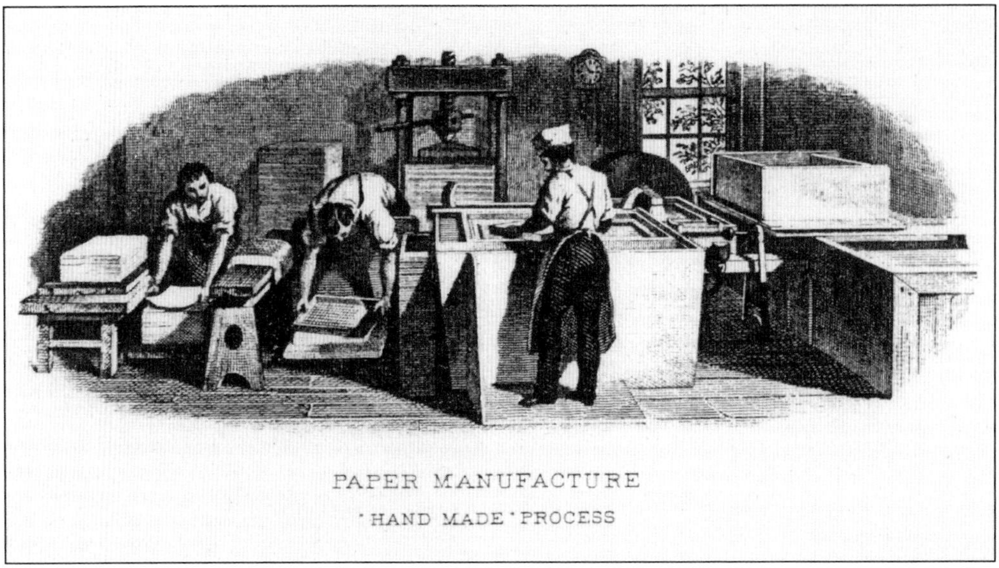

Paper was still almost exclusively made by hand. Women were hired to cut up the rags that arrived at the factory in bundles to remove excess dust and to sort the rags by color. Men would operate the Hollander beater—a large, wooden tub that had a spiked cylinder over which the rags would roll so their fibers would be broken down. In the next stage, a skilled vatman would immerse a two-tiered frame and mold into the pulp mixture. When he lifted the frame, water would drain, and he would then shift the mixture back and forth into an even sheet with the desired thickness.

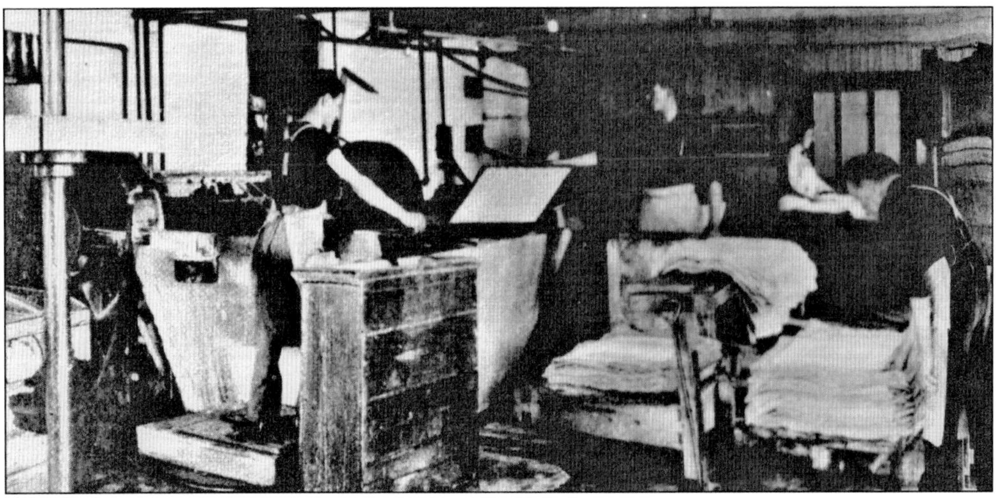

Another perspective of papermaking by hand comes in this photograph of the L.L. Brown Paper Company in Adams, the last of the Berkshire paper manufacturers to operate a hand process. In this photograph, the vatman is actually a woman who has just dipped her framed mold into the mixture. The man on the right is stacking the paper sheeting that has just emerged from the mold. In 1901, the *New England Stationer* carried a story on William Brown and his son Walter who carried on this tradition of handmade paper for the small market who desired this quality.

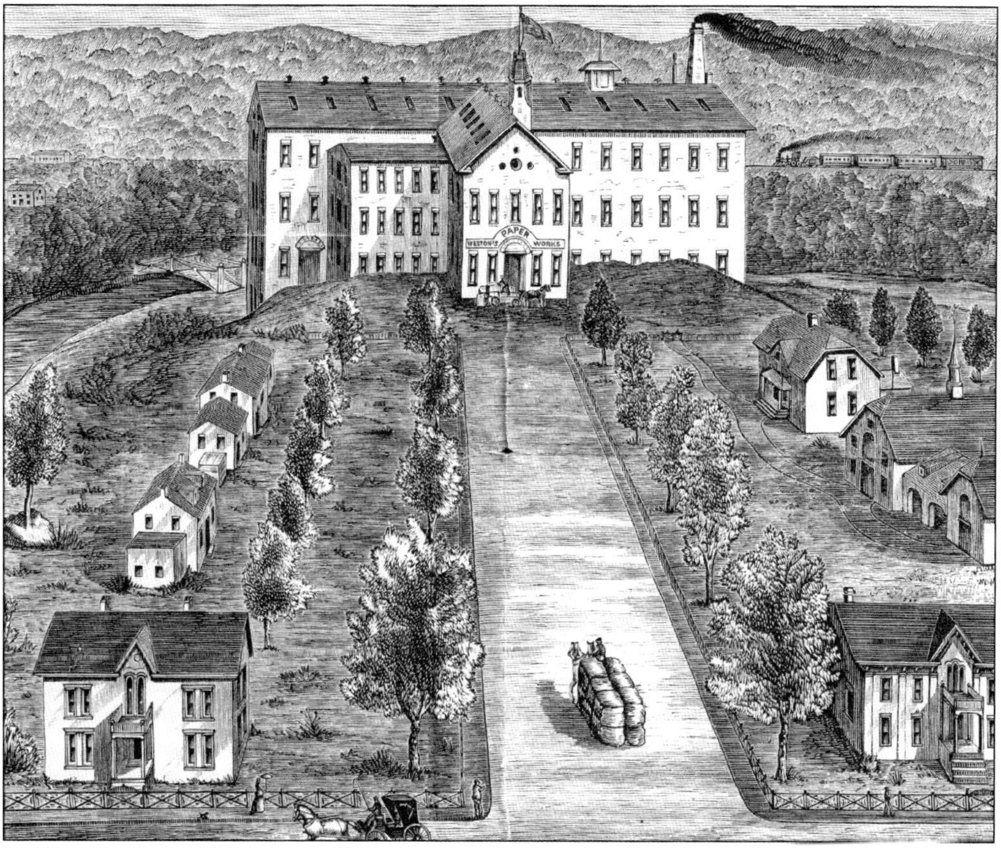

In a pattern that would repeat itself throughout the 1800s, ownership splintered and divided. Zenas Crane sold his stake in the factory to devote time to finding new clients and markets. David Carson, who had worked as a hand papermaker in Crane's factory, joined forces with Joseph Chamberlin in 1823 to build the Defiance Mill in Dalton. With only one vat and one beating machine, the factory produced 126 sheets of paper a day. By the 1860s, after a fire, Byron Weston bought and expanded the Defiance Mill to the point where it was producing over two tons of paper a day. Weston's house stands in the lower corner, within walking distance of his mill.

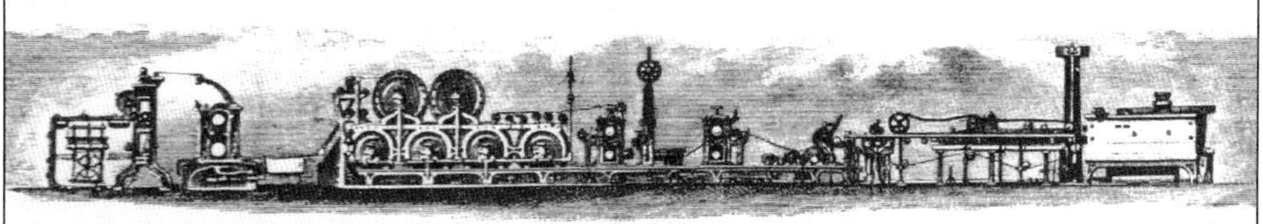

FOURDRINIER MACHINE

Byron Weston grew up in Dalton around the local papermaking process, but moved to Saugerties, New York, to become an apprentice in his uncle's factory. That company was one of the first to import from England a papermaking machine named after its inventor, Henry Fourdrinier. This continuous papermaking machine replaced the skilled but tedious operation of the frame and mold handling. It required a lot more water and space to house the machine. Owners had to expand their buildings and even branch out to other sites to accommodate these new machines that could produce much more paper than the hand processing.

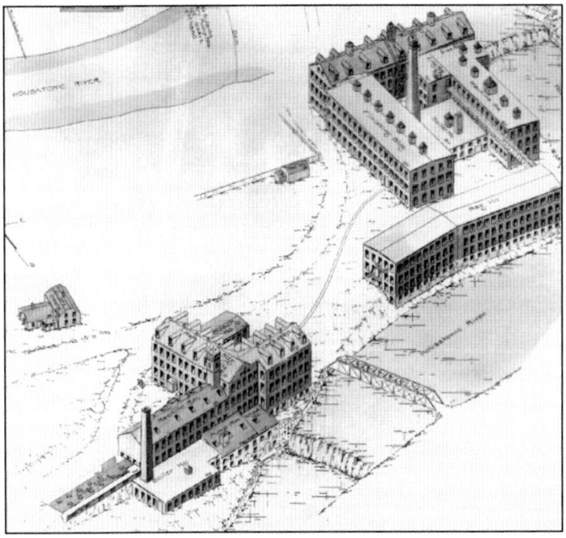

With the success of his Defiance Mill, Weston bought the old, failing Centennial Mill that had been built by Albert Chamberlin 20 years earlier and had gone through various owners and tenants, including the Crane family. After a fire in 1875, Weston purchased the old mill building, which he greatly expanded over the next two decades. This Associated Mutual Insurance drawing shows both of his mills, strategically placed at a bend in the Housatonic with two dams to supply water. Always in search of pure water to improve the quality of his paper, Weston dug two deep artesian wells that together could flow at the rate of over 500 gallons per minute.

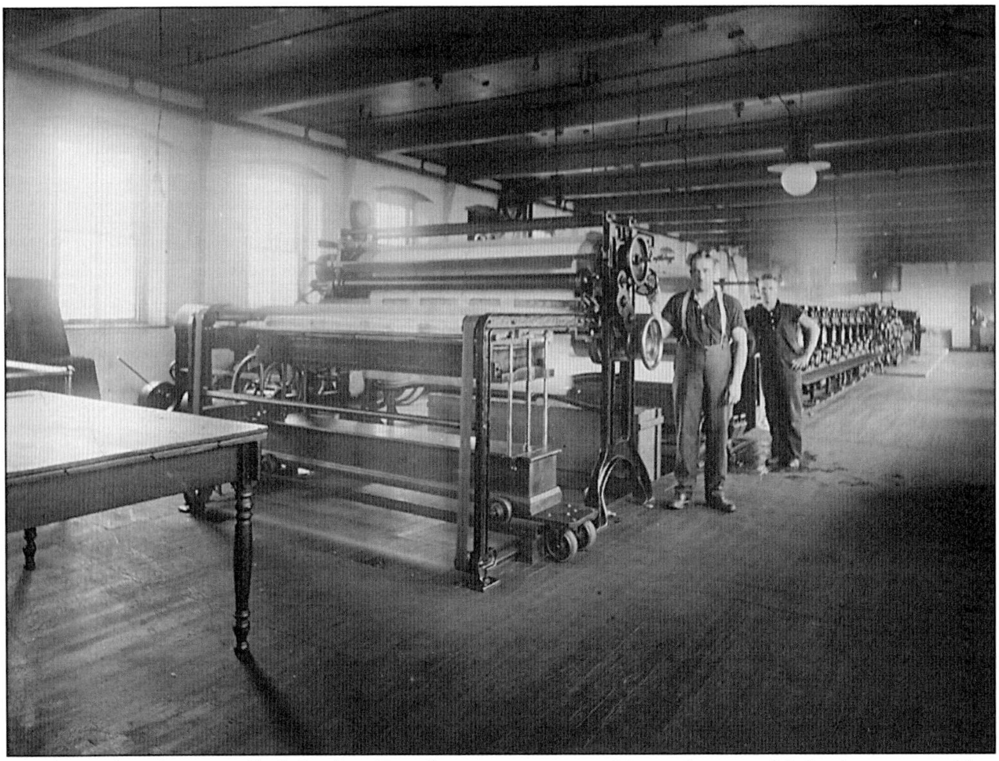

Stephen Thatcher installed the first Fourdrinier in western Massachusetts. He had convinced his former employer Zenas Crane to invest in a new mill on farmland that Thatcher's family owned in East Lee. That mill proved so successful that Thatcher was able to buy out Crane within a couple of years. Thatcher incorporated the latest machinery and processes into the mill. This 1890s photograph shows two employees of the Crane Mill standing near the finished rolled paper produced on the Fourdrinier after making its way through the long sifting, shaking, and flattening of the pulp.

After more than four decades of papermaking, Zenas Crane stepped down as owner of the greatly expanded Red Mill in Dalton. He turned the business over to his sons Zenas Marshall Crane and James Brewer Crane. In need of more space to house the large machines, the two sons built a new mill made of stone in 1844, just two years after taking over the company. The Stone Mill doubled paper production for the Cranes until 1869 when it burned. Today, the rag room of the Stone Mill survives as the iconic home for the Crane Museum of Papermaking.

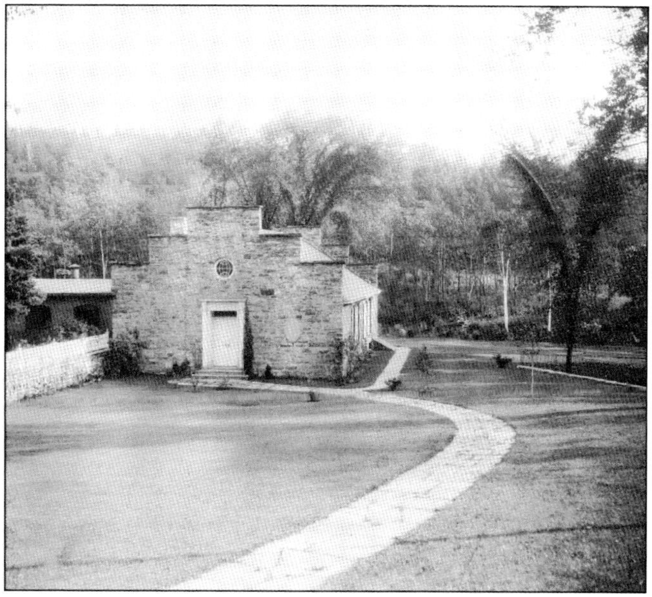

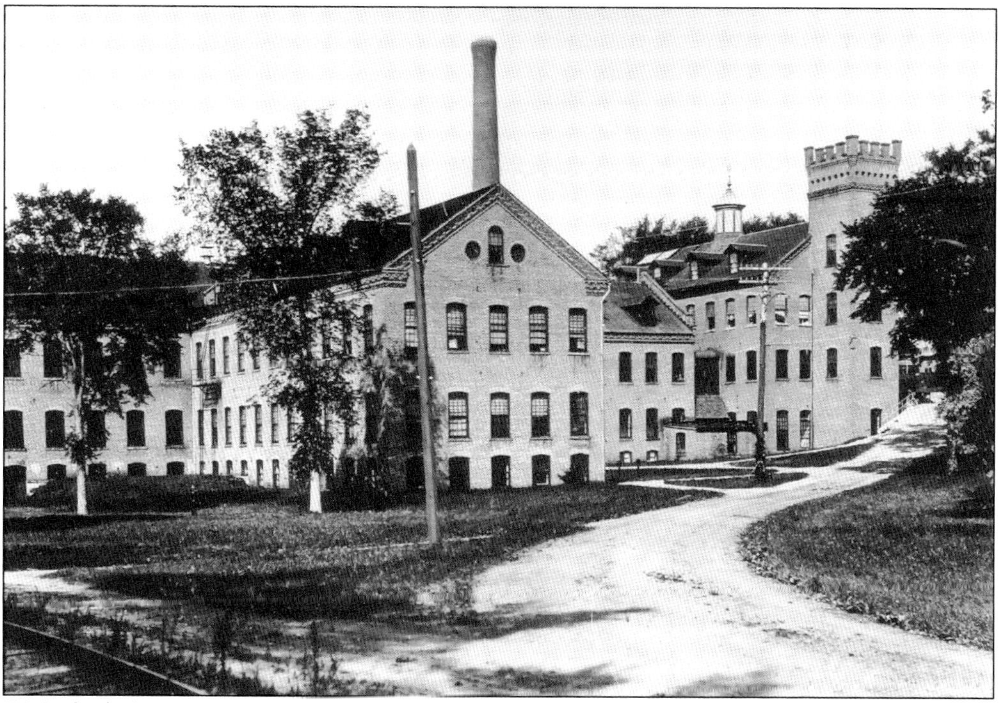

With the help of his brothers as silent partners, Seymour Crane, the third of the founder's sons, bought Ashuelot Manufacturing, an old woolen mill in Dalton in 1851. He converted the facility into a papermaking operation, but he did not enjoy the success of his brothers, however. The company failed in 1857, and a year later, his brothers bought up the mill situated further upstream. They changed the name to Bay State Mill, and after a fire in yet another Crane facility in 1877, they rebuilt it. This early-1900s photograph shows the mill that is still in operation today.

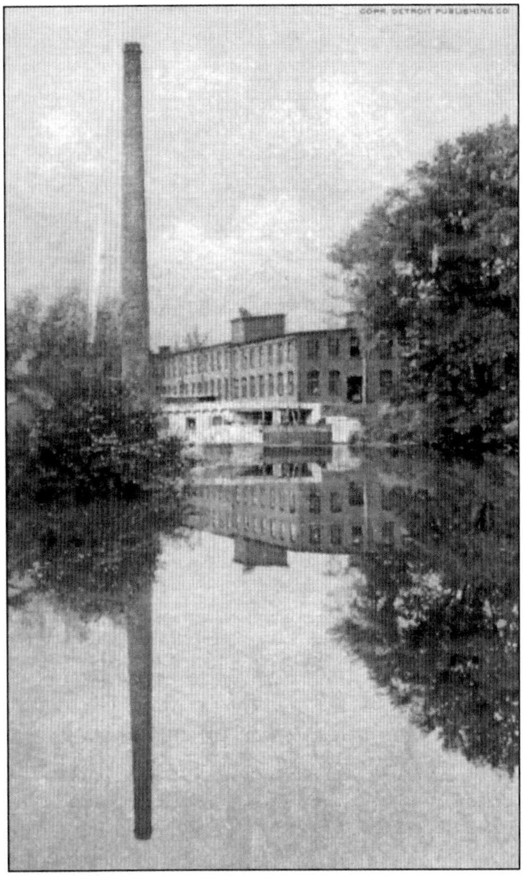

In 1879, Winthrop Murray Crane, the grandson of Zenas Crane, secured a contract with the US Treasury to produce the paper for currency. Crane identified a vacant paper mill just over the town line in Pittsfield, downstream from the other Crane mills. Shut down during the Panic of 1873, the Colt Paper Mill had operated since 1847 on the site of an old tannery. Thomas Colt had purchased the facility in 1851, where he dug the first artesian well in western Massachusetts to ensure the quality of his paper. Here is a postcard of the Government Mill that the Cranes built to replace the Colt facility after a fire in 1892.

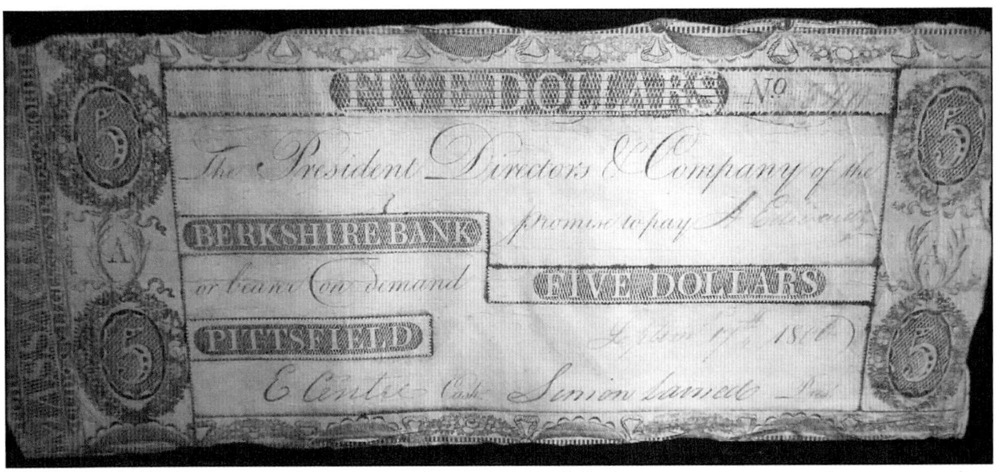

Before the US Treasury printed money, banks printed their own paper notes that promised to pay customers the amount noted. The first bank in Berkshire County had this $5 bill printed at Zenas Crane's original factory in 1801. The unscrupulous director of this bank, Andrew Dexter, convinced the bank to place large sums of their deposits in Boston, which he promptly used to build a hotel and office space for the state's exchange office, which regulated banks. The Berkshire Bank failed in 1810, and several of the local directors landed in the Lenox jail. (Courtesy of Crane Museum of Papermaking.)

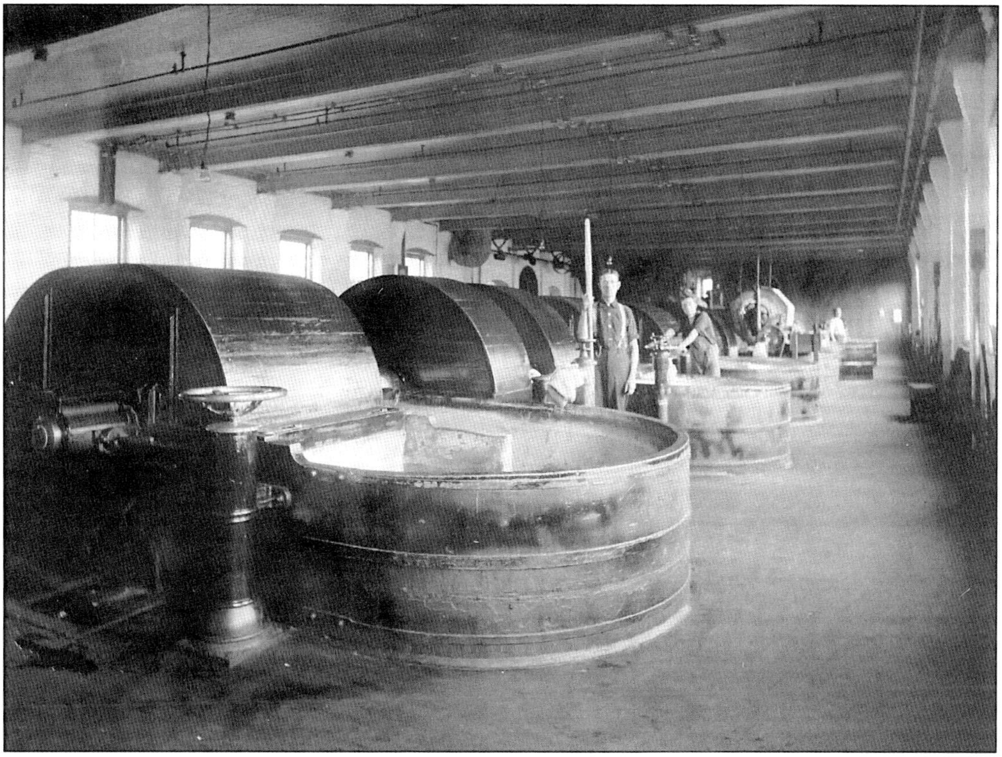

In this beating room, workers operate vats that turn over and pull apart the cut and cleaned rags into pulp, using large quantities of water. It is estimated that for every ton of paper produced, 100 tons of water are needed to prepare the pulp. Lime and other chemicals are added to clean and bleach the pulp. In the background, one worker turns the water valve for the second vat while his colleague stands beside the front vat with a heavy wooden pole used for stirring the pulp and breaking up and unclogging any large chunks. (Courtesy of Crane Museum of Papermaking.)

In this 1890s photograph of the drying room in one of the finishing buildings of Crane's mills in Dalton, individual sheets of paper are hung to dry. After the pressing of the pulp, the paper moves to a cutting area before arriving here for drying. Until machines were introduced for drying, sheets of paper were hung in heated rooms. This worker is separating and stacking the individual sheets that would then move on to the next phase of coating the sheets with sizing. (Courtesy of Crane Museum of Papermaking.)

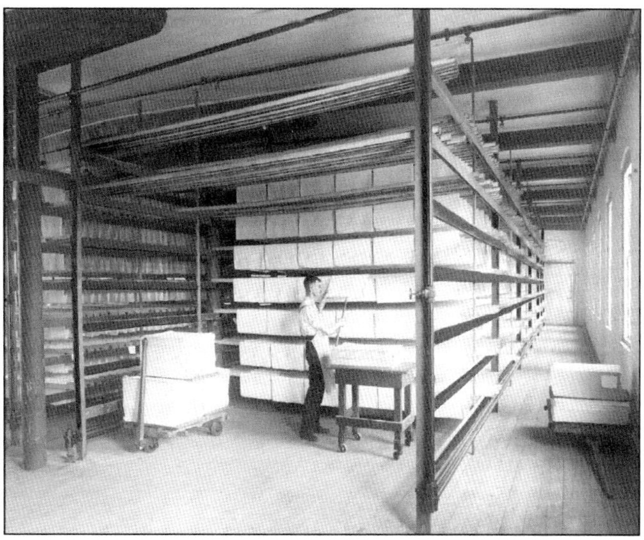

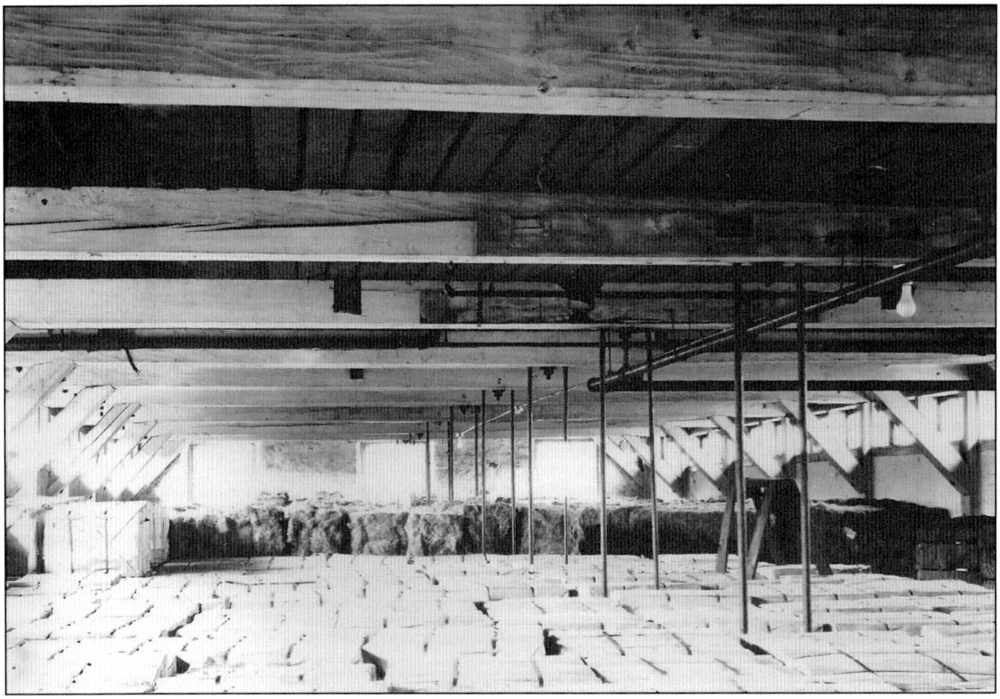

The interior of the large storage area at the Bay State Mill holds both wrapped pulp, probably from wood, and bales of rags waiting for processing. The large wrapped cubes of pulp are brought in on rail and stacked in the warehouse. In winter, they arrive frozen, making them easier to move and stack. Crane facilities produced paper for all uses: parchment, tracing, architectural drawing, and deed recording. Such paper had to be of the highest quality to withstand the wearing and aging of important legal documents. In addition, Crane perfected dyeing techniques to produce the finest ladies' stationery, using tints that had come from France in the production of silk there.

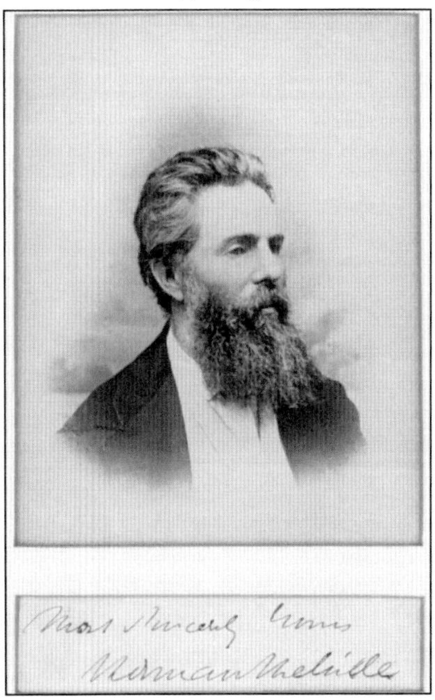

Herman Melville moved to Pittsfield in November 1850, bringing with him a draft of a book about a whale. His need for paper to complete the book led him to visit Crane's Red Mill in Dalton, Massachusetts. He later described the mill in the short story "The Tartarus of Maids," which appeared in *Harper's Magazine* in April 1856. "Where stands the mill?" he wrote. "Suddenly a whirring, humming sound broke upon my ear. I looked, and there, like an arrested avalanche, lay the large whitewashed factory." Sounds a little like a whale.

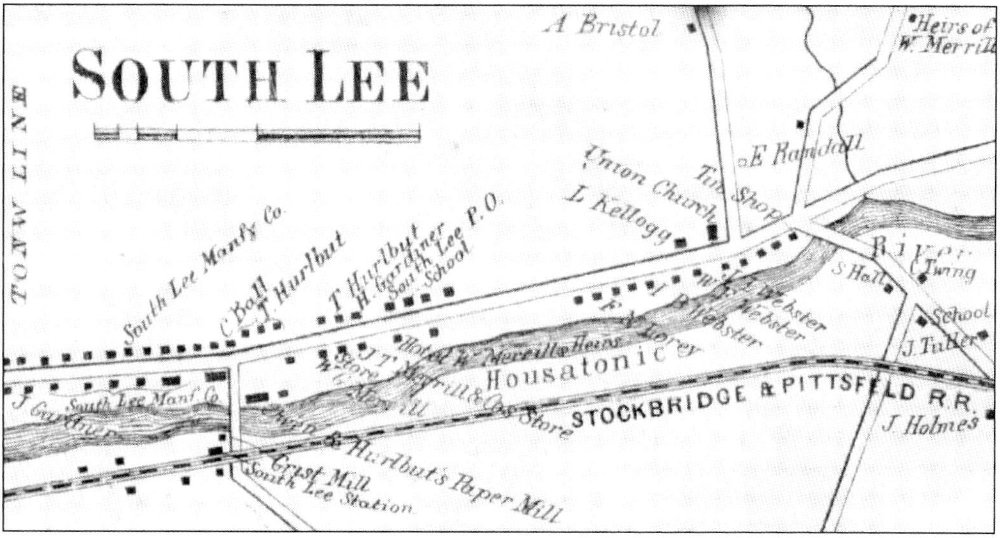

The second paper mill in Berkshire County was built in Lee in 1806. Fifty years later, the town, in its three villages, could boast 25 paper mills and produced more paper than any town in the country. In 1806, Samuel Church, who learned papermaking in Connecticut, moved to Lee to branch out on his own, building a two-vat complex in South Lee that he called the Willow Mill. He sold the mill in 1822 to a new company started by Charles Owen and Thomas Hurlbut; it was renamed by mid-century to South Lee Manufacturing Company. This 1858 map of South Lee shows the complex, which includes housing for workers and the railroad station that opened in 1848.

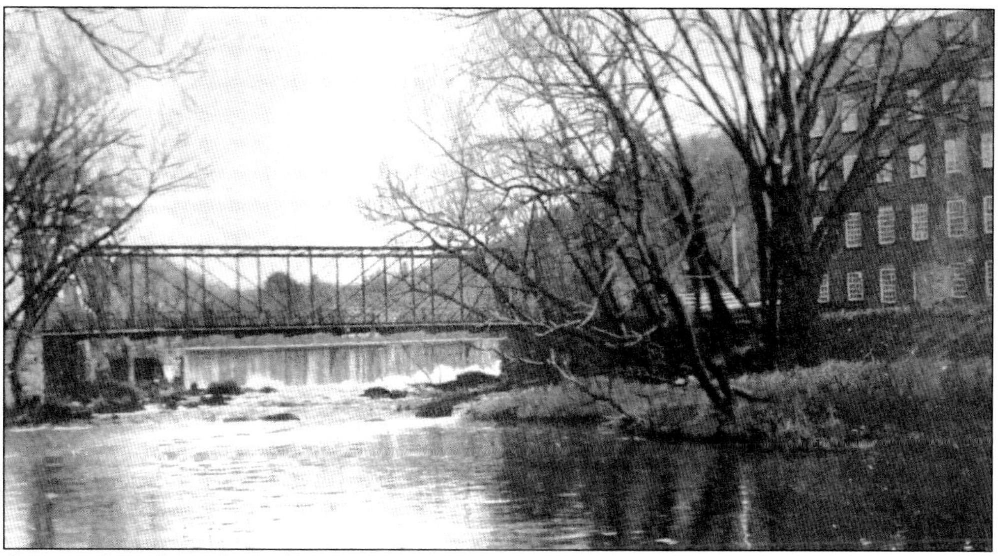
Owen and Hurlbut rebuilt the original Willow Mill, giving it an apt new name, the Phoenix Mill. By 1860, Owen decided to focus his business interests elsewhere, so he sold his share of the mill to Hurlbut and his sons. A year later, the elder Hurlbut died, but his sons continued to expand the business. Near the Phoenix, in 1872, they built a large four-story mill, measuring 373 feet in length that could produce 10,000 pounds of writing paper a day. The importance of water for paper production is clearly shown in this Christmas card of the new Hurlbut Mill.

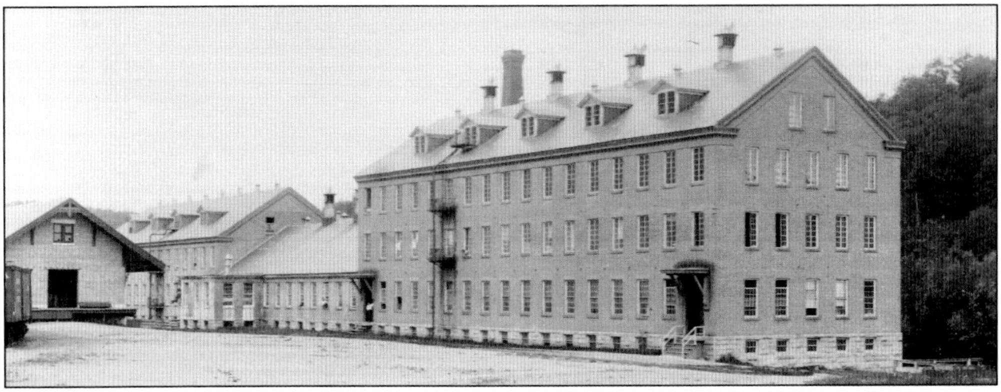

When the Phoenix Mill burned in 1883, the Hurlbuts decided not to rebuild that mill. Their new building was all they needed to meet their customers' orders. Four solitary workers are barely visible in the doorway and windows of this massive plant in this 19th-century photograph, which had to have been taken on a Sunday or holiday given the absence of the bustling activity expected during a normal workday. On the extreme left near the warehouse is the front of a railroad car on a spur to load and unload materials and finished product.

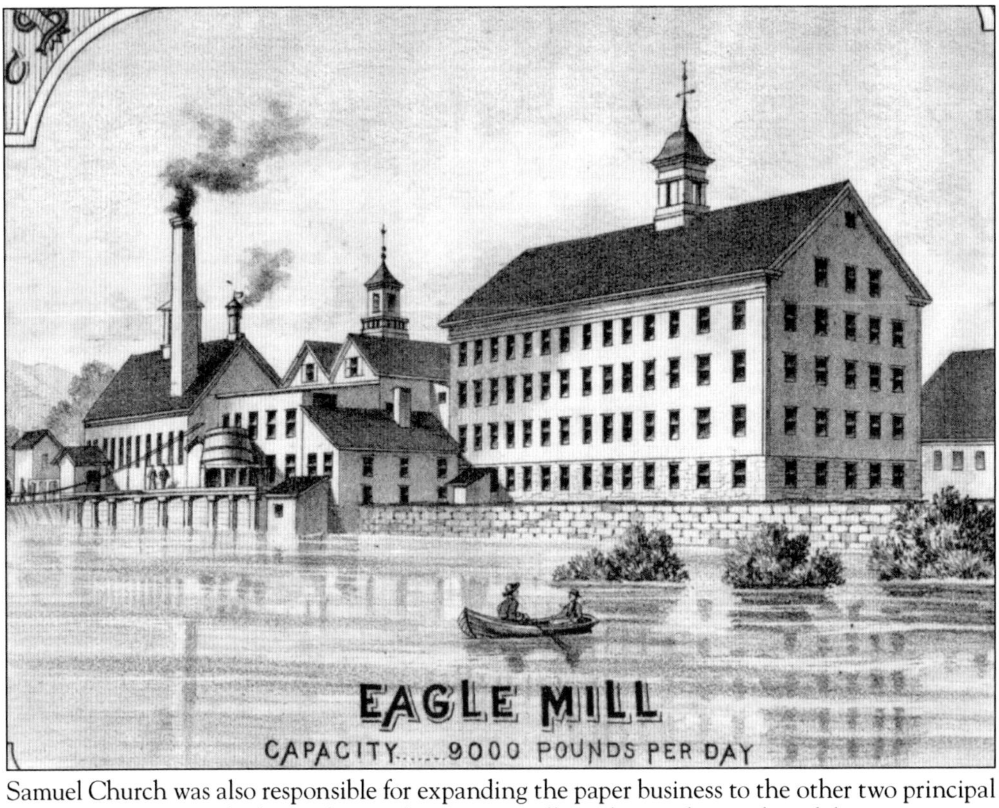

Samuel Church was also responsible for expanding the paper business to the other two principal sites in Lee. In 1808, he located a site for a paper mill on the northern edge of the town center, upstream on the Housatonic. There, he built the Union Mill that his two sons, Joseph and Leonard, would buy and operate for 20 years. A third son, Luman, bought an old carriage shop adjacent to Union Mill and converted it into a paper mill. After the devastating Panic of 1837, the brothers sold both mills to George Platner and a young Elizur Smith, who changed the name of Luman's original mill to the Eagle Mill.

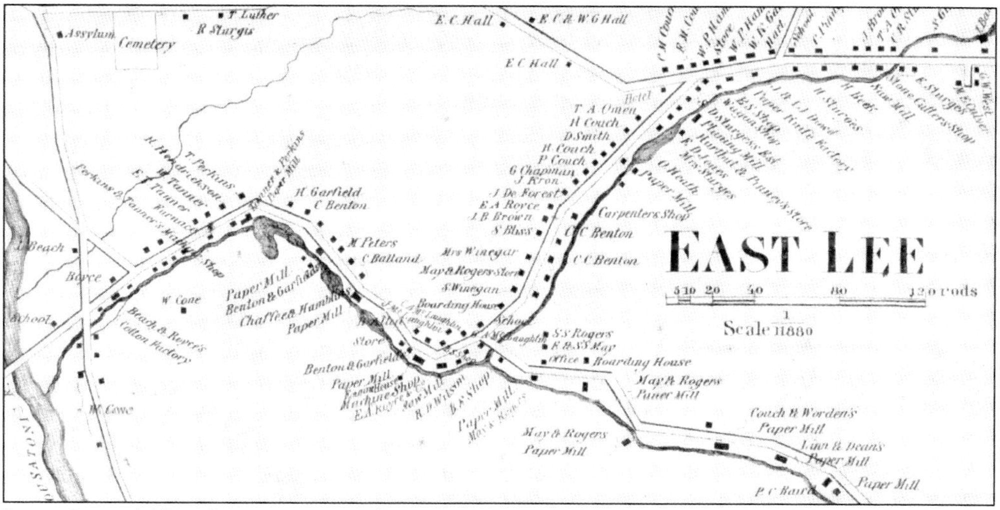

It was Samuel Church's son Luman who opened up East Lee for the papermaking business, building the Forest Mill, undoubtedly named for the surrounding woodlands, in 1819. On the Lake May Stream feeding into the Housatonic, Church placed an overshot waterwheel 30 feet in diameter. His two brothers operated the mill, making high-quality writing paper. By the time this Walling map was drawn in 1858, Caleb Benton and Harrison Garfield owned the Forest Mill, marked just to the left of the map center.

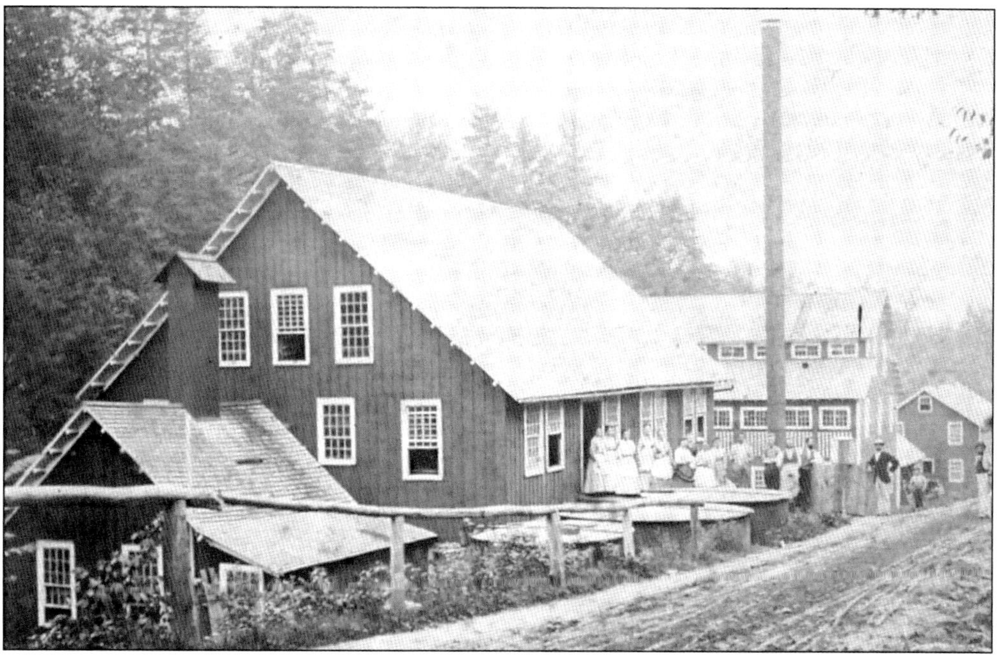

East Lee soon became the hub of papermaking activity, outstripping the rest of the town for the number of active mills. Two streams fell over 500 feet, lending enough waterpower for a dozen mills. After purchasing the Forest Mill, Caleb Benton and Harrison Garfield went on to build a mill upstream, calling it the Upper Forest Mill, and eventually owned two other mills along the same stretch of river, Mountain Mill and Washington Mill. They sold Upper Forest Mill to P.C. Baird. In this photograph of the Baird Mill, a small group of women and men workers stands outside the wood-frame building, behind the large vats that store water for the papermaking process.

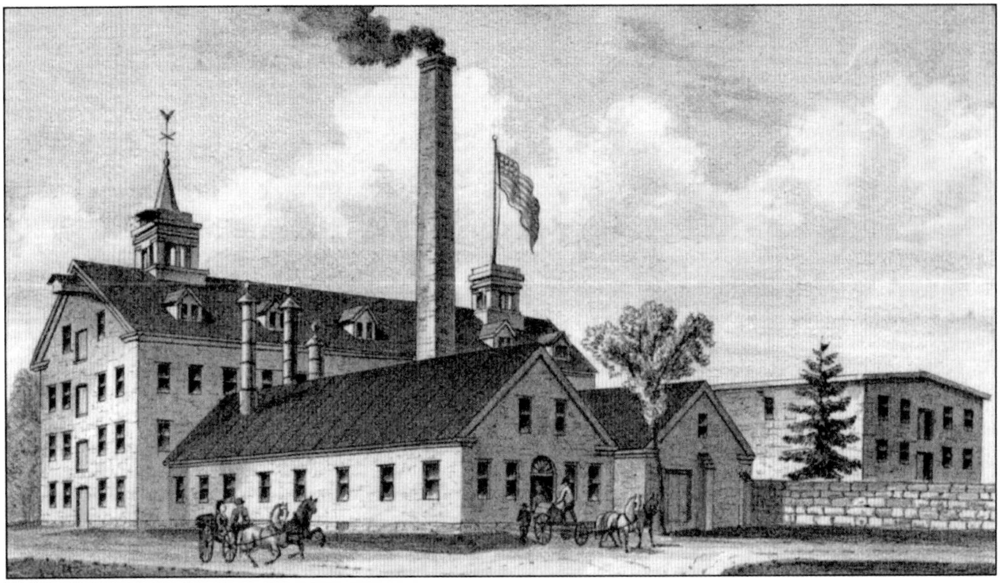

When residents objected to repeated accidents coming from an explosives factory that Walter and Winthrop Laflin had built, the brothers converted their plant north of the Lee town center into a paper mill and called it Crow Hollow. Several fires and several owners later, the plant landed in the hands of the reigning papermaker in Lee by mid-century, Elizur Smith, who also owned the Union Mill just downstream. Smith changed its name to the Columbia Mill. It was here, under the supervision of his son Wellington Smith, that paper was made from wood pulp for the first time in the United States.

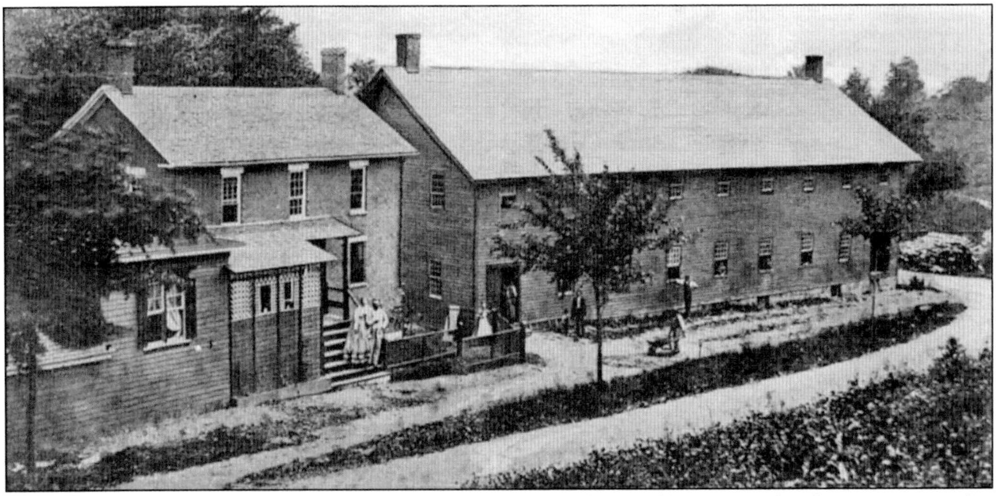

By 1868, the 35 paper mills in Berkshire County needed 28 million pounds of rags to meet the growing demand for paper, newsprint, containers, and even clothing, such as hats and collars. A family of German immigrants decided to set up a small operation in Stockbridge to grind wood into pulp for paper production. Alberto Pagenstecher and his nephews built a large wooden mill in the Curtisville section of Stockbridge. They enlisted a German engineer by the name of Friederich Wurtzbach to set up the Volker wood-grinding process they had learned in Germany. In the dead of night, the Pagenstechers sent their first shipment to the Columbia Mill under orders from Wellington Smith, who wanted to keep the new method a secret. (Courtesy of Stockbridge Library Museum and Archives.)

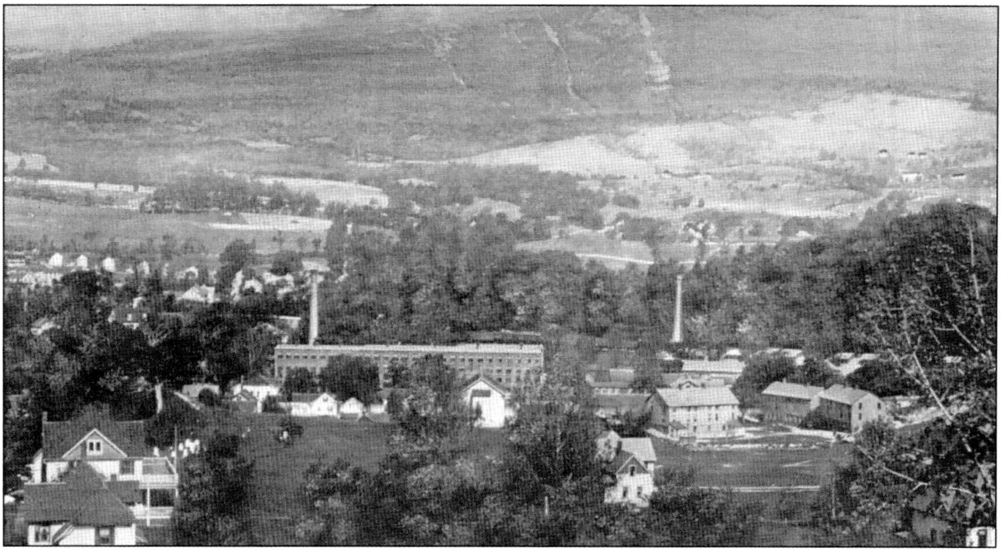

Only a few mills in the county served as both textile and paper mills. The L.L. Brown Mill in Adams had originally been built as a cotton mill by William Plunkett and Russell Brown. With nearby houses for workers, the mill continued to produce cotton print cloth until 1861, when it was bought by Levi L. Brown. Having learned the paper business at the Crane mills in Dalton, Levi started making paper in a small mill just to the north of this cotton mill. By the time this postcard was printed, the complex had grown to include 15 factory buildings in addition to the worker housing.

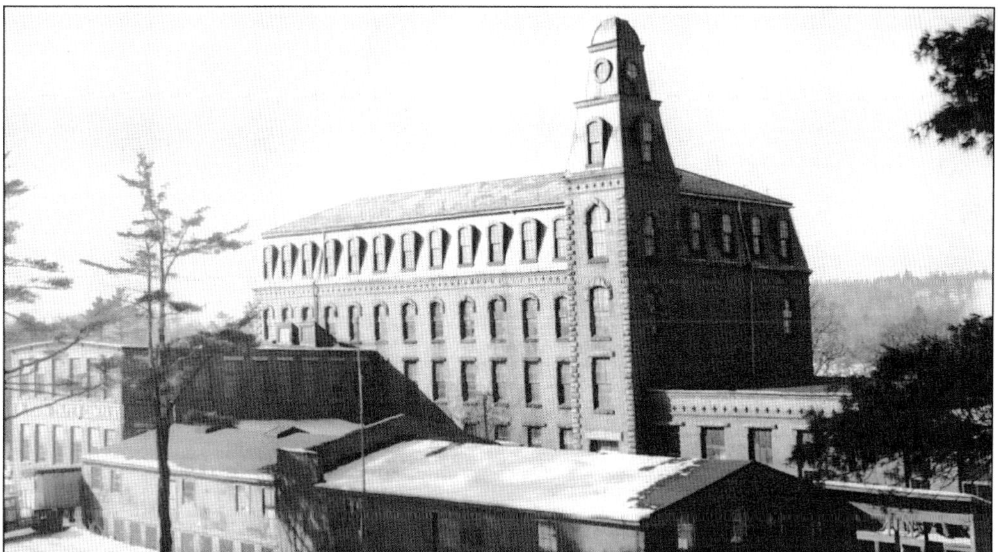

In 1852, on the site of an old sawmill, Henry Potter built a dam on the Housatonic River just north of the town of Great Barrington. After Potter erected a large wood-frame building and installing a waterwheel and machines to start his own paper mill, the structure burned. A lengthy period of ownership under the Owen family, who owned paper mills in Lee, ensued before the site's manager, Henry Cone, bought the company in 1873. Cone launched a plan for a brick structure that would dwarf all other mills in the county, calling it Centennial Mill. With failed investments elsewhere, Cone stopped work on the building, pictured here half complete.

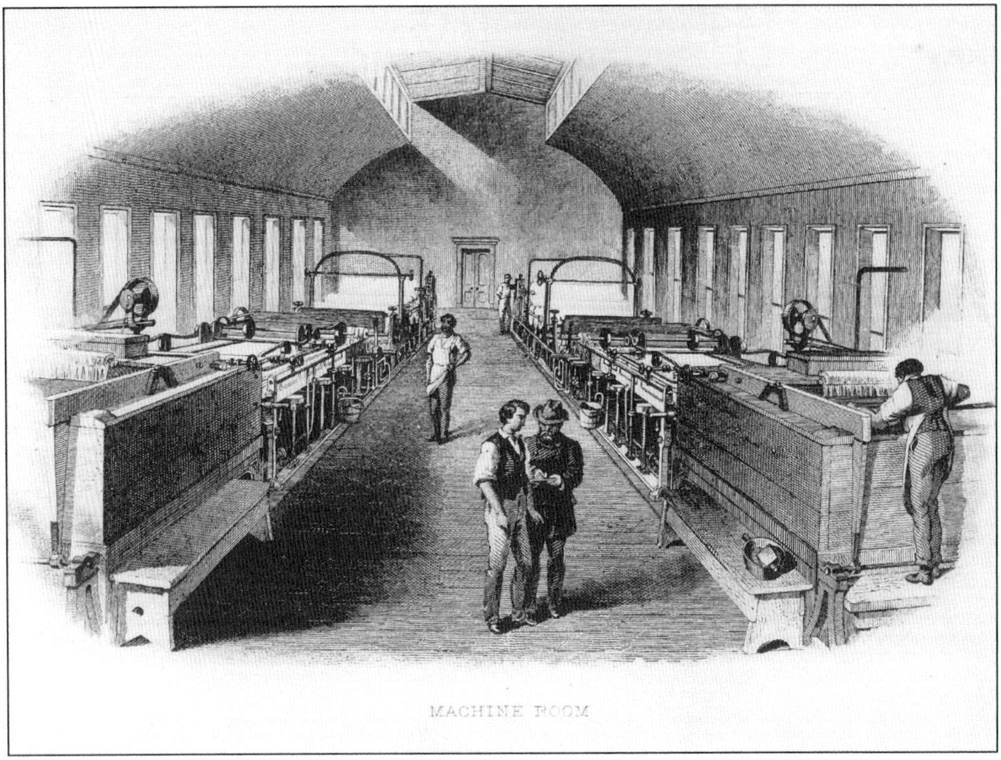

Only in 1899 under the leadership of Bradley D. Rising was the Centennial Mill finally completed, opening in 1900 and employing over 300 people. At its height, the mill was able to boil 12,000 pounds of rag at a time, mixing in chemicals of lime and soda to bleach out and remove impurities. This drawing shows the inside of the connecting block at Rising Paper Mill where the Fourdrinier machines integrated several processes, including removing water from the pulp, felting the fibers together, and rolling them out to form sheets that are then cut.

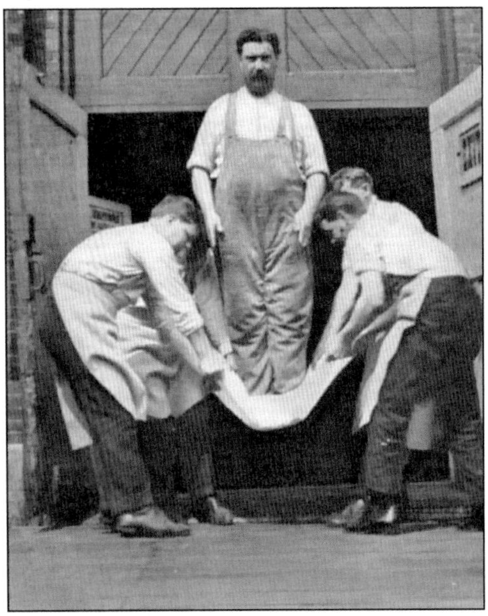

The paper produced at the Owen Paper Company had a reputation for its strength. To demonstrate, John Barker, a paper cutter at the factory who weighed 275 pounds, stood on a sheet of the rolled paper held by four coworkers. Recognition of the quality of Owen paper products extended far and wide. In 1876, Owen paper was awarded first prize at the 1876 World's Fair held in Philadelphia.

Two articles appeared in *Scientific American* ten years apart. In 1871, the journal ran a cover story on the Owen Paper Company called "An Example to Manufacturers." Ten years later, in a supplement on industry, praise rained on Henry Cone, who "made it a specialty to manufacture only first class paper, made from the best linen and cotton fiber . . . [and] large orders being received from abroad, frequently without solicitation."

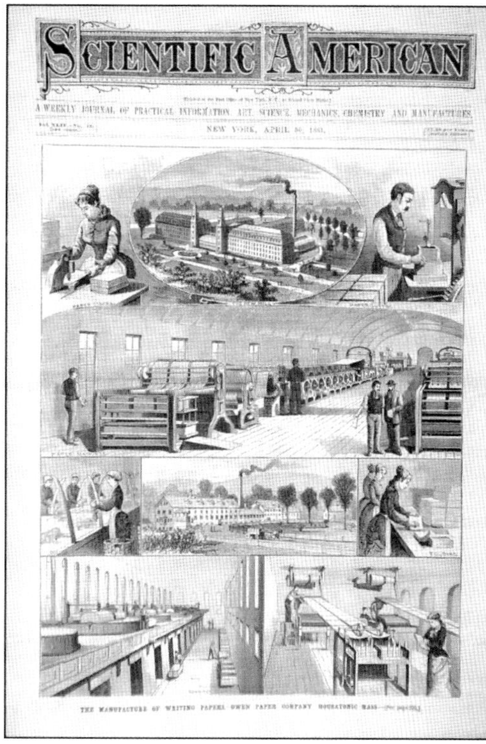
SCIENTIFIC AMERICAN

A WEEKLY JOURNAL OF PRACTICAL INFORMATION, ART, SCIENCE, MECHANICS, CHEMISTRY AND MANUFACTURES.

NEW YORK, APRIL 30, 1881.

THE MANUFACTURE OF WRITING PAPERS. OWEN PAPER COMPANY, HOUSATONIC MASS.

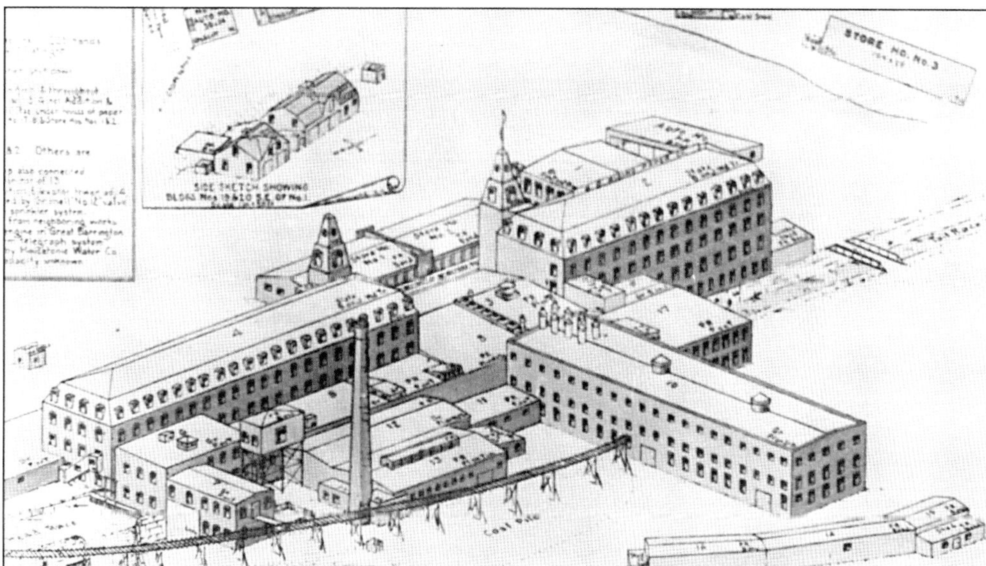

The Rising Paper Company turned its predecessor Owen Paper into one of the largest paper mills in the nation, with over 20 buildings on the site. Its twin towers separate two long blocks, each of which had four stories. They were connected by a third block, two stories tall. Each building housed the different functions of papermaking. In the right block, the rags were received and processed; they were transferred to the center connecting block where the long integrated Fourdrinier machines transformed the wet fiber into sheets. These were then dried and cut in the large block on the right.

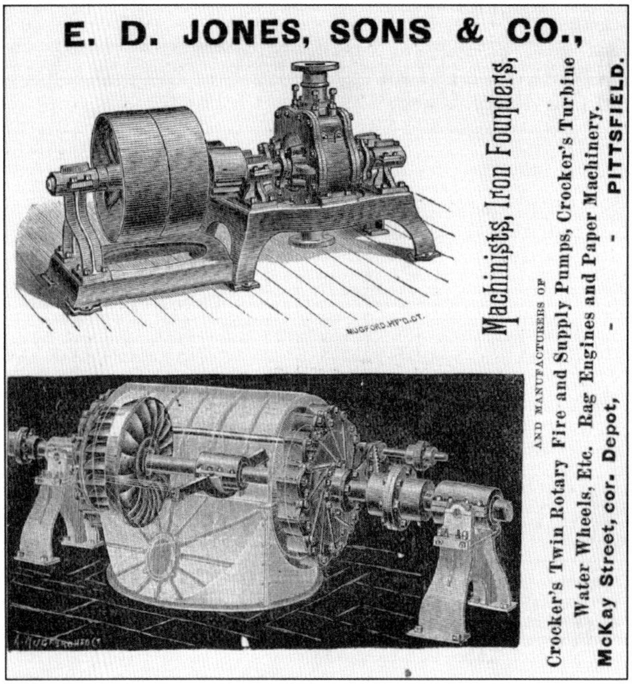

The paper mills spawned a whole industry to develop and maintain the complex equipment in the many paper mills in the county. In 1866, Edward Jones, a young engineer who had started producing machinery for mills in Lee, bought the old Duckworth Loomworks building in Pittsfield, a prime location right near the rail station. There, he and his sons operated E.D. Jones & Sons, a successful foundry and machinist operation to produce the gears and shafts as well as machines like beaters and dusters for the mills. This advertisement in the *Pittsfield City Directory of 1893* depicts water turbines that the company sold to run the paper machinery it also built.

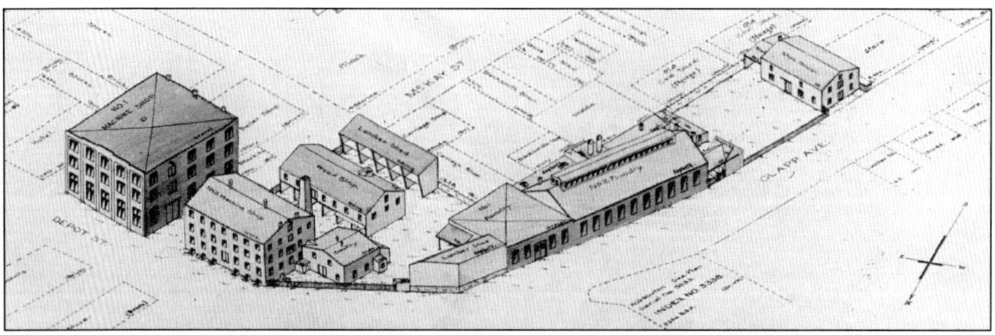

With the town of Lee producing more paper than any in the country, the demand for Jones's machinery continued strong. When he bought state-of-the-art boring equipment, he discovered that his buildings were too small to house the new turning machinery. So, in 1894, he built the three-story machine shop at the left-hand side of this insurance map. By then, entrepreneurs were contracting with the company to build their entire operations. One, the Eli Terry Clock Company, was located a few blocks away, but E.D. Jones was selling equipment around the world.

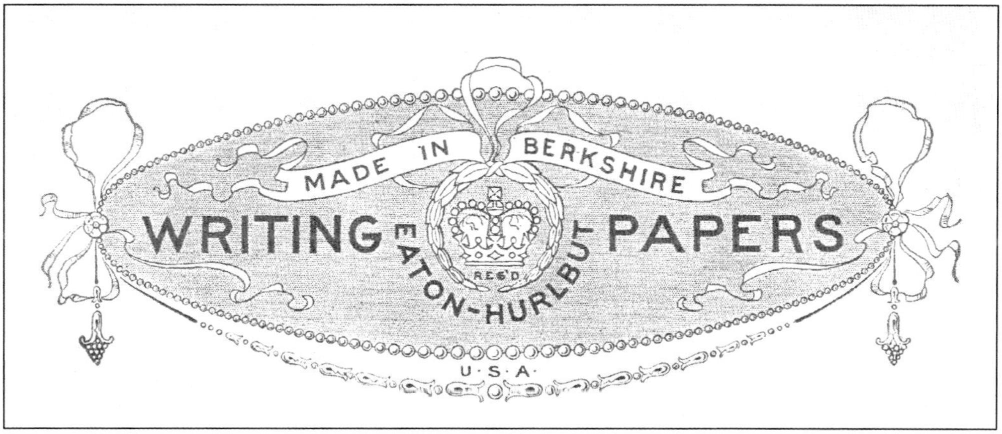

Pittsfield had textile mills, but apart from Crane's Government Mill, the paper industry had no foothold in the county seat. That changed in 1893, when Arthur Eaton, a general manager for Hurlbut Paper Manufacturing, bought the Terry Clock Company building in downtown Pittsfield. Hurlbut had enjoyed success with a new line of stationery called Arthur's Linen and wanted to expand into fine-quality stationery. The company already owned several paper mills in Lee but needed additional space to produce the writing paper in a new firm, using this exquisitely designed label for its stationery.

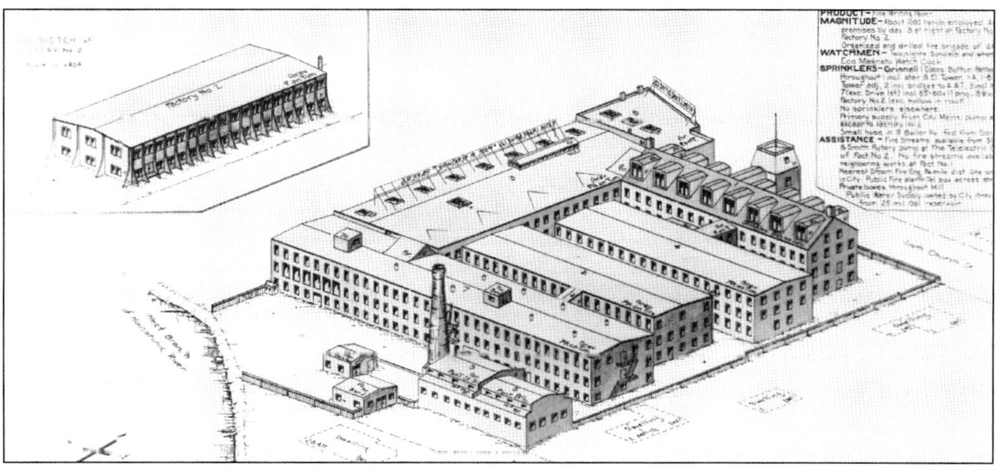

By 1899, Arthur Eaton was able to outright purchase the company from the Hurlbuts of Lee. He changed its name to Eaton-Hurlbut and moved quickly to expand operations. He hired 450 employees to produce not only the fine writing paper but also the envelopes and the sturdy, elegant boxes holding both. In 1908, after Eaton's daughter married Winthrop Murray Crane Jr., the Crane family bought into the firm. This insurance map from 1912 shows a greatly expanded complex overshadowing the clock tower.

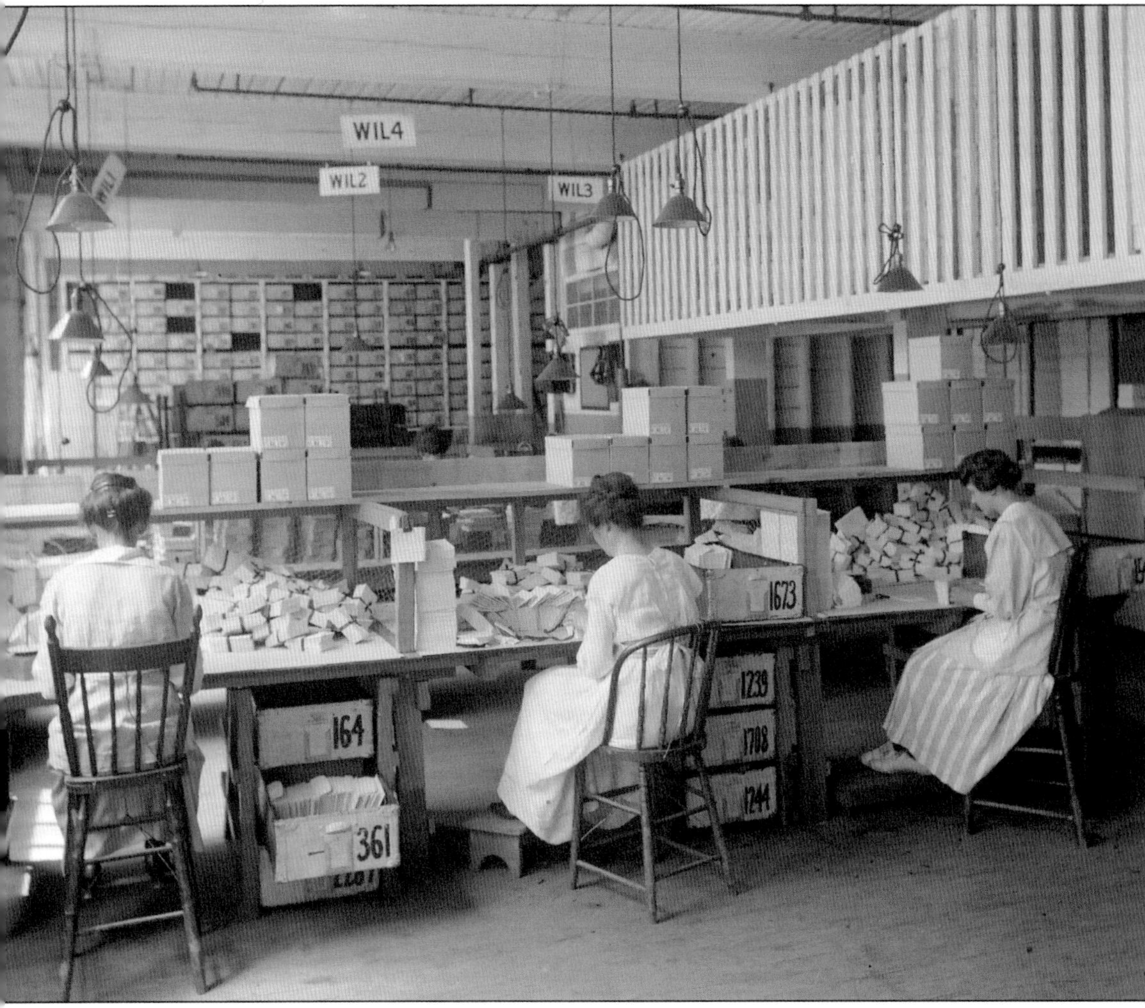

The new Eaton, Crane & Pike produced 1.5 million sheets of stationery and sold them across the country and in Europe and Latin America. It was also the first firm to produce airmail paper, reflecting the growth of the air industry in postal services after World War I. Across the large complex, workstations were busy with employees concentrating on the many different work processes involved in stationery production, from cutting paper to folding envelopes, preparing cardboard boxes, and pasting labels on the finished products. In this photograph from the early 1900s, women are counting and tying ribbon around envelopes.

Four

Iron, Glass, and More

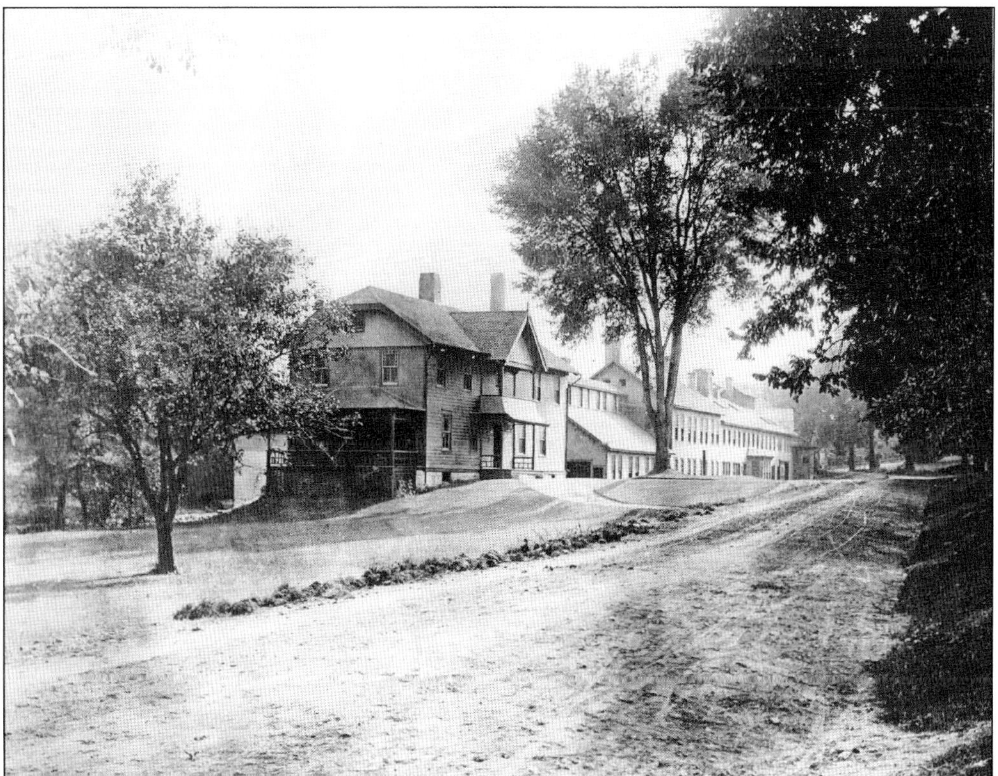

Industries cropped up in almost every town in the area, ranging from large enterprises to small family-owned businesses. Some supported the textile and paper mills, such as the Spencer Mill in West Stockbridge, pictured here. Others proved to be leaders with their own markets, in iron and glass most notably, but also in making products as diverse as shoes, rakes, and axles. In this mill, John Spencer produced rolls that fit on calender machines for pressing and flattening paper.

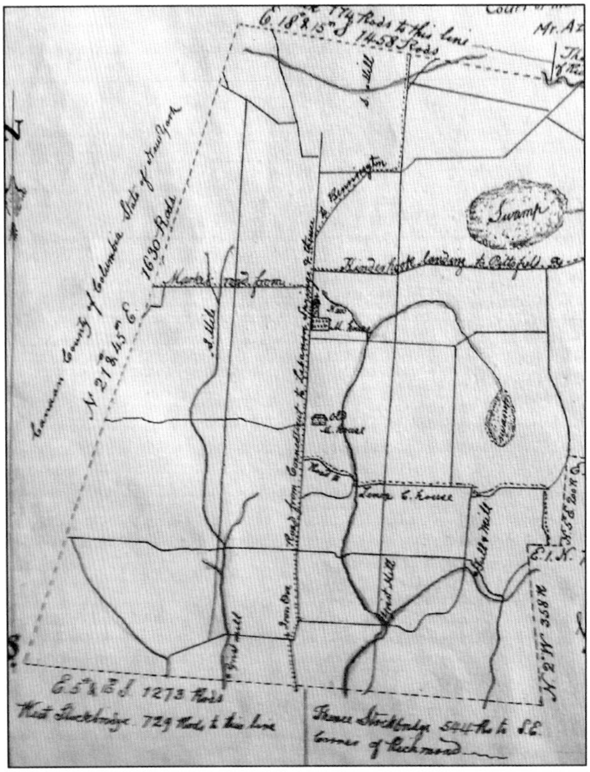

The earliest settlers in Berkshire County were aware of large iron ore deposits in the region. Unfortunately, the iron deposits were too deep to exploit before the 1800s. This 1794 map of Richmond places the iron ore at the lower center of the map in the general vicinity where the Richmond Iron Works was eventually located. Whatever iron was extracted went to small forges in West Stockbridge and Glendale, and later to a larger blast furnace in Lenox that was built in 1765.

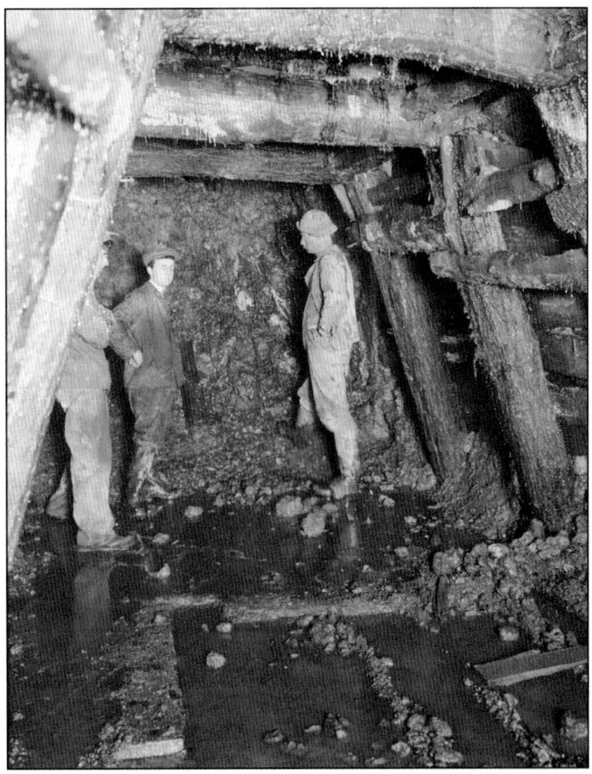

Richmond was not the only Berkshire town where major iron ore deposits were discovered. The towns of Adams, West Stockbridge, Lanesborough, and Cheshire also developed mines to extract iron ore. Even the Shakers operated an iron mine on their property in Pittsfield. New deposits rich in high-quality ore discovered in Richmond propelled the shift from surface mining to pit mining by the early 1800s. This photograph of a mine controlled by Richmond Iron Works highlights the nature of the work—wet, dirty, and dangerous. The foreman on the right is Mike Troy. The company grew to operate and buy ore from as many as 17 mines in this area.

With the new Cone Open Pit Mine at the southern tip of Richmond, local resident Samuel Gates joined with several iron mining representatives from Connecticut to form Gates, Pettee & Company. In 1829, the company built the first iron furnace that was 32 feet high. Seneca Pettee, who had a stake in the Connecticut mines, moved north to become the first ironmaster in Richmond. During the first year in operation, the blast furnace produced 800 tons of iron at the rate of more than 2 tons per day. In 1843, the company was incorporated as the Richmond Iron Works.

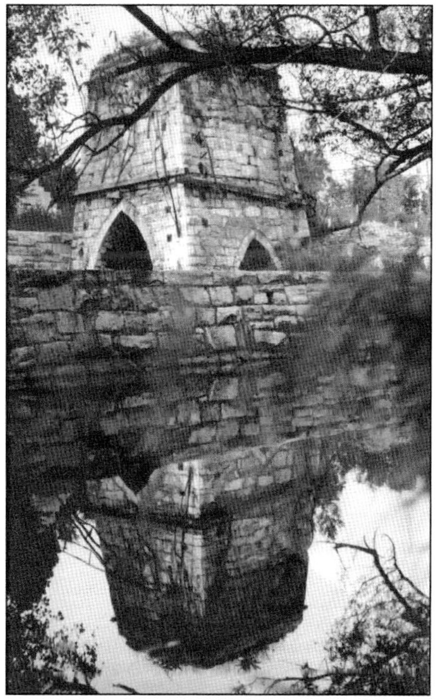

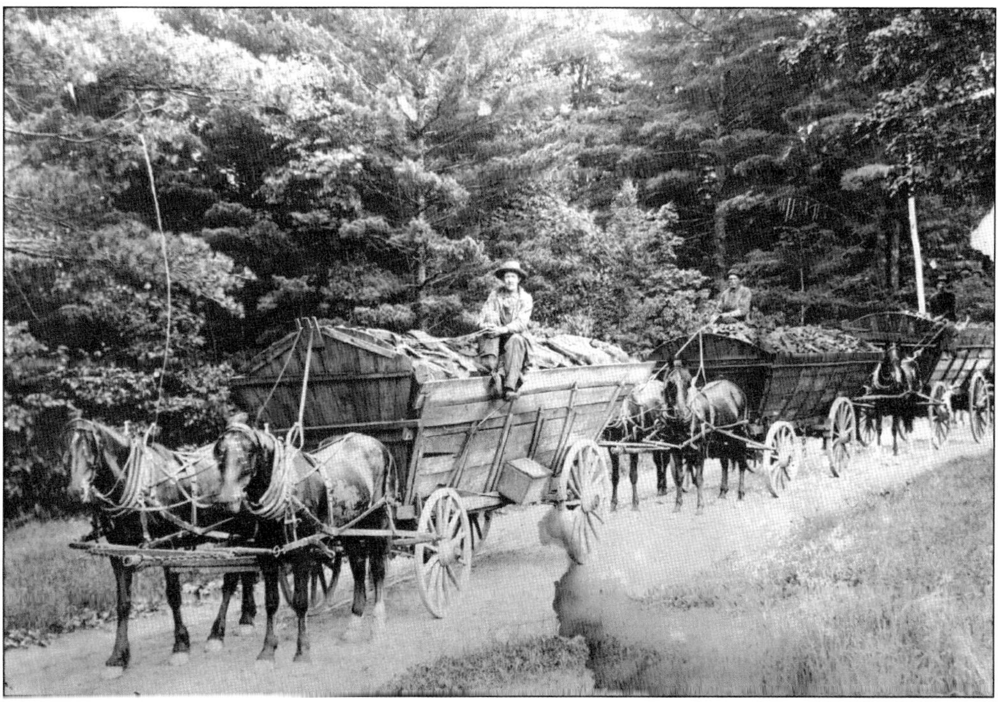

In order to separate the iron from the ore, the furnace burned charcoal that was produced by local farmers who cut down vast swaths of the forest around Richmond and burned the wood in earth-covered pits that smoldered until the wood turned to charcoal. It is estimated that 125 bushels of charcoal were needed to produce one ton of iron. Gates, Pettee & Company located the furnace near what is now called Furnace Brook and used a waterwheel for the air blasts needed to burn the charcoal at the high temperatures to smelt the ore.

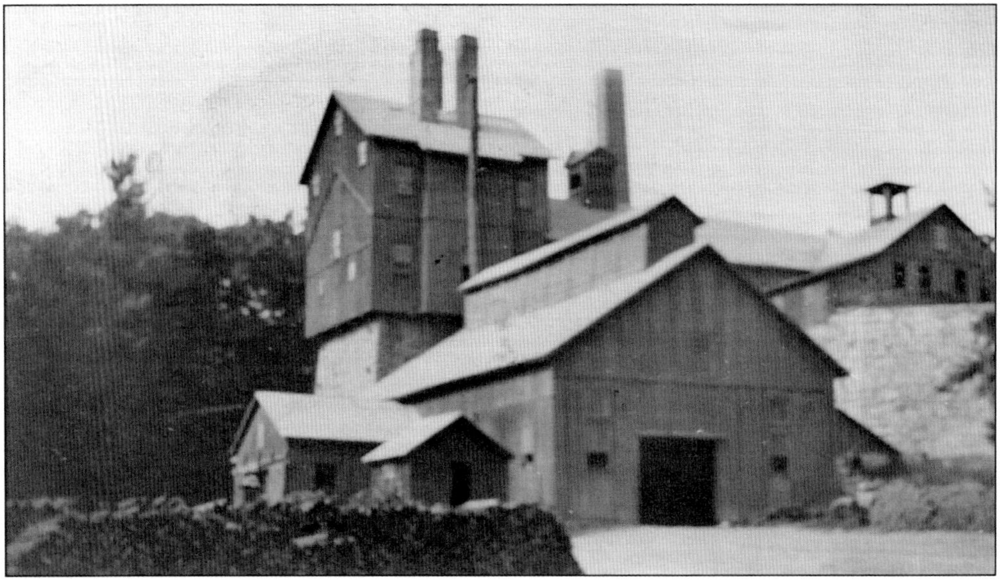

The advent of the railroad era made profitable the mining of iron in the deep deposits in Richmond. Iron produced here made its way into the rail lines and carriages for railroads. Business grew quickly as the iron ore was determined to be of superior quality, especially for products that required strength for load bearing. Then, when the Boston-Albany line was finally completed in May 1841, the railroad passed through Richmond and a side spur was laid directly to the ironworks. This picture shows the growth of the complex, with the stone furnace under a top house for charging the fire. The long building in the front is the casting shed.

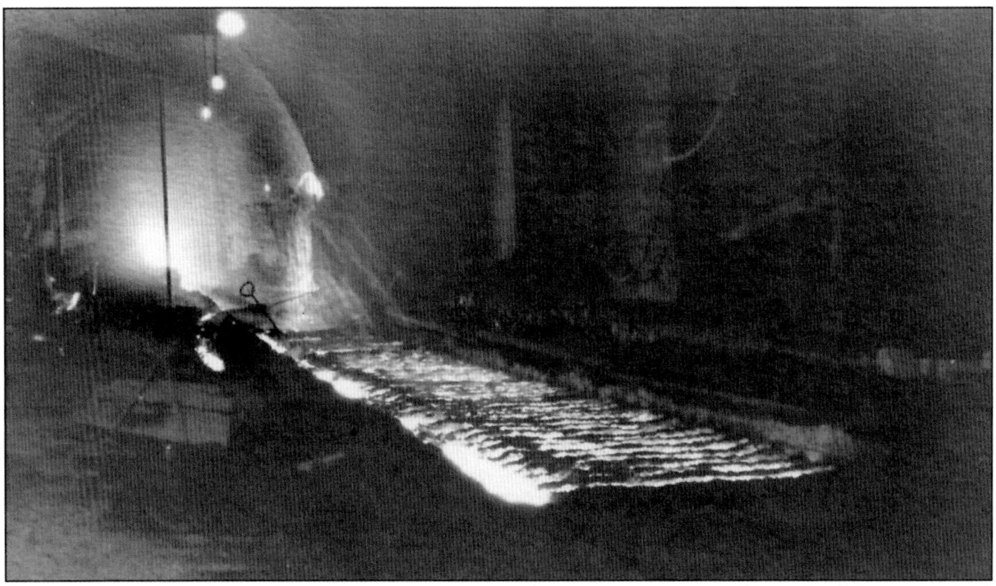

The rail line allowed ease for raw material to get to the company, especially as the log cutting had reduced the forest in the immediate surroundings. Lime from local deposits was brought in and used as an acting agent that, in the high heats of the furnace, attached itself to the impurities in the ore, separating out the iron. Here is the interior of the casting shed, which extends on a lower level than the furnace. Once heated, the impurities would rise to the surface and be skimmed off. The iron in liquid form flowed into sand molds.

In 1834, one of the original investors in Richmond, John C. Coffing, branched out on his own and led the team building an iron furnace on a bend in the Williams River, just before it reaches the Housatonic in Van Deusenville. By 1844, Richmond Iron Works had acquired the Van Deusenville operation and, in 1857, upgraded the furnace there. The increased demand for iron during the Civil War meant that by 1865, the furnace employed 90 workers and produced 1,566 tons of iron per year.

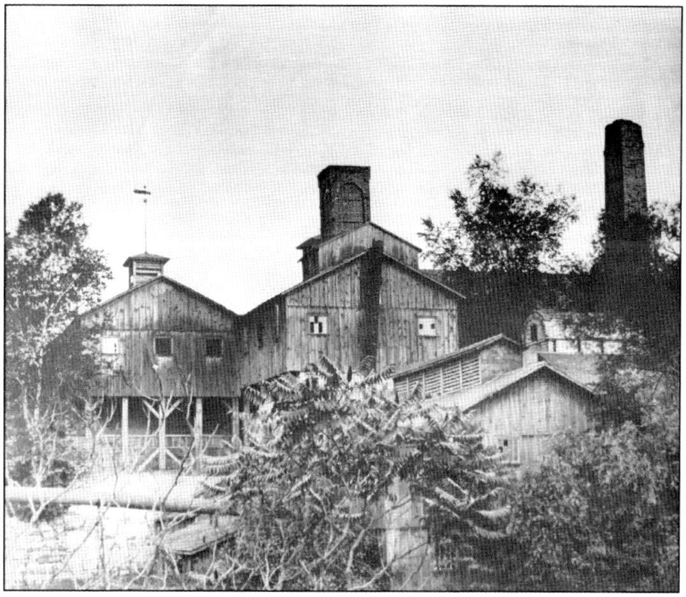

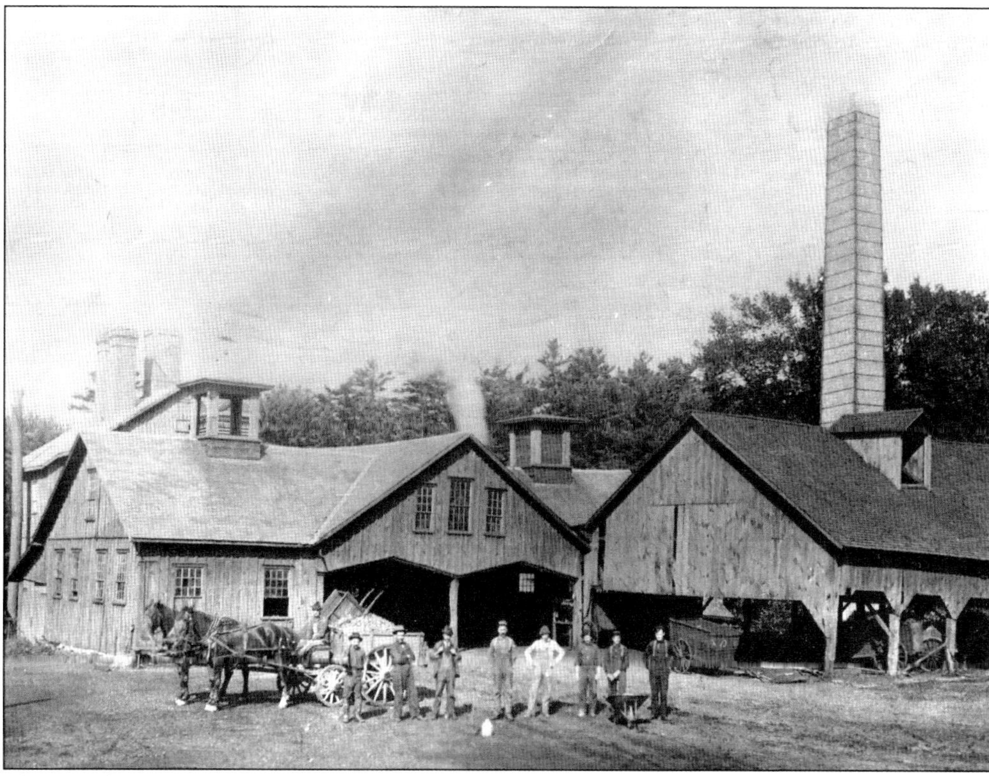

The population in Richmond grew as a result of the iron business from as few as 844 in 1820 to over 1,100 in 1840, with many immigrants coming from England, Scotland, Wales, and, after the potato famine, Ireland. The company built a boardinghouse in 1832, shortly after it started operations in order to accommodate the influx of workers. It also relied on a herd of over 100 draft animals that were used for hauling the raw materials and finished products. Workers were allowed to use the horses on Sundays in the farm plots they were encouraged to till.

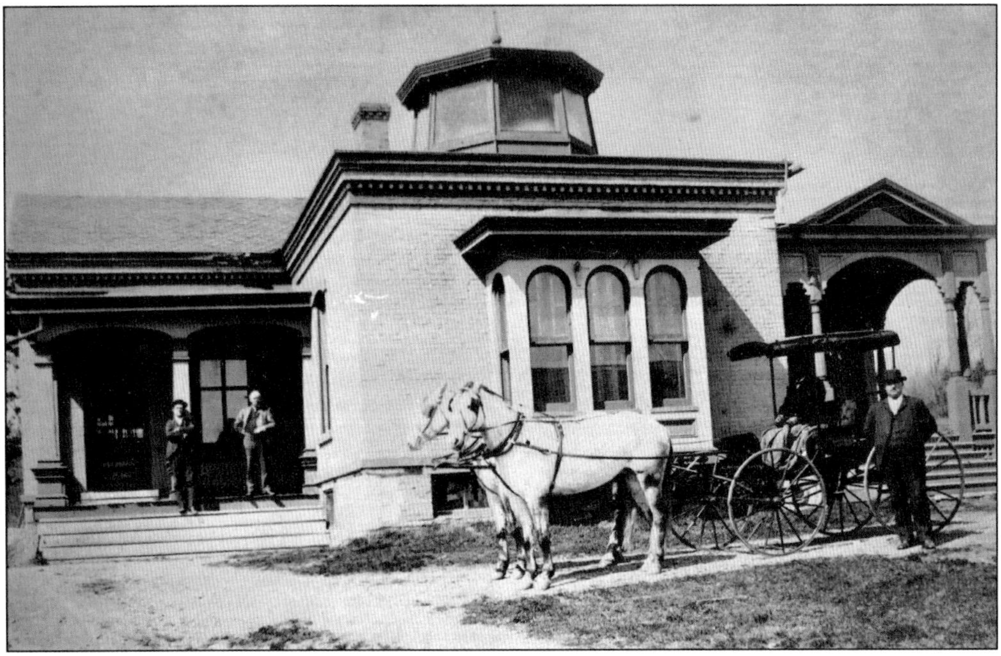

The Richmond site grew, eventually encompassing during its long history 28 buildings and another 100 other structures. Not far from the furnace complex, an office was built in 1862; it was the most ornate structure on the site. In it, the company concluded all administrative functions from payroll to accounting and purchasing. In this photograph, standing in front of the carriage is Elisha Williams, a wood agent for the company.

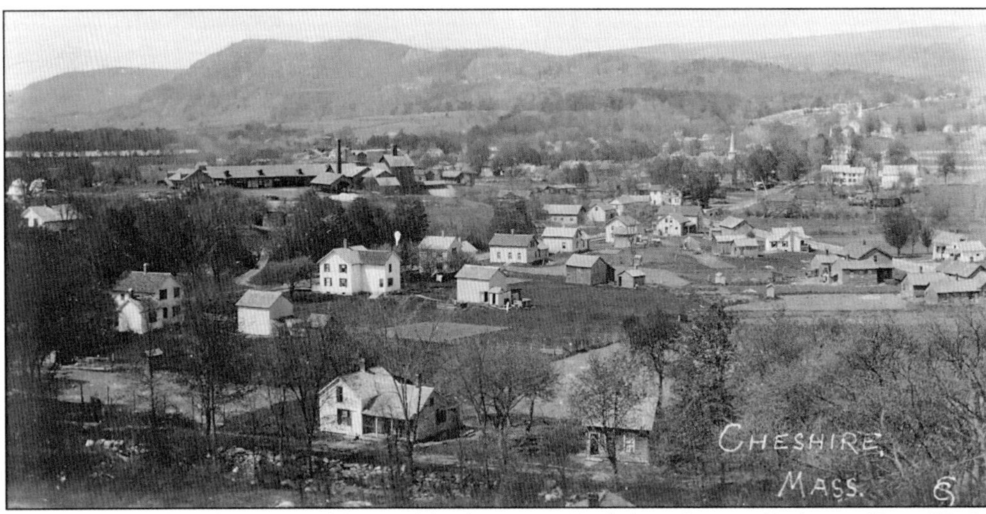

The Civil War sharply increased demand for the iron in Berkshire County. Richmond Iron Works installed a steam-blowing engine that allegedly ran continuously for three years and fourteen days during the war. Much of the iron from Richmond went into the production of Rodman guns that were used on the new Union ironclad boat the *Monitor.* Iron from Richmond may also have found its way into the production of the iron plates for the ship. The ironworks also acquired the Cheshire blast furnace that had started operations in 1848. The Cheshire works can be seen in this photograph in the center of the town, dominating the landscape.

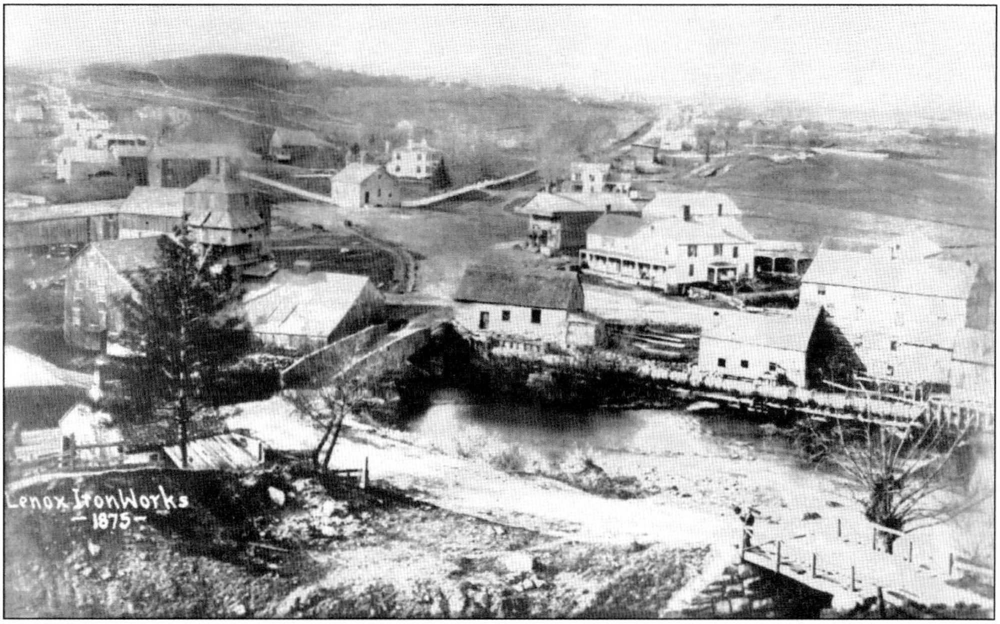

The large furnace at Lenox Iron Works is obscured by one of the few trees in this 1875 photograph. Tapping into the same vein as nearby Richmond, Capt. Job Gilbert and Judge William Walker first launched their ironworks company near the Housatonic River in the late 1700s. Burning charcoal to make 14 tons of pig iron each year helped give the small village the name Lenox Furnace. It was not until 1848, though, that the Lenox Iron Works was incorporated and ran at a profit through the Civil War. The company closed shortly after this image was taken in 1877, when Smith Paper Company from Lee took over the site. (Courtesy of the Lenox Library Association.)

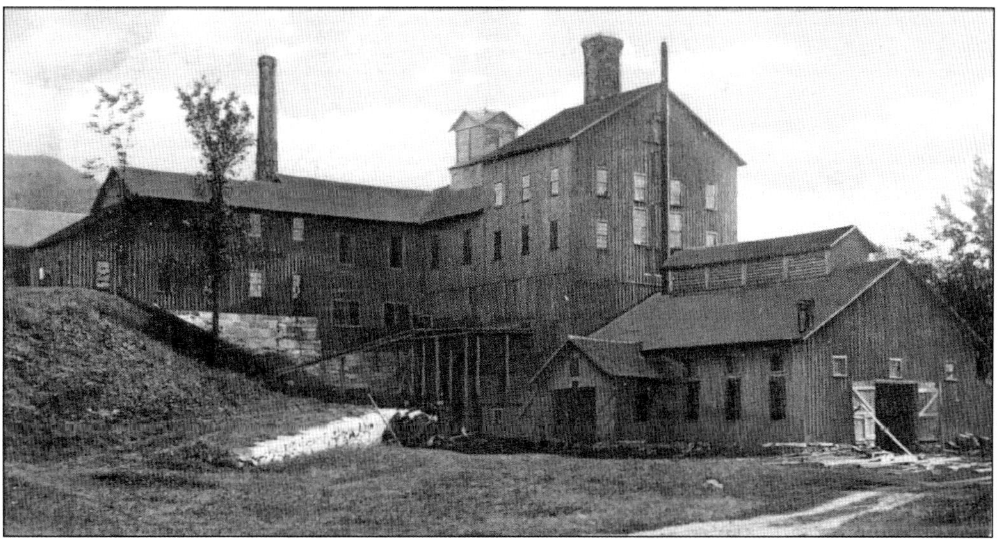

The Civil War spurred not only increased production in Richmond, Lenox and Van Deusenville, but also expanded operations for the company to open up a furnace in the heart of Cheshire. Construction imitated the other furnaces with a top house above the stone furnace, and a casting shed was attached where the heated iron would flow once the impurities were removed. By the 1880s, all three sites were responsible for the production of 12,000 tons of iron per year, with a payroll of 700 employees.

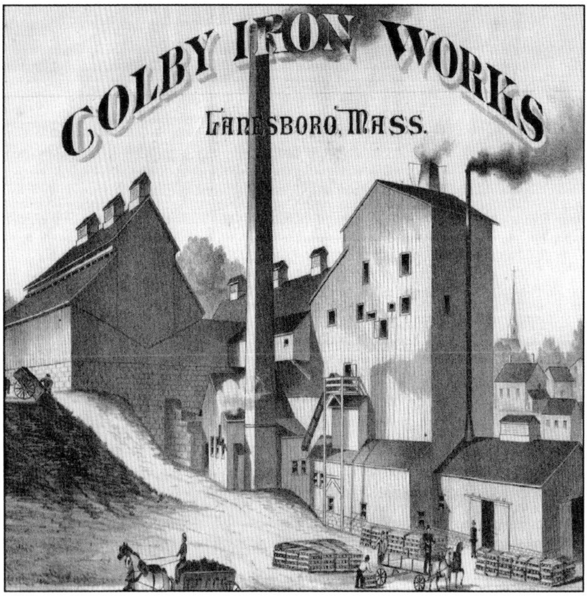

Iron was so prevalent in the geological composition of the region that furnaces were able to bring profits for their owners despite the dominance of Richmond Iron Works in the market. In Lanesborough, Thomas Pingree established Briggs Iron Works with its single furnace in 1847. Fifteen kilns were set up to burn down the wood needed for charcoal to heat the iron. J.L. Colby of Pittsfield bought the furnace in 1864, and with around 200 men on the payroll, the company produced at full capacity 12 to 15 tons of iron a day. Plagued by market swings and two debilitating fires, the company went out of business shortly after Colby's death in 1888.

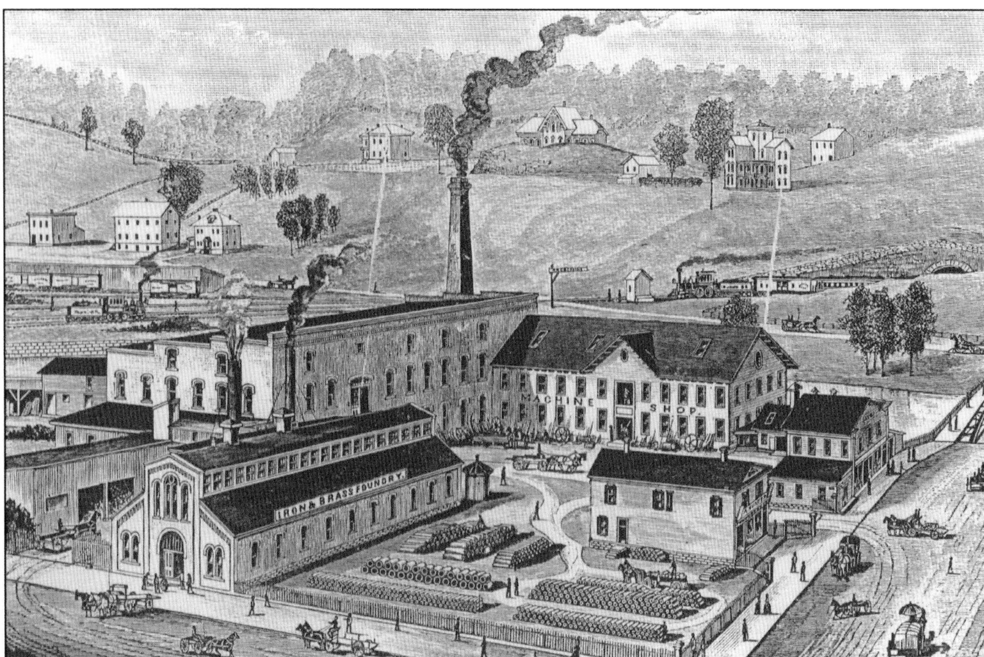

One year after helping build Greylock Cotton Mill in the northern section of Adams, James Hunter decided to leave his position as a finisher in a textile mill. In 1847, he bought an old iron furnace that was strategically located in the center of North Adams. Snug up against the Hoosic River and the railroad, Hunter and his sons turned the foundry into one of the largest in the county. With his son, the company moved into the machine business, building entire mills and filling orders for soaping and wetting machines for mills.

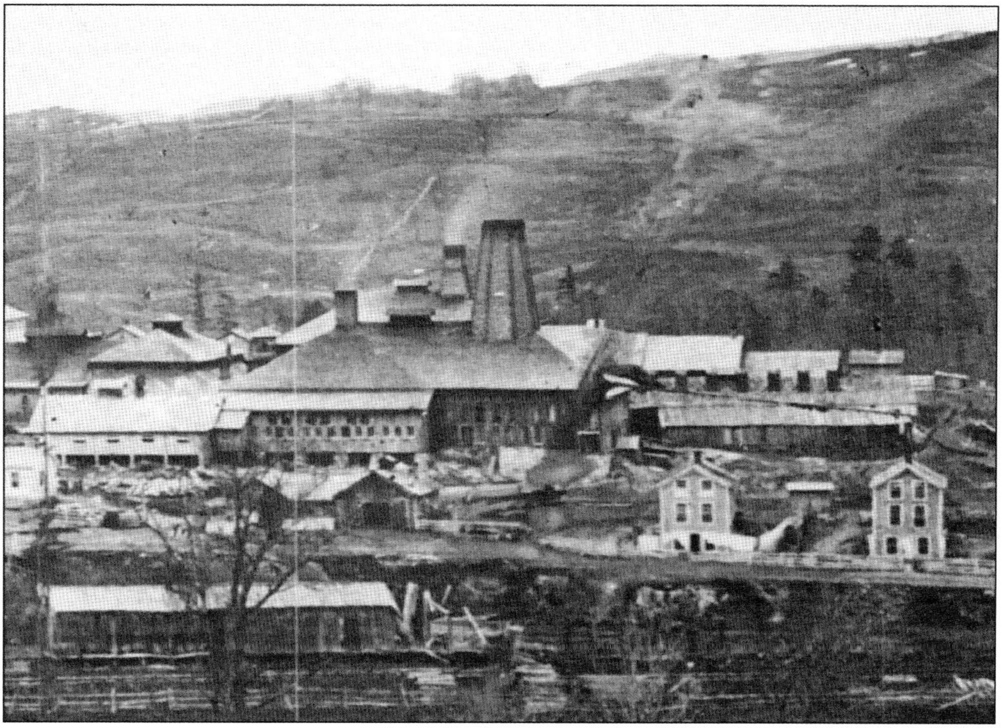

In 1809, the Cheshire Glass Manufactory became the first company in Massachusetts to incorporate to make glass. Whether it ended up actually making glass is unknown; however, in 1812, the Cheshire Crown Glass Company went into production, but only for three years due to the cost of transporting the sand needed. It took another 30 years to realize that the original company had been sited on top of one of the finest sand deposits in the country. In 1849, Samuel Smith, William Linn, and William Filley launched the Berkshire Glass Company, but it took the owners until 1853 to build their factory, which is pictured here after expansion in the 1870s.

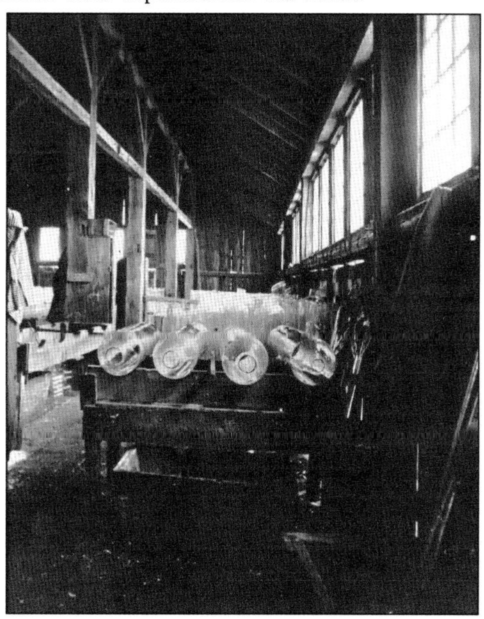

With one eight-pot furnace and 47 employees, the new company started making glass cylinders that were then reheated and rolled flat. After being cut into standard sizes, they were crated and shipped around the county and then farther afield, taking advantage of the new rail links. Within a few short years, the company was selling 3,000 feet of glass each day, making about $8,000 a month. Pictured here are cylinders at the Berkshire Glass Company that have been capped and are cooling on top of a cart.

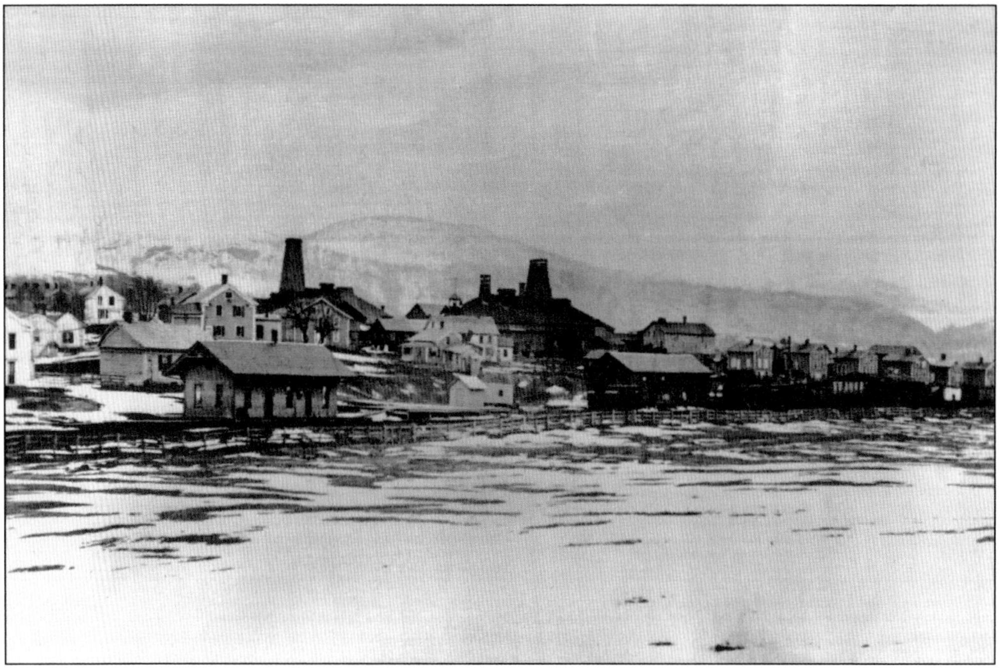

The Panic of 1857 hit the Berkshire Glass Company hard and forced its sale. One year later, Harrison Page and James Robbins, who owned a glass company in Boston, bought the Berkshire operations and reestablished the production of glass. Because of the distance from the nearby towns of Pittsfield, Cheshire, and Lanesborough, the owners purchased additional land in order to build housing for their workers. According to the 1860 census, Berkshire Village had 341 people living in it. The workforce expanded so that by the end of the Civil War, the company had hired 130 people. Most were hired locally, but immigrants from Canada, Ireland, and Germany were brought on as well.

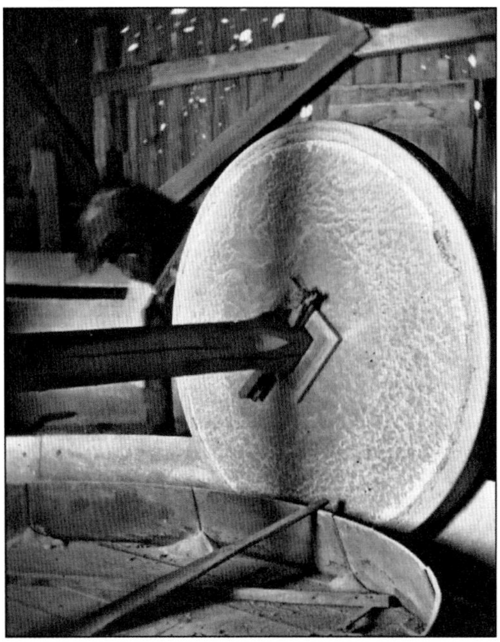

It was not long before Berkshire Glass started producing flat glass, heating and pouring the molten mixture onto a flatbed. It was just up the road that artisans at Cheshire Glass became the first in the United States to roll flat glass in the early 1800s. Clay pots were constantly needed to mix and melt the raw materials for glass production. Berkshire Glass made its own pots, using clay shipped from as far away as Missouri and shards of clay that gave the clay pots firmness and consistency. In this photograph, an upright stone wheel crushes clay shards for mixing into a water and alkali solution called a grog.

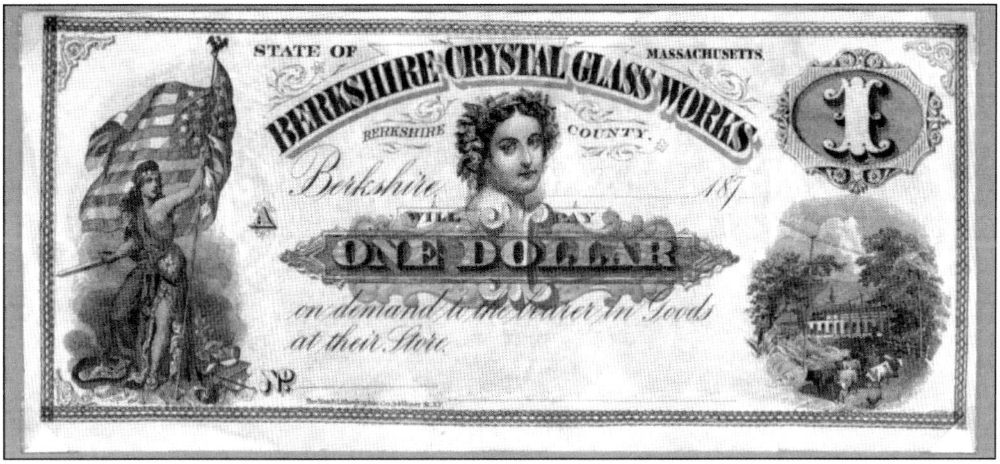

A young Williams College graduate, William G. Harding, joined the company in 1861, and just two years later, he became William Page's partner, managing the day-to-day operations. Harding made recruiting trips all the way to Belgium to hire specialized glassworkers there. With a workforce of 200, Harding expanded the village to include 70 different tenement buildings and a store for the 500 people who lived in Berkshire Village. He paid his employees in his own paper currency that could be exchanged in the village store or at other stores at a discount.

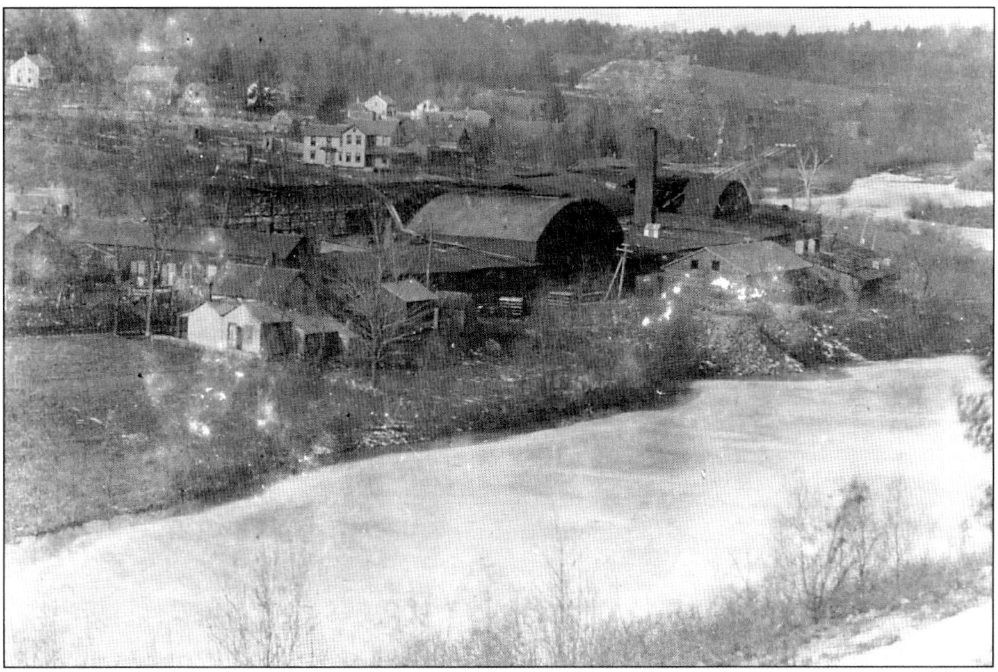

The owners Page and Harding survived through the economic panics and heavy indebtedness of the 1870s. By 1885, they took over the largest competitor in the county, the Lenox Plate Glass Works. That company had started in 1853 as an offshoot of Lenox Iron Works. The owners enlisted first Hiram Pettee and then his brother Seneca—two men familiar with working iron—as superintendents to run the glass works in Lenox. Like with so many other Berkshire industries, fires, and economic downturns took their toll on Lenox Glass Works, and the parent company went through cycles of closures, sales, and restarts for the next 20 years before being leased to Page and Harding from Cheshire. (Courtesy of the Lenox Library Association.)

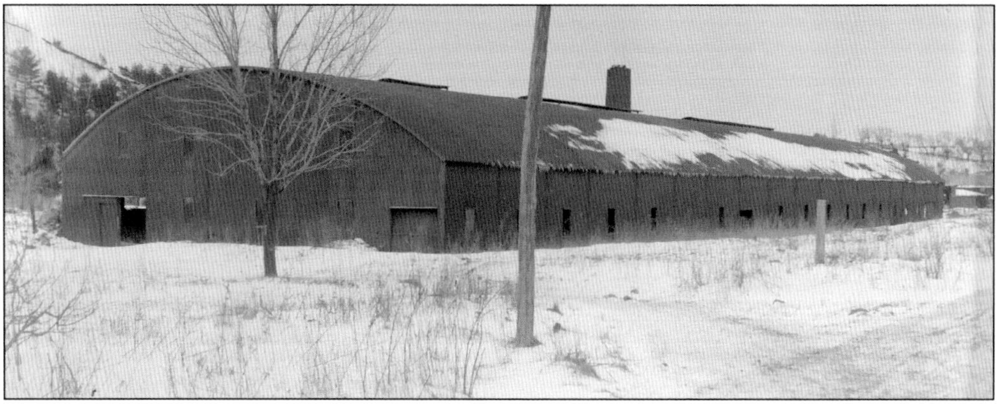

One of the owners of Lenox Glass was the father of a future president of the United States. After a fire destroyed the property in 1862, the owners built a new structure, claiming it was the largest building in the world, measuring 600 feet long by 100 feet wide. Eventually, the company divided in two, with one producing rough plate glass and another producing cylinder glass. In 1872, the company was sold off, with Smith Paper from Lee purchasing one division for a new paper plant and investors from New York, James and Theodore Roosevelt Sr., buying the other. Future president young Theodore Jr. accompanied his father on a visit to the glassworks to see this large complex. (Courtesy of the Lenox Library Association.)

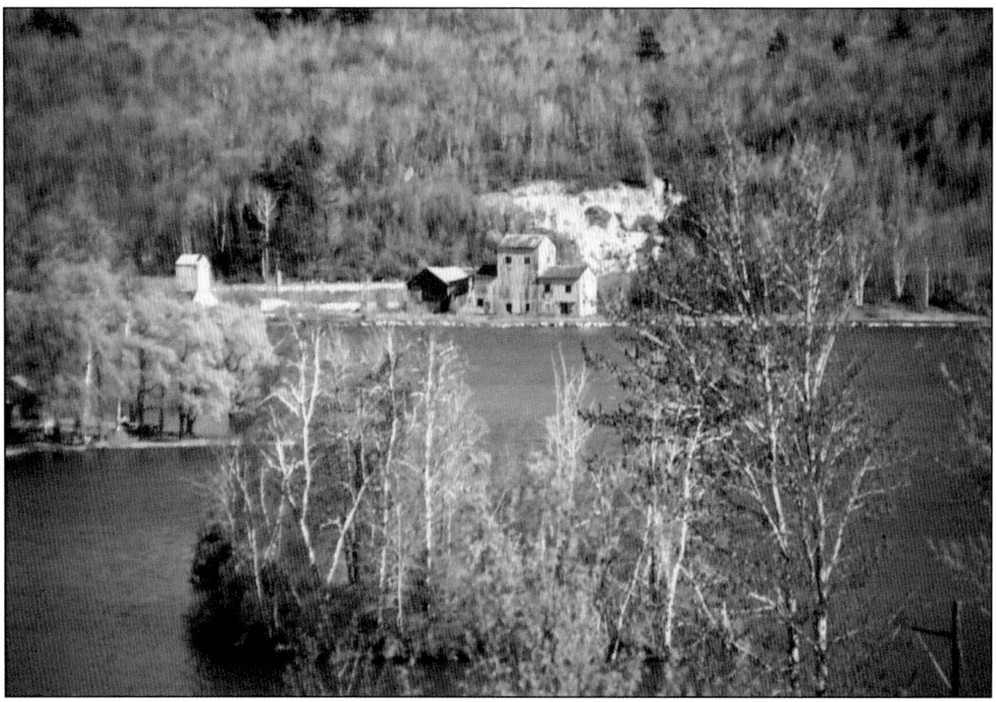

While the production of glass moved from Cheshire, quarries in and around the town continued to yield the rich, high-quality sand for glass in Lanesborough, Lenox, and beyond. The introduction of the north-south rail line, going right through Cheshire, made transport of this sand more cost-effective. George William Gordon bought the sandworks and operated the quarries until 1877, when the Berkshire Glass Sand Company was formed. It shipped 10,000 tons of sand a year around the country by the mid-1880s. The quarry and now abandoned buildings pictured here continued to operate until 1958. (Courtesy of Barry Emory.)

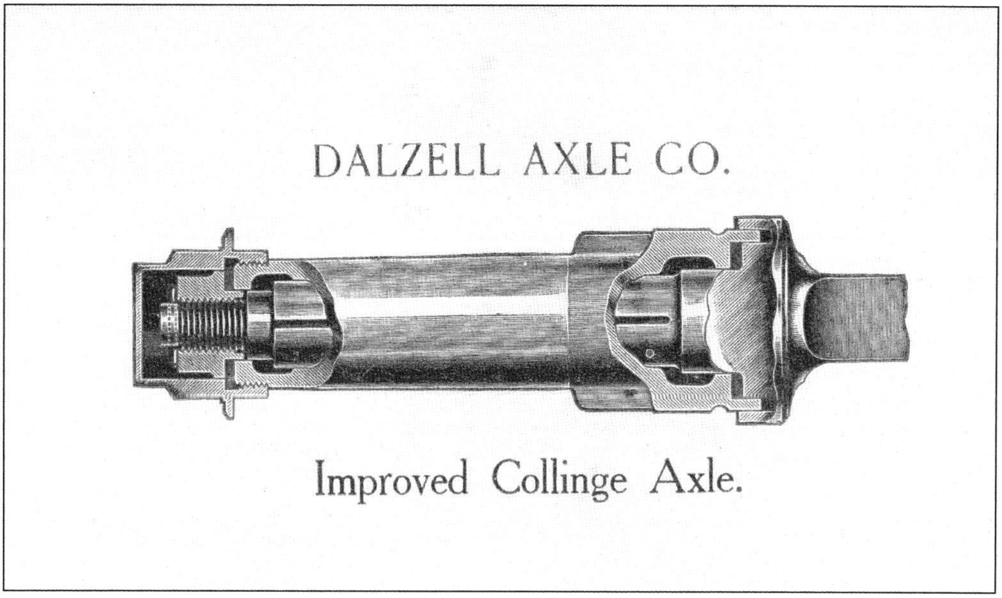

One company that undoubtedly drew on the iron furnaces of Berkshire County was the Dalzell Axle Company in South Egremont, which operated successfully with clients across the United States for almost 65 years. David Dalzell, who had apprenticed in a carriage "trimming" business in New York, bought out a small carriage-making business in South Egremont in 1845. Five years later, he focused his business on producing carriage axles, taking advantage of the extensive iron furnaces nearby. His two sons entered the business and expanded it to the point where the company employed 60 men and turned out 12,000 axles a year.

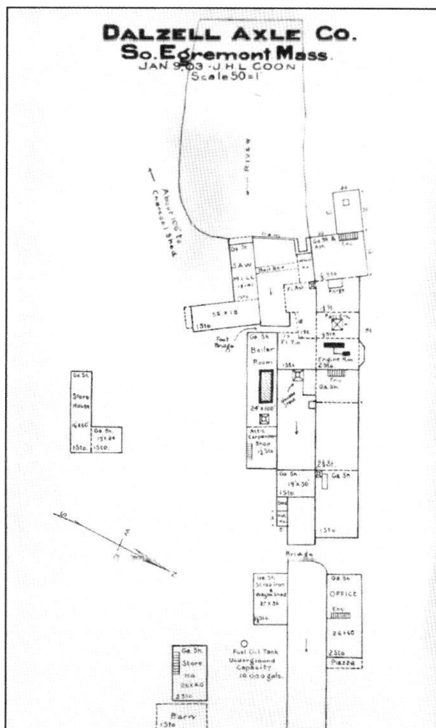

The Dalzells developed several patents for innovations that increased demand for their products. The quality of their axles came from a design that was made out of one solid, continuous iron bar proved better than welded-together pieces, which would make axles and collars weak and susceptible to breaking. For the Philadelphia Exposition in 1876, the Dalzells produced a "Centennial Axle" that won several awards. The company was slow to adapt to the introduction of the automobile and had to close its operations in 1909.

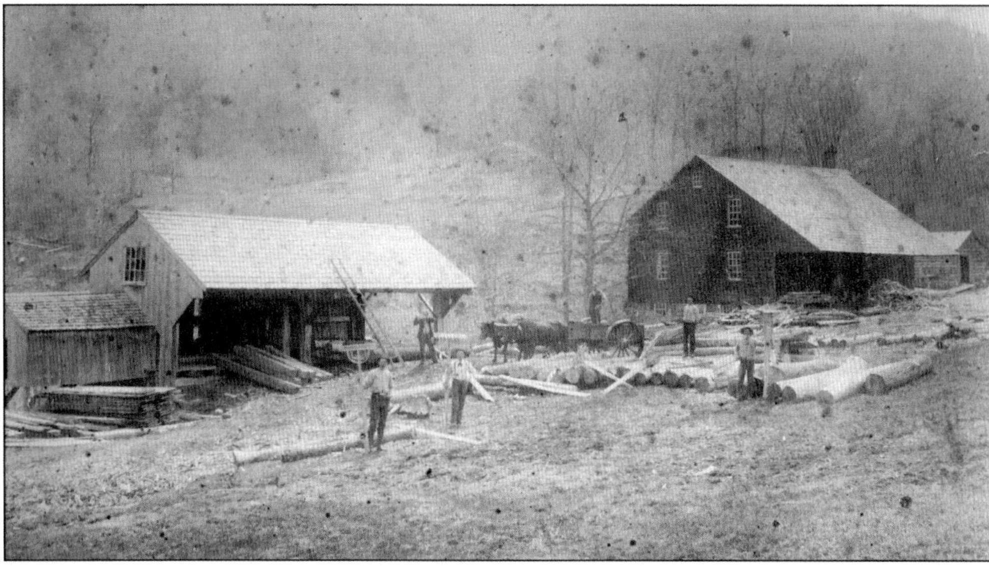

With all the plastic and metal rakes now, it is hard to imagine that once these essential farm tools were made out of wood. Tyringham produced these rakes for 160 years, selling them across the country. In 1818, William Stedman set up shop in the Sodom section of the town. Ten years later, he installed a machine to cut the wooden teeth for the rakes. When he died in 1858, his son Martin Van Buren Stedman took over the business. In this photograph taken around 1880, Martin Stedman (left) stands with several employees in front of the rake factory and sawmill.

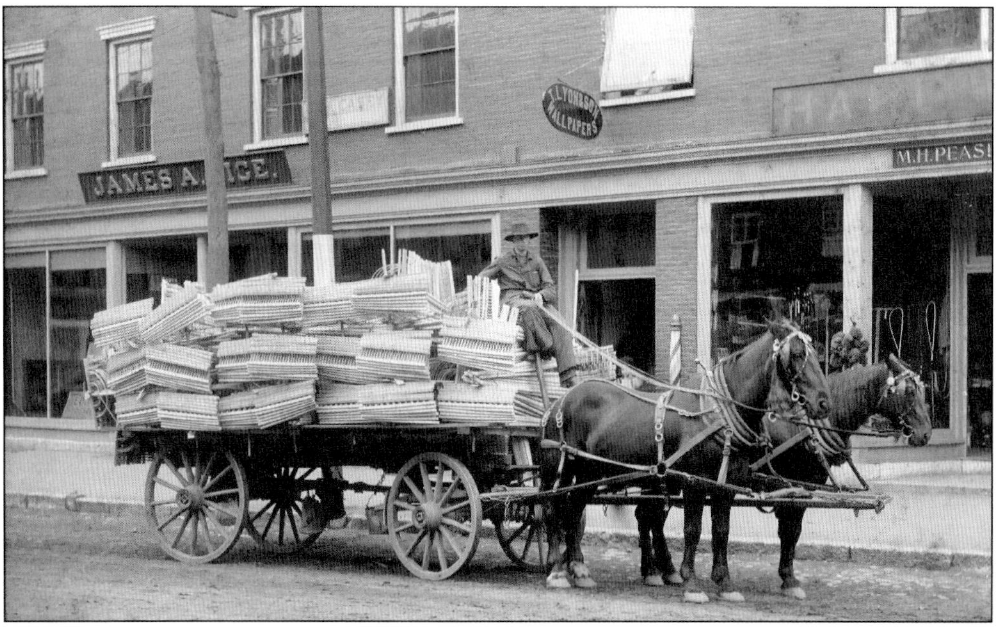

To get his rakes to markets along the Eastern Seaboard and beyond to the Midwest, Stedman used the closest rail line in Lee. Here is a 1903 photograph of a wagon full of bundles of wooden rakes on their first leg of the journey to Lee, where trains would take these rakes down to New York for further distribution. The teamster in the wagon is identified as Charles Williams. Annual production seemed to hold steady at around 25,000 rakes a year, with a staff of 25 employees at its peak.

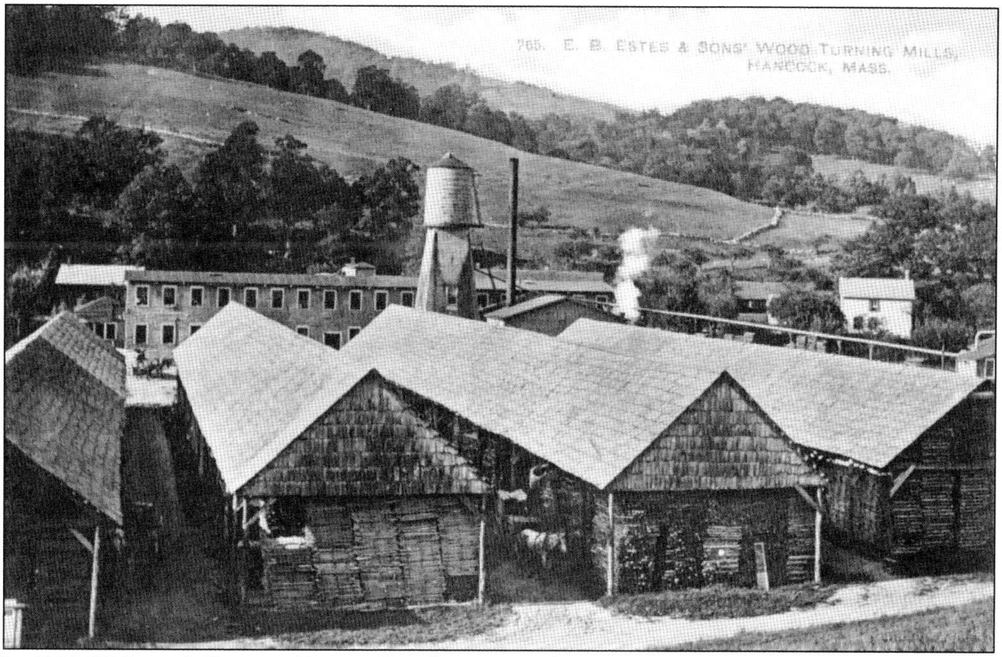

In 1904, Webster C. Estes and his son Beechum opened a woodturning mill in Hancock, reputed to be the largest in the world and employing over 100 people. Using machine saws and lathes, lumber was fashioned into many fine wood products that were painted and polished before shipments to markets around the world. In this photograph, stacks of sheet lumber lie protected in large open-air drying sheds. Horse-drawn carts can be seen moving the lumber to the main turning building. The Estes ran the mill until 1928, following the deaths of both the father and the son.

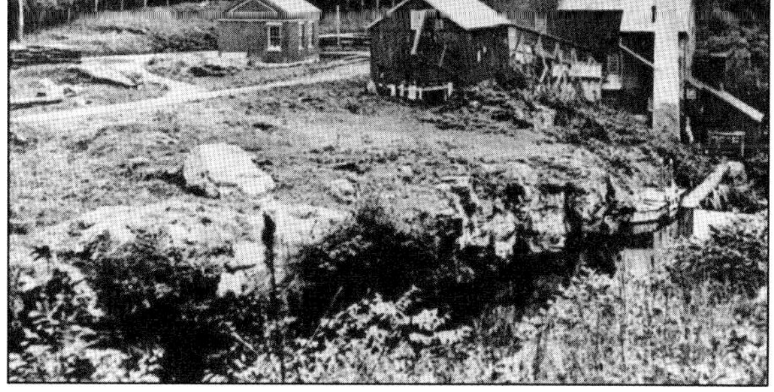

With its small population of under 2,000 people at the end of the 19th century, West Stockbridge was home to quarries, mines, iron furnaces, lime kilns, and a paper mill. Nestled in along the Williams River was the Rockdale Mill that ground all manner of grains—wheat, corn, oats, and rye. Rebuilding a dam that powered one of the early iron furnaces, Charles Platt and Thomas Barnes opened the new mill in 1847. Destruction from three separate fires did not deter the pair, who rebuilt and passed ownership on to Erwin Barnes, who kept the flour operation in business until 1921.

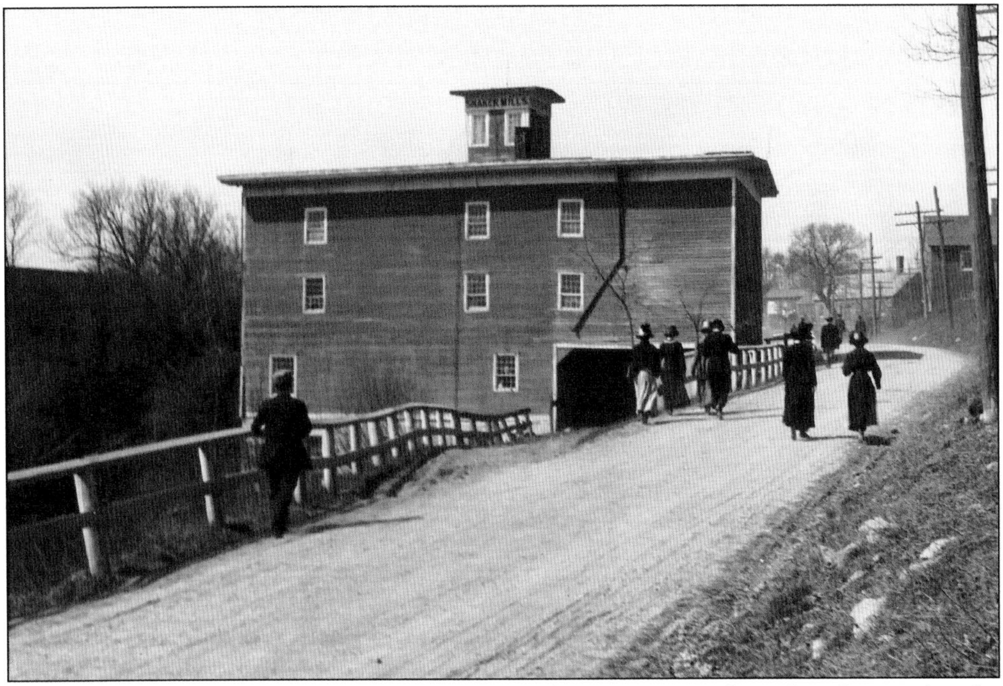

Many gristmill owners sold their water privileges to the new paper and textile industries, but the Shaker communities in Hancock and Tyringham retained their flour mills and had a steady demand for their services. The gristmill shown here across the town line in Pittsfield was built in 1823 on land using a water privilege the Shakers bought from Daniel Stearns, who was setting up his own woolen mill in West Pittsfield. The Shakers ground flour here until 1916, when the building burned. With their "hands to work and hearts to God" philosophy, the Shakers ventured beyond the spiritual into manufacturing, taking advantage of the volunteer labor of their members.

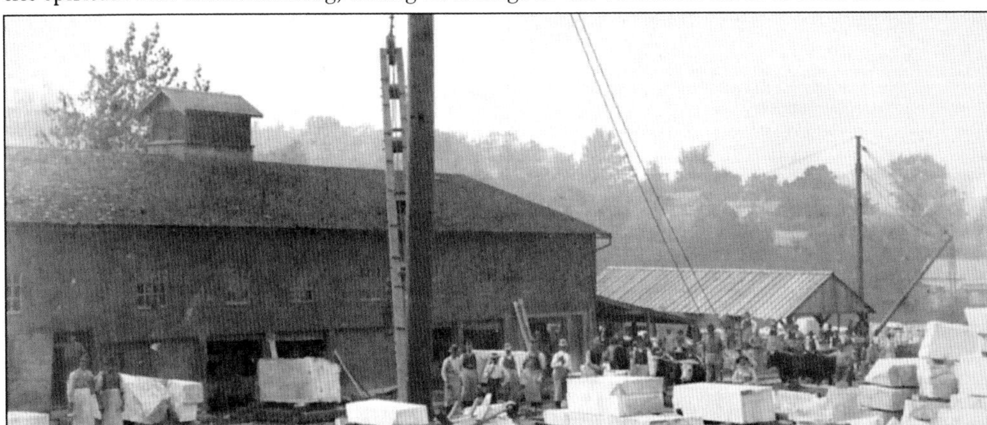

Lee, known as "Paper Town" for its two dozen paper mills, was also the site of one of the nation's richest geologic formations of bedrock containing marble, limestone, and granite. In 1852, the first quarry for extracting marble was established. The high-quality marble found customers around the country, including firms that built St. Patrick's Cathedral in New York and that added a wing on to the Capitol in Washington. In this photograph from 1887, workers at the Gross Brothers Marble Works stand amidst a system of pulleys and cranes that lifted the large slabs of fine white marble. (Courtesy of the Lee Public Library.)

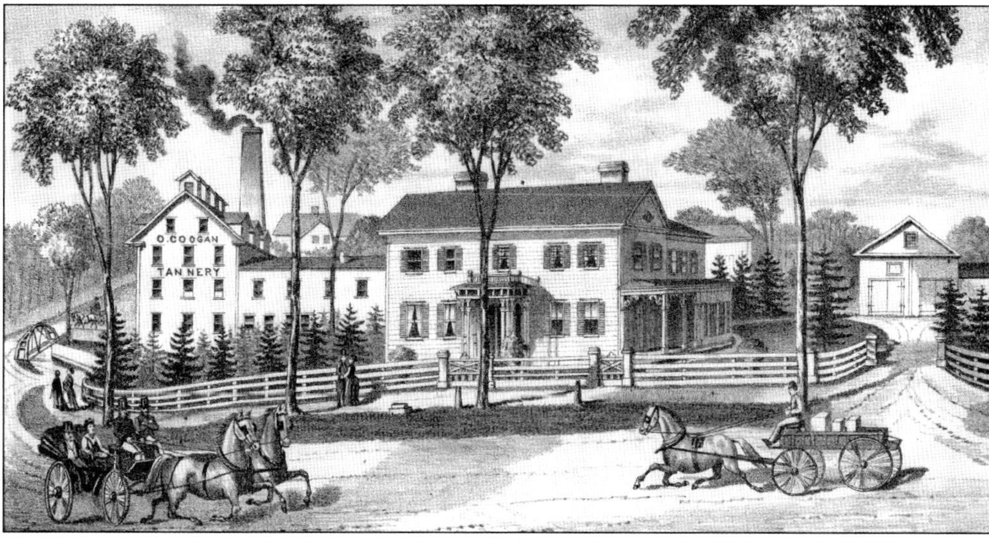

The first Pittsfield dam built for textile production was at Elm Street on the east branch of the Housatonic River. Here, James and Simeon Brown set up their tannery in 1790. Owen Coogan purchased the property in 1850 and quickly expanded it, employing 30 men, tanning 15,000 hides each year by the 1880s. Owen passed his business on to his sons who continued operating until 1927. Their house and tannery stood prominently on Elm Street, as depicted in this Beers map engraving. In 1950, the A&P grocery chain bought the site to build a store that served the town for decades.

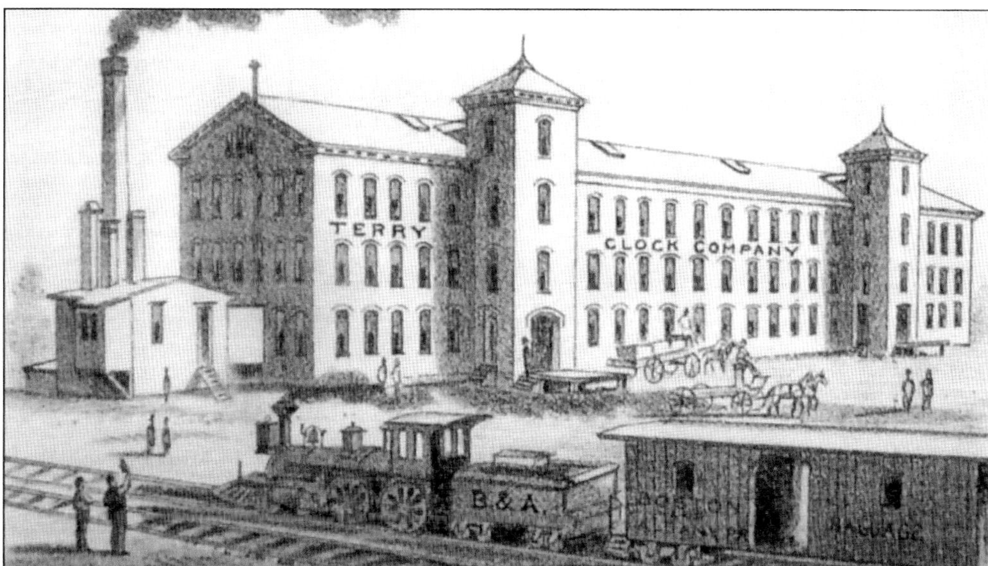

The Berkshires were slow to adopt coal and steam power. The abundance of falling water made power generation cheap, less expensive than the transport of coal to the region in order to drive the steam engines. However, with water rights locked in by a small number of wealthy business leaders, entrepreneurs increasingly looked to coal and steam for power generation. When the Kellogg Steam Power Company opened in 1873, one of the early tenants in Kellogg's new steam plant was a clock maker named Eli Terry, who had moved north from Connecticut to expand his operations. (Courtesy of the Berkshire Athenaeum.)

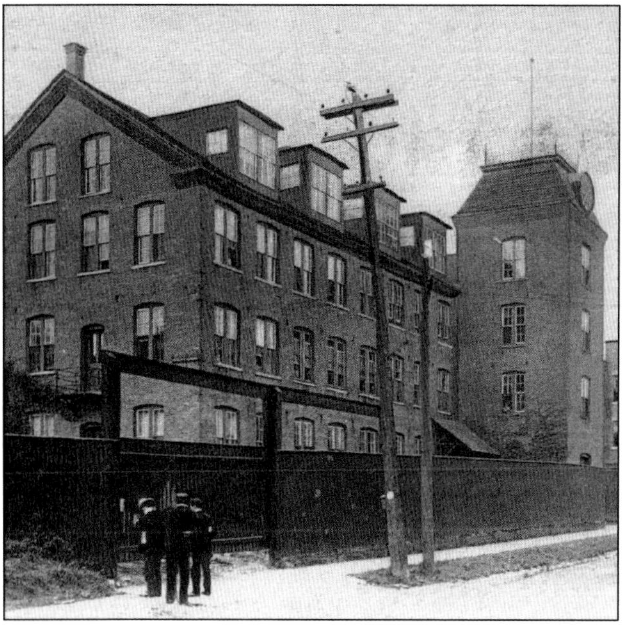

Eli Terry did not stay long in Kellogg's leased space and joined forces with machinist E.D. Jones to build his own plant in 1883, not far from Pittsfield's Park Square. At its height in the 1890s, the company employed 120 people with a daily output of 350 clocks. Its success was short-lived, as the building was sold 10 years later to Hurlbut Paper Company from Lee who converted the building to produce fine stationery. Instead of the usual bell tower on earlier mills, Terry appropriately placed a clock, which still adorns this building that is now condos, offices, and home to the *Berkshire Eagle.*

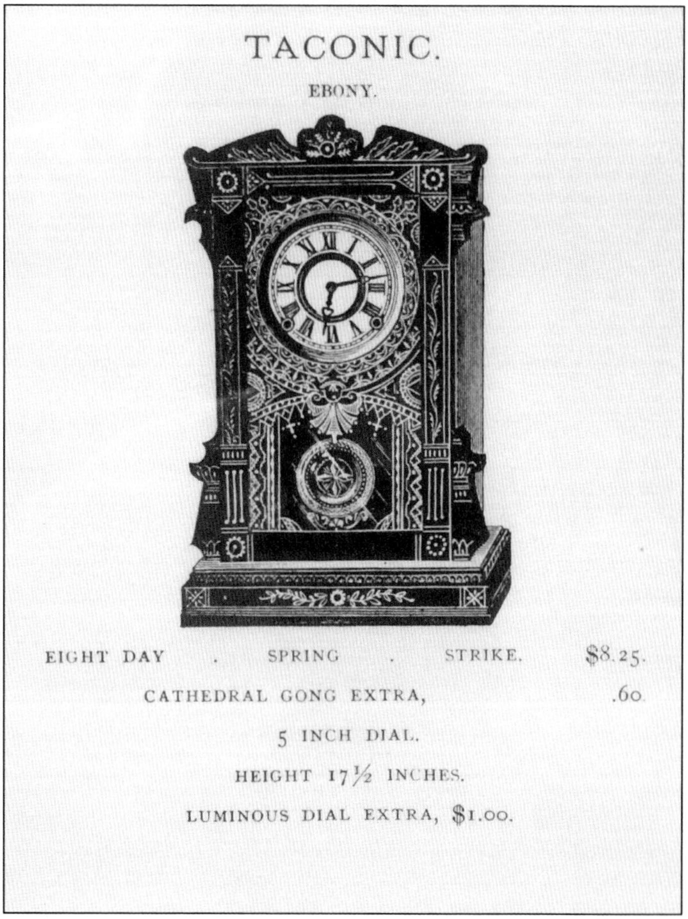

A Terry Clock catalogue describes the features of this Taconic clock, appropriately named for the region where it was built. With over 150 different styles of clocks, names were adopted from far beyond the Berkshires. Terry invented clocks that could receive and send telephone signals, establishing a unique niche in the business. The company made its clocks with different kinds of wood, sizes, and additional features such as a face that lit up. This clock sold for just $8.25, but Terry clocks fetch upwards to $2,000 on eBay now.

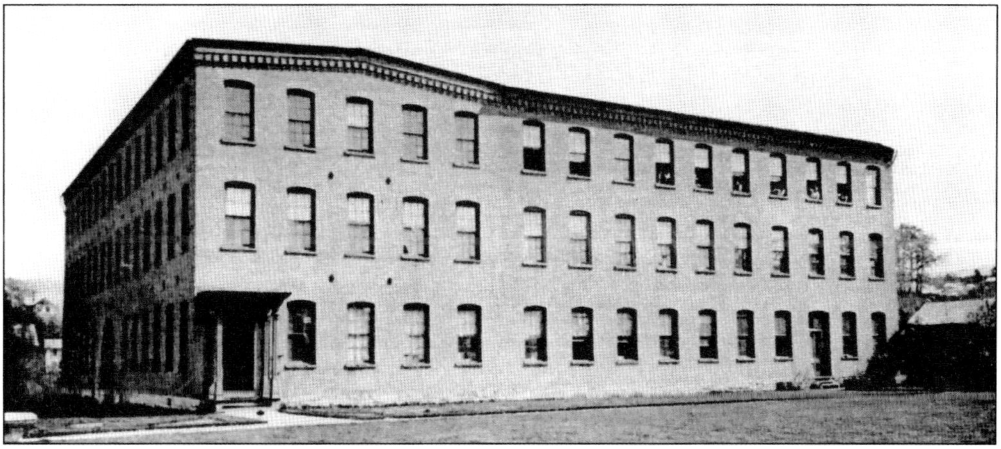

In the 1840s, North Adams saw the beginning of shoe manufacturing on an industrial scale, making it the leading industry in town through the 19th century despite all the textile mills. In 1850, a young Calvin Sampson moved to North Adams from Vermont to sell shoes with a cousin. Sampson proved so successful, he branched out on his own—first with a store and then with his own manufacturing business. Over the next 40 years, Sampson continued to expand and innovate, bringing in new technology to make his shoes more efficiently. (Courtesy of the North Adams Historical Society.)

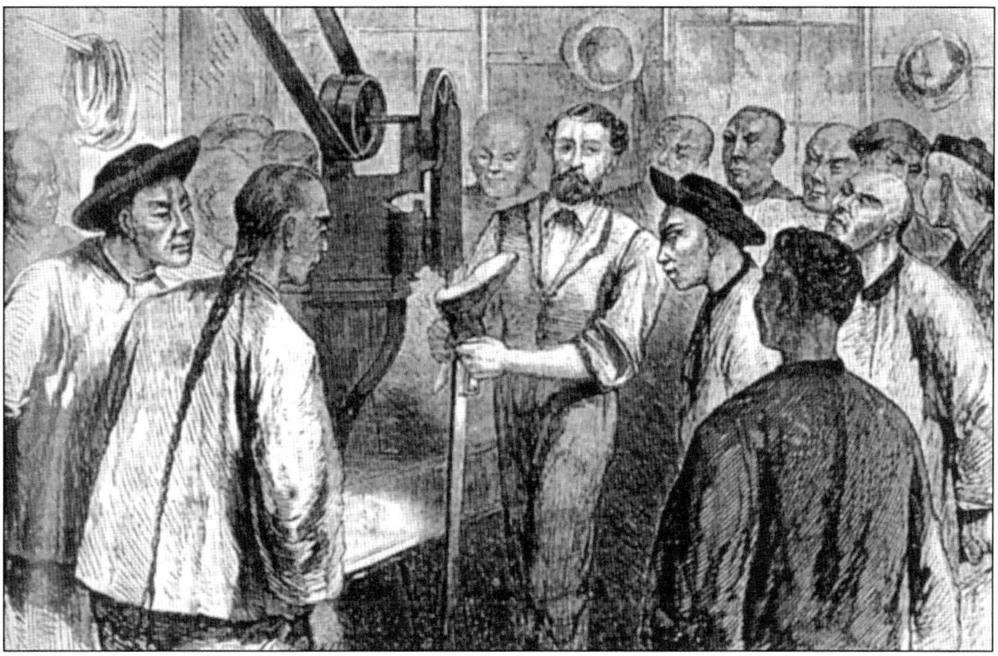

After the economic panic of 1857 and the Civil War, Sampson faced growing labor unrest in his factory, stemming from a new organization, the Knights of St. Crispin. With no laws to protect the rights of workers, Sampson was able to fire organizers and rehire outside workers, but they too quickly joined the union. When workers objected to new machinery in 1870, they decided to strike. Sampson brought in Chinese laborers from California under a three-year contract to replace the striking workers. After a few years, they returned to California and local residents were once again hired, bringing the workforce to 350 by 1885. (Courtesy of the North Adams Historical Society.)

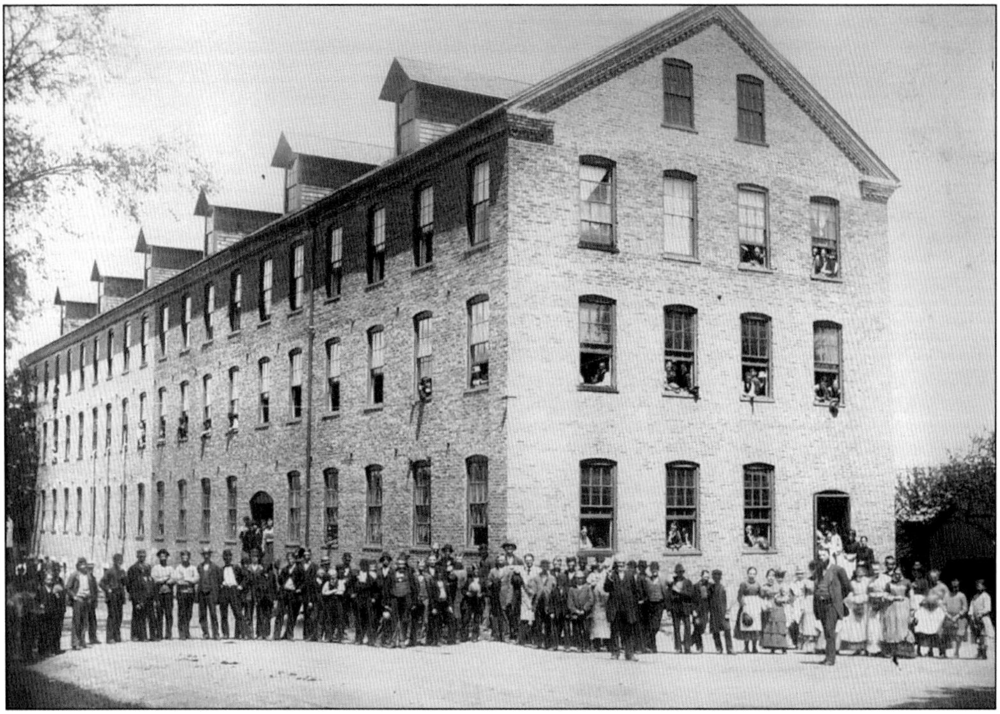

Workers hang out the windows so that they can be included in this photograph of Robbins and Kellogg Shoe Company, situated not far from downtown Pittsfield, on Fourth Street. Among its 450 workers were women and children. Built in 1870, the shoe company only lasted for 30 years, but at its peak, it was producing 1,800 shoes per day, with machinery powered by a 40-horsepower coal-burning engine. By 1900, the company was forced to close, but the building survived, mostly as a storage facility for General Electric and then for England Brothers, Pittsfield's premier department store.

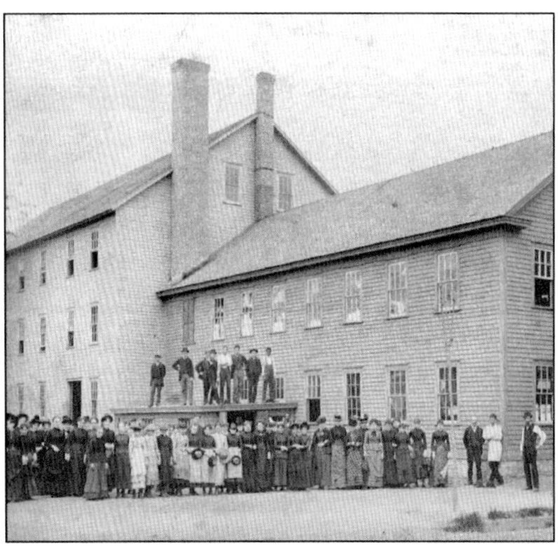

Some textile mills in Pittsfield sold their unfinished products directly to other companies who cut and sewed the reams of cloth into clothing and other products. Brothers Martin and Arthur Sprague joined Edric C. Brimmer to launch a shirt manufacturing business in 1880. Situated near the train station in Pittsfield, the company expanded from 15 to 200 workers, necessitating the three-story addition in the rear of this photograph. Hiring mostly women, the Sprague Brimmer Shirt Company produced over 400 dozen shirts per week. In 1895, a fire destroyed the factory, and a year later, the company was sold to a Boston firm that moved the equipment out of Pittsfield.

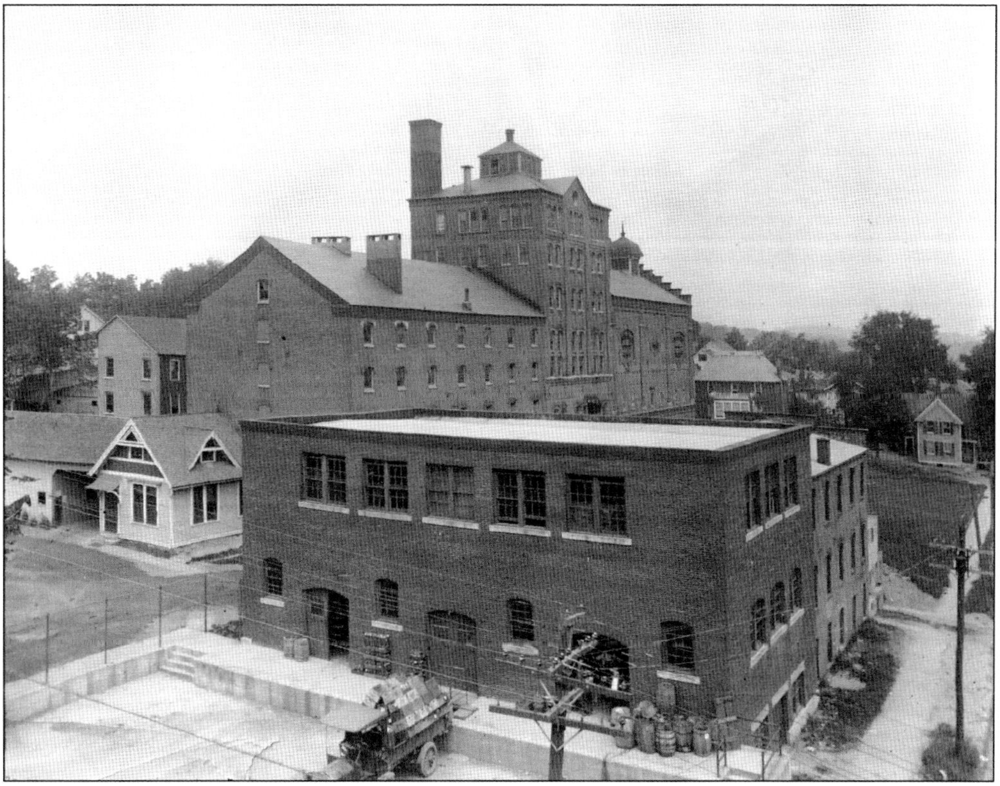

A pair of German immigrants moved to Pittsfield after the Civil War and worked in the Taconic Mill. In 1868, Jacob Gimlich and John White left the mill to buy out a small brewery in the town, producing about six barrels per day. Initially, their factory was located near North Street, but as the business expanded, they moved several blocks away, tapping into an outlet from Onota Lake. Their five-story brick factory, built in 1880, stood out on the Pittsfield skyline and took up an entire city block at the corner of John Street and Columbus Avenue.

Jacob Gimlich and John White's business grew fast, and shortly after moving to the new site, the two founders turned the company over to new owners who changed the name to the Berkshire Brewing Association. Its lineup of beers sound like the finest craft beers of today: Lenox Half Stock Ale, Greylock Ale, Mannheimer Lager, and India Pale Ale. It was a short horse ride down to the train station to pick up supplies and deliver the finished products for distribution as far away as South Carolina.

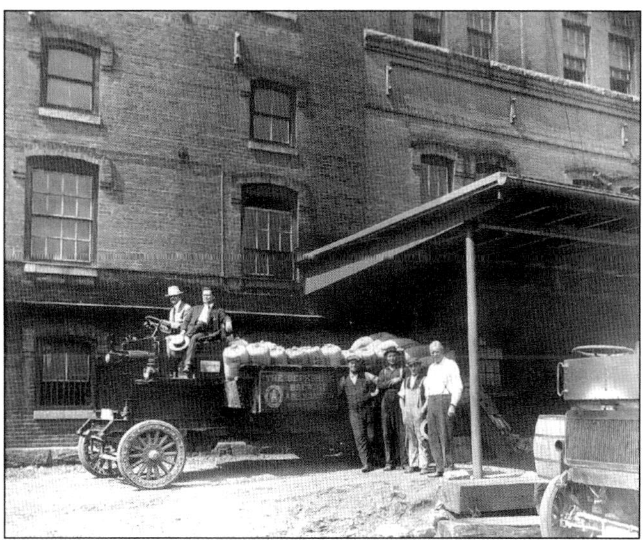

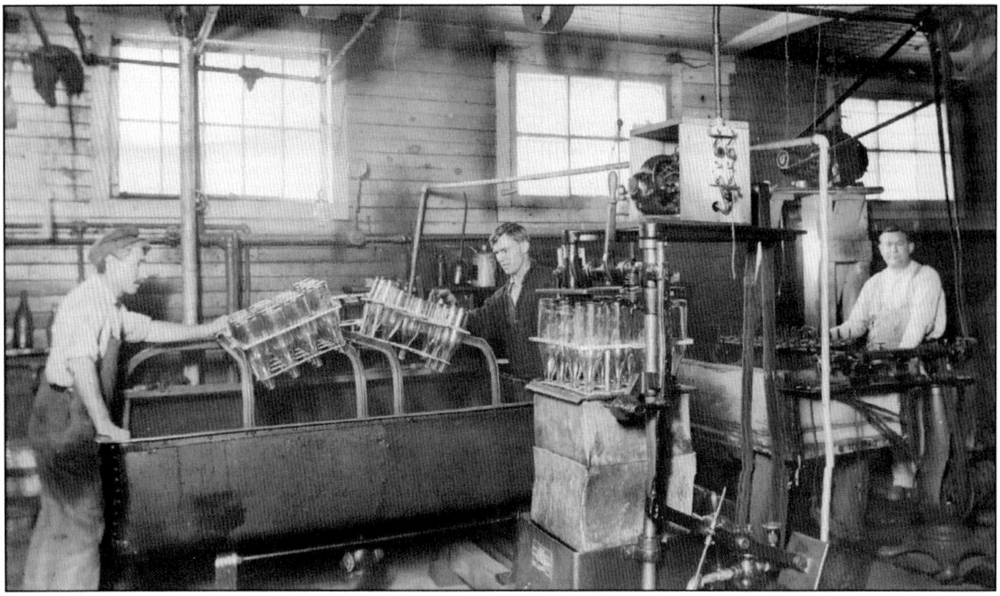

By 1890, Berkshire Brewing employed 100 people and produced 300 barrels a day. Advertisements for the beer appealed to those "summering and touring in the Berkshire Hills" and praised the "pure bracing air and pure water" of the region. Besides beer, the company also produced soda and mineral water. It is likely that the brewery bought the glass bottles from the nearby glassworks in Cheshire and Lanesborough. Here, workers clean the returned bottles. These can now be bought on eBay for as high as $400.

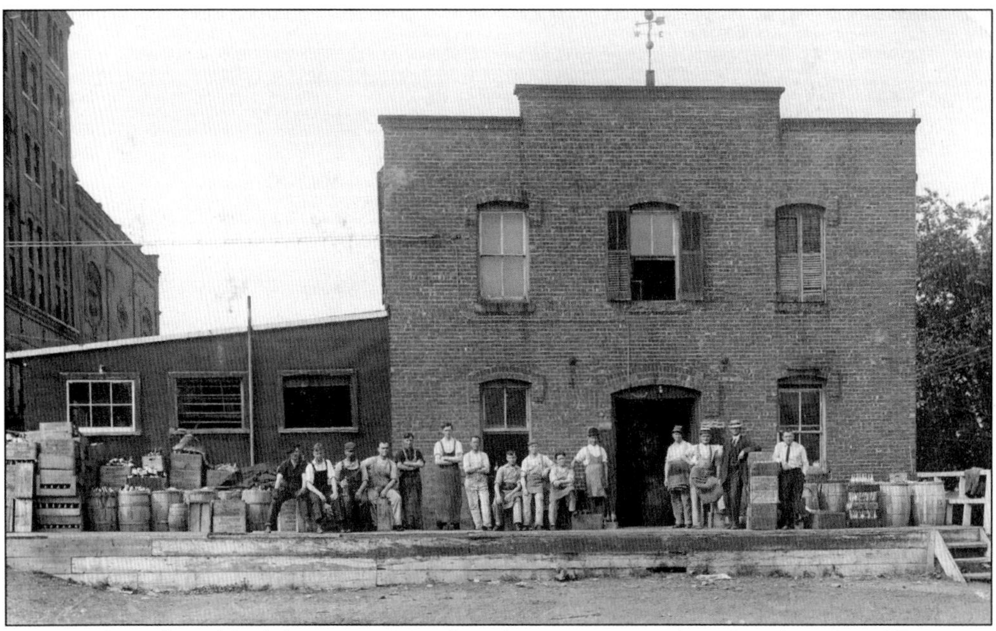

Business thrived until Prohibition in 1919, when the company was forced to close. Siegel Furniture Company later bought the complex and turned the plant into a warehouse and showroom. The large building stood until the 1970s when the city bought the property and as part of urban renewal razed the complex. In this postcard, brewery workers stand on the loading dock in an outbuilding adjacent to the main plant.

Five

OWNERS

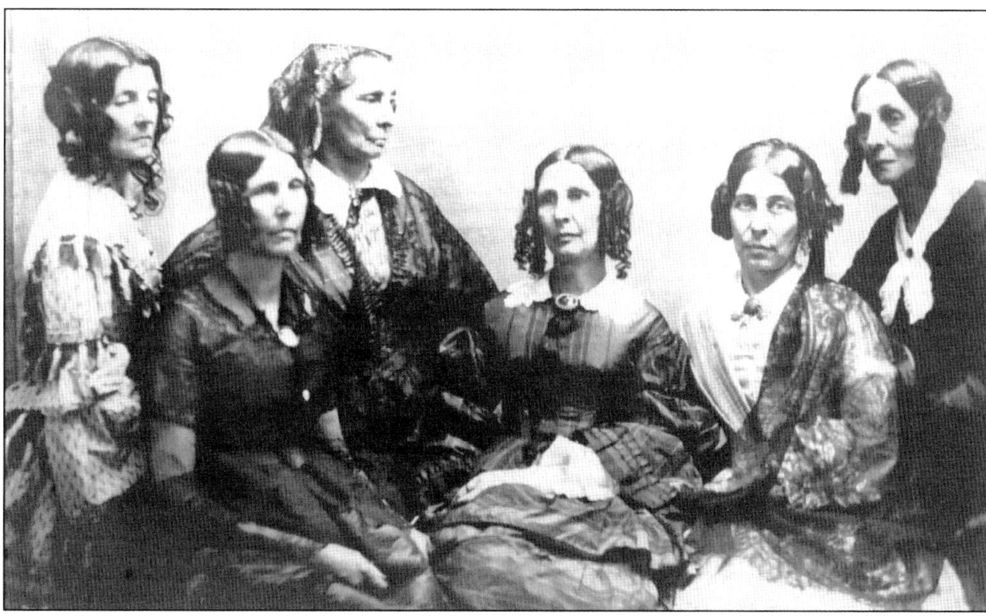

The entrepreneurs, owners and managers of the mills and factories around Berkshire County in the 19th century were exclusively men. Their wives, daughters, and sisters played little active role in business. A few, such as Caroline Campbell, inherited shares in their father's business, but in her case, she turned her stake in the Pontoosuc Woolen Mill over to her husband, Ensign Kellogg. Women were involved in the civic and social life of the communities, promoting medical care and, during the Civil War, caring for soldiers in the Ladies Soldiers Aid Auxiliary. This photograph shows the sisters and daughters of Theodore Pomeroy, who inherited textile mills in Pittsfield from his father.

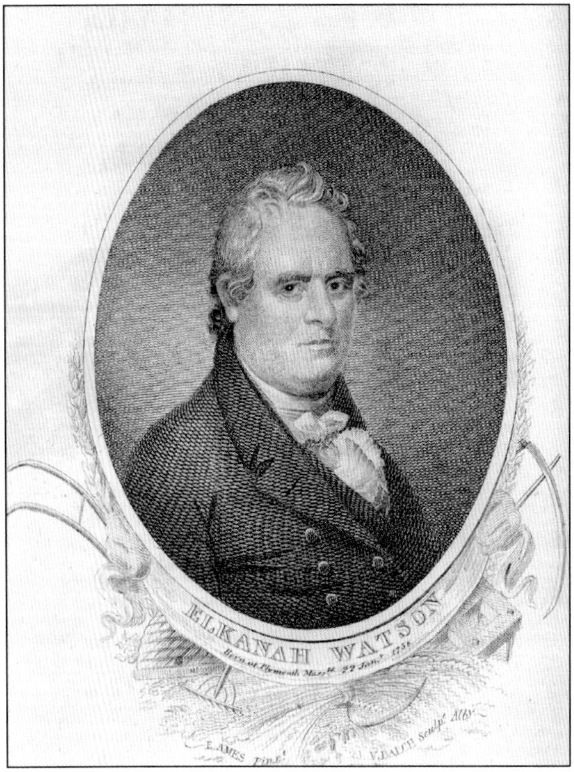

The man who introduced merino sheep to the Berkshires moved to Pittsfield at the end of a life that intersected with many of the main events of the new nation. Born in Plymouth, Massachusetts, Elkanah Watson became indentured to the Brown family from Rhode Island, who helped start cotton factories there. He was involved in slave transactions for Moses Brown and, during the Revolutionary War, he was sent to France with dispatches for Benjamin Franklin. At war's end, Watson decided to take up farming and, in 1807, brought a new brand of sheep imported from Spain to Pittsfield. Their high-quality wool helped boost the new mills just starting. (Courtesy of the Berkshire Athenaeum.)

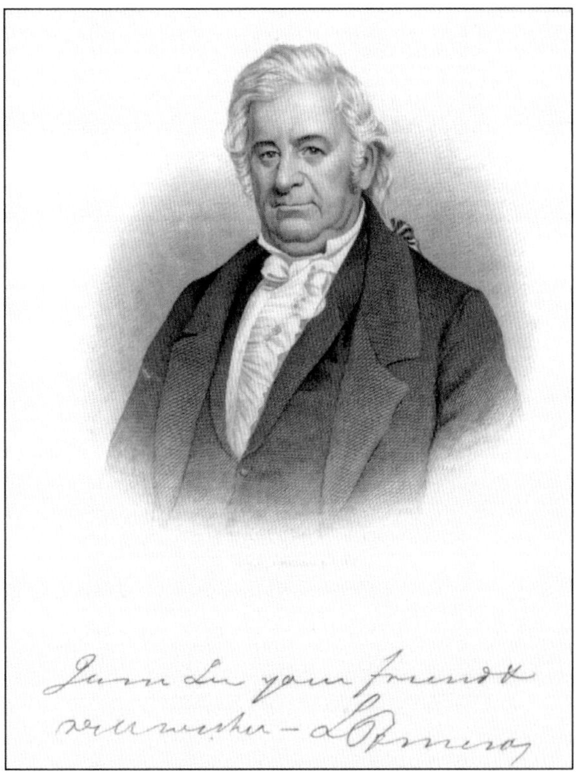

With his astute business skills and civic leadership, Lemuel Pomeroy epitomized the early mill owners in Berkshire County. Pomeroy came to Pittsfield in 1799 from the Connecticut valley with experience as a blacksmith. After a fire destroyed his own shop, Pomeroy purchased a gun shop on the site of the old Whitney forge north of the center of town. When the War of 1812 started, he filled a government contract to produce 2,000 muskets a year. Pomeroy saw another business opening in the production of textiles and built a mill close to the town center.

By the time Lemuel Pomeroy died in 1849, he had already brought his sons into the business and changed the name of his textile mill to L. Pomeroy & Sons. Only Theodore, pictured here, had the interest in and talent for running such a complex. Like his father, his business interests extended to other mills where his investments helped launch Taconic Mill and the Pittsfield Woolen Mill, as well as a large stake in the Greylock Mill in North Adams. He and his father were also original shareholders in the new rail line contemplated for Pittsfield that would greatly ease transportation of their textiles to markets in New York and beyond.

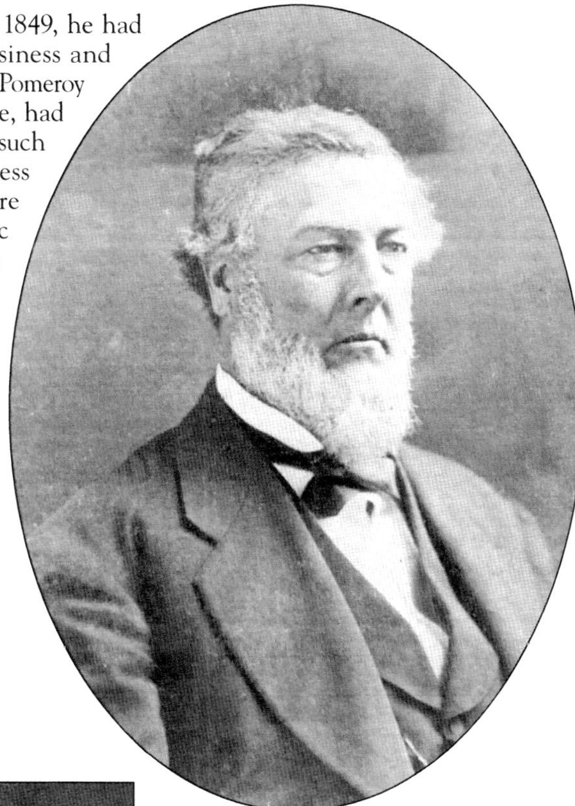

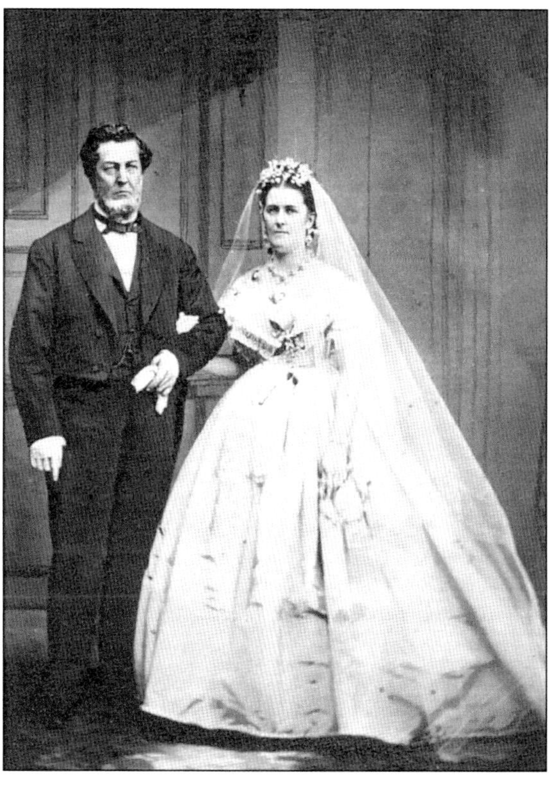

As successful as he was in business, Theodore Pomeroy was unlucky in love, as his first two wives died young. His first marriage to Fannie Bacon lasted 15 years before she passed away in 1851. A year later, Theodore married Mary Harris from New York, and they had six children before she died in the middle of the Civil War in 1863. Three years later, he and Laura, pictured here, married; they had two children.

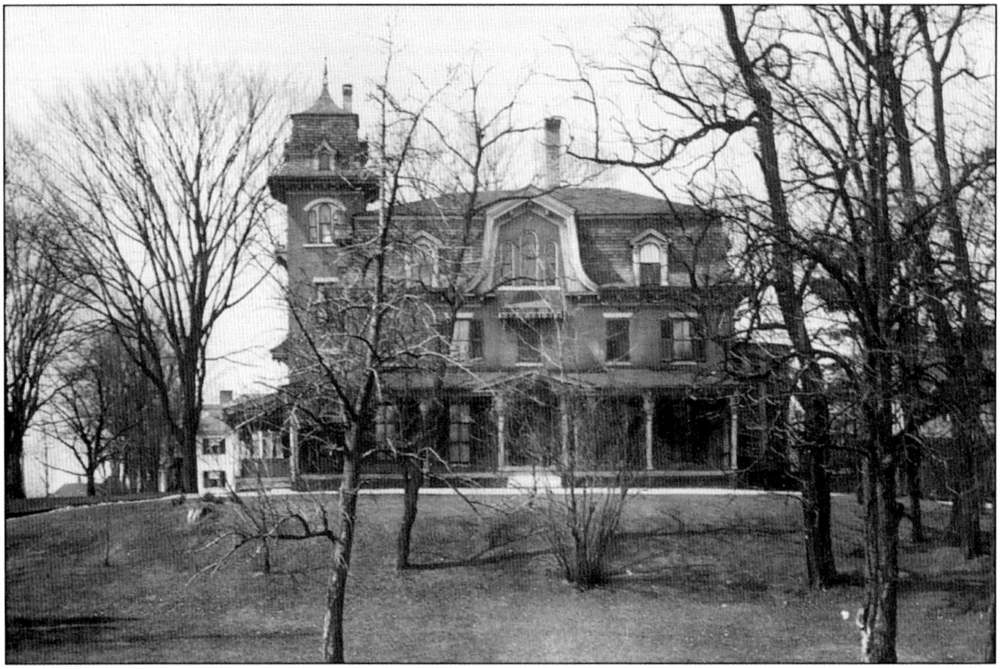

Not far from the mills he owned and ran, Theodore built a large mansion for his growing family. It was not uncommon in the early years of textile mills for owners to live within walking distance of their factories and their workers. Gradually, with the introduction of railroads and both horse-drawn and electric trolleys in the towns, workers and their managers moved farther away from their work and lived in different parts of the town.

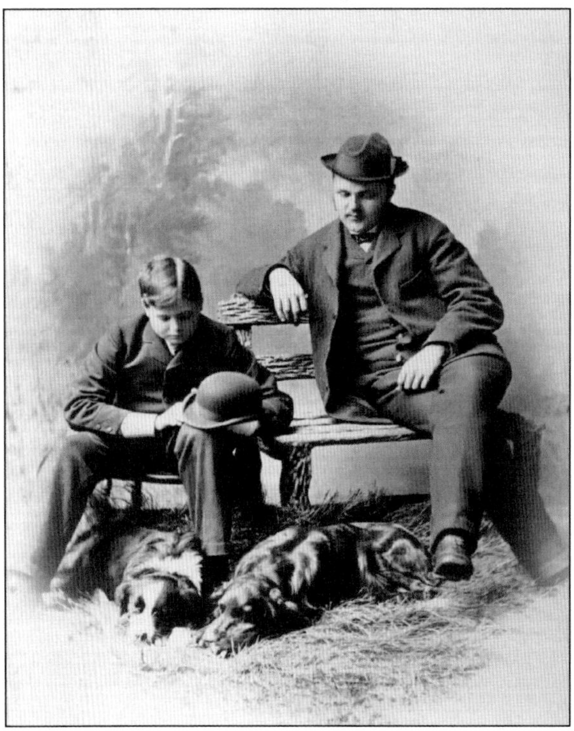

The two sons of Theodore Pomeroy were destined to carry on the business their grandfather had started. Theodore (left) and his older brother Silas were groomed from a young age in the affairs of the textile operations. When the boys' father passed away, a group of trustees helped run the mills until Theodore turned 21. He and his brother carried on the business for more than a decade.

It was a small clique of men who ran and owned the textile mills in mid-century Pittsfield, using their personal and family connections to expand their interests into new areas. Ensign Kellogg became president of Pontoosuc Woolen Mill after he married Caroline Campbell, the daughter of one of the first investors of the mill. In addition to a coal-powered company, Kellogg had his hand in politics, as a Republican state legislator who supported Abraham Lincoln in his 1860 bid for the presidency.

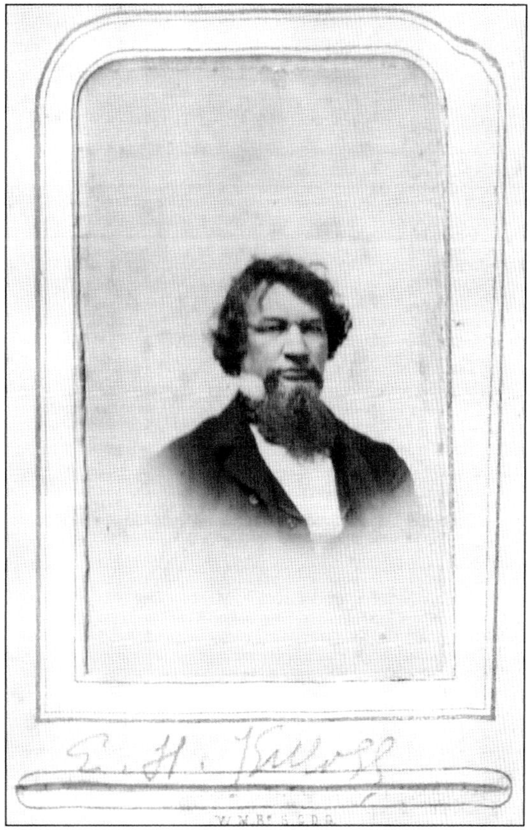

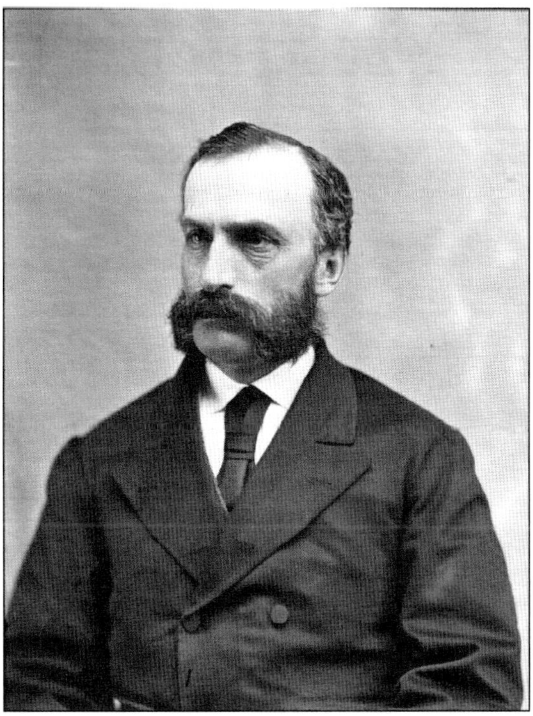

Jabez L. Peck was the middle of three generations of Pecks who owned and operated the two mills along Onota Brook in Pittsfield. It was his uncle Elijah who was the driving force behind the initial construction of the mill that produced cotton warp in 1844. Jabez's father had bought out Elijah's partner and then passed it along to his son 10 years later. By 1864, Jabez was sole owner of the mills, having purchased his uncle's stake in the company.

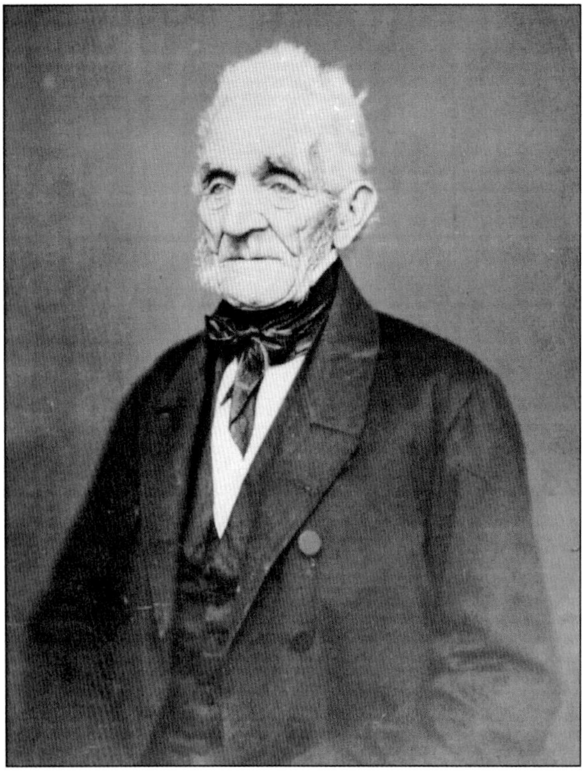

At an age when most people consider retiring, Jabez Peck continued expanding the two mills he owned for the next three decades through major economic "panics" that saw rival mills close and change ownership. Jabez ran the operation well into his 90s and then turned the business over to his son Thomas. Seen here is "Grandfather Peck" shortly before his death in 1895 at the age of 96.

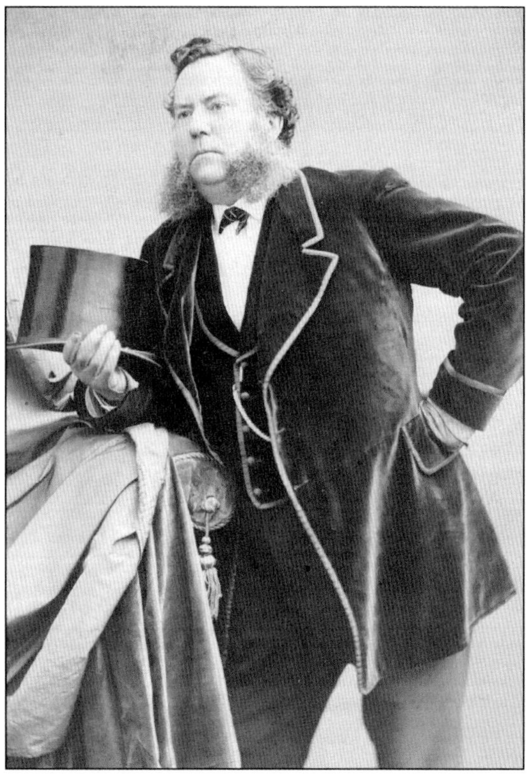

Thaddeus Clapp Jr. grew up around textile weaving, as his father had first come to Pittsfield to be the general superintendent of the first textile mill in the city, the Pittsfield Woolen and Cotton Company. When the Pontoosuc Woolen Mill started in the late 1820s, the elder Clapp moved over to supervise operations there. Shortly before his father died in 1865, young Thaddeus became general agent and superintendent of the mill and served as its president until he died in 1890.

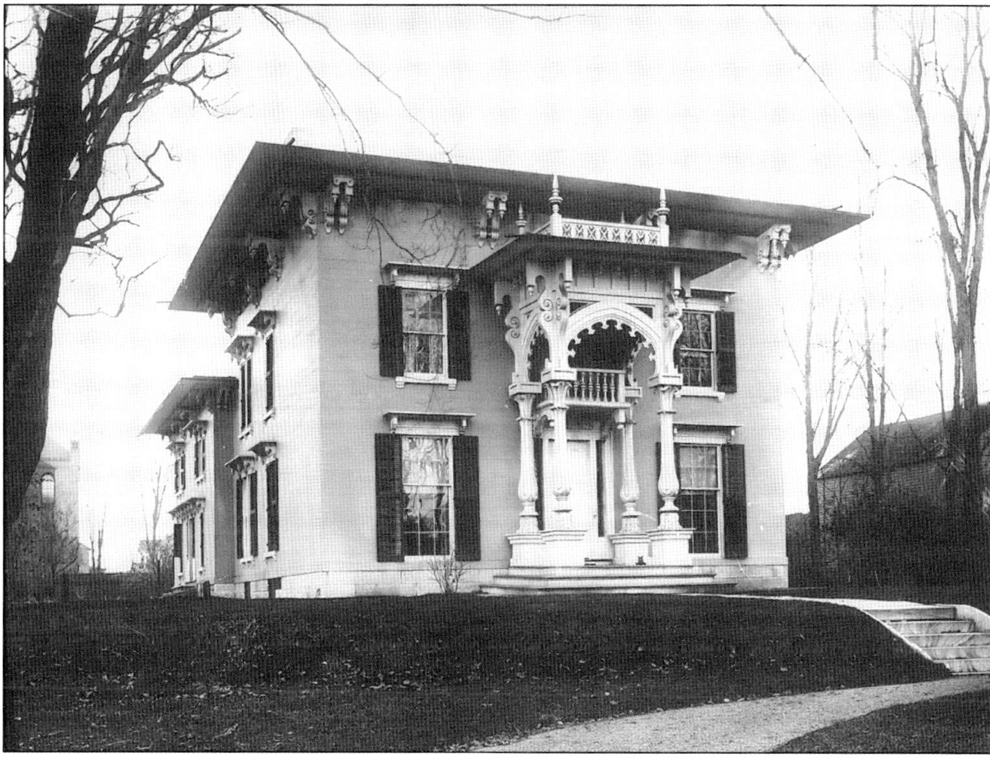

The Clapp family had residences all over the city. In the 1850s, they lived out near Pontoosuc Woolen Mill to be close to the daily operations of the mill. The introduction of horse-drawn trolleys in Pittsfield, and much later electric trolleys, allowed both managers and workers to move away from the mills. Thaddeus Clapp Jr. built this ornately decorated house closer to the town center, on East Street. There, he would find as his neighbors a growing number of prominent Pittsfield businessmen, such as Ensign Kellogg and Julius Rockwell.

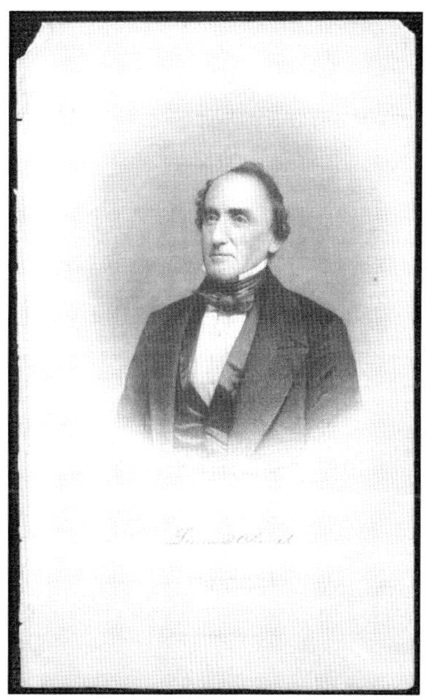

Mill ownership and management was often a family affair. Leonard Church was born into a papermaking family in 1800. He moved to Lee at the age of 6, when his father built the second paper mill in the county and the first one in the town. By the age of 19, Leonard was running the Forest Mill, built by his older brother, Luman. Like many industrialists of the era, Leonard became involved in banking and politics. He served in the Massachusetts General Court, and after accepting the presidency of a local Lee bank, he left the papermaking business. (Courtesy of the Lee Public Library.)

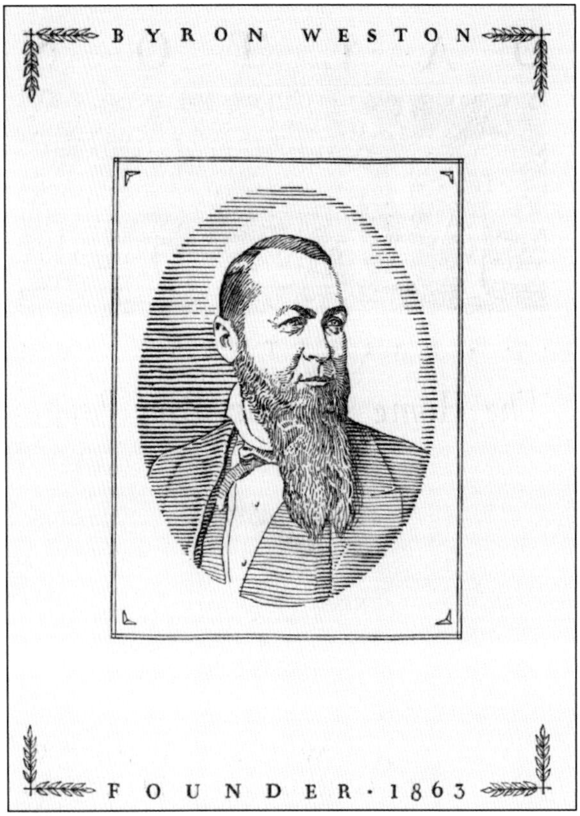

Byron Weston was born in Dalton in 1832. After school in Easthampton, Massachusetts, and Beloit, Wisconsin, he went to work in his uncle's paper factory in Saugerties, New York. During the Civil War, he signed on as a captain in the all Berkshire County Regiment, the Massachusetts 49th, which saw action in the Battle of Port Hudson. After the war, with the help of his uncle, Weston bought the Defiance Mill and began his papermaking business. (Courtesy of the Berkshire Athenaeum.)

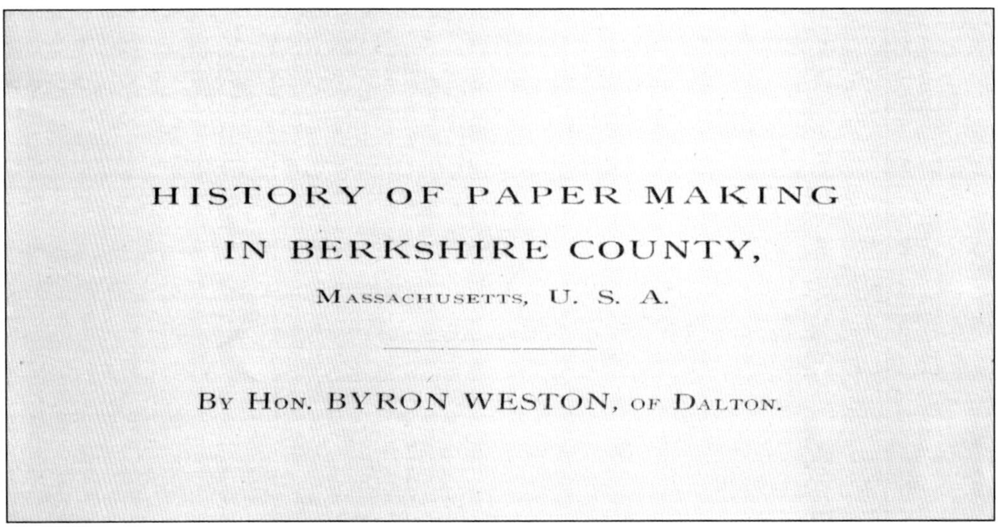
HISTORY OF PAPER MAKING

IN BERKSHIRE COUNTY,

MASSACHUSETTS, U. S. A.

BY HON. BYRON WESTON, OF DALTON.

Like many successful industrialists in the latter half of the 19th century, Weston turned to public service and philanthropy. He ran as a Republican for the state senate and won, leading to his nomination for lieutenant governor in Massachusetts. With the wealth he accrued, Weston donated money for the construction of Grace Episcopal Church in Dalton and athletic fields at Williams College that still bear his name. Before he died of a stroke in 1898, Weston had recorded his business contributions in a short pamphlet, *The History of Papermaking in Berkshire County, Massachusetts, U.S.A.* (Courtesy of the Berkshire Athenaeum.)

Zenas Marshall Crane entered the family business of papermaking in Dalton. Born in 1815, young Zenas grew up learning all facets of paper production, and he and his brother James became partners in the company in 1836 and full owners when their father retired in 1842. Zenas developed a process of embedding silk thread into paper that gave his company an edge in making paper for currency. When he died in 1887, he had already passed the company on to his son Zenas Crane Jr.

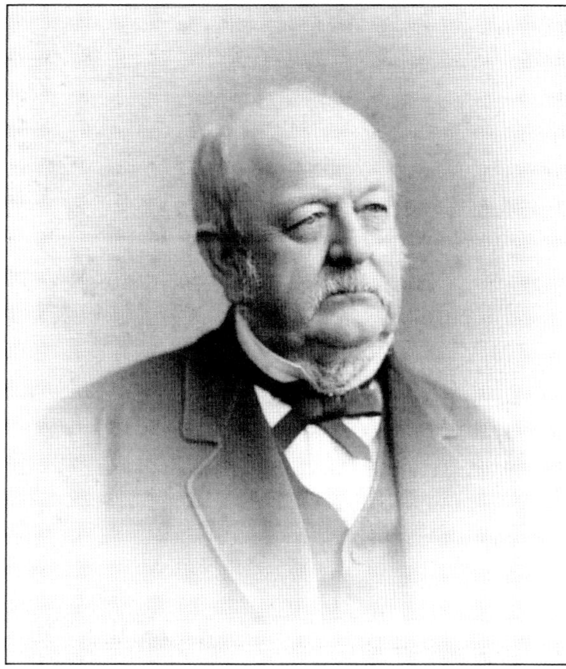

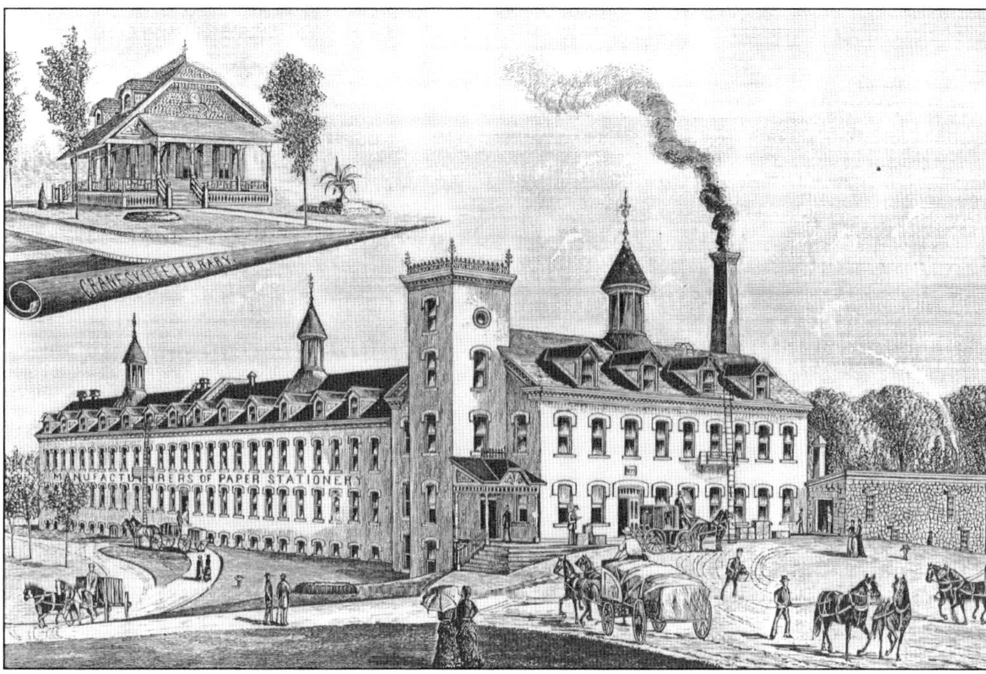

Civic leadership was also good for business. In 1882, Zenas Crane Jr., grandson of the founder of the paper company, decided to build a public library in Dalton. With 500 volumes and magazine subscriptions, his workers had an outlet that was less disruptive than other pursuits that the owners frowned upon—especially alcohol. The library also served to start assimilating the new immigrants who would find their way to work in the paper mills. Crane's generosity preceded the first library built by Andrew Carnegie by four years. This Beers map drawing shows the Old Berkshire Mill, with the inset of the library.

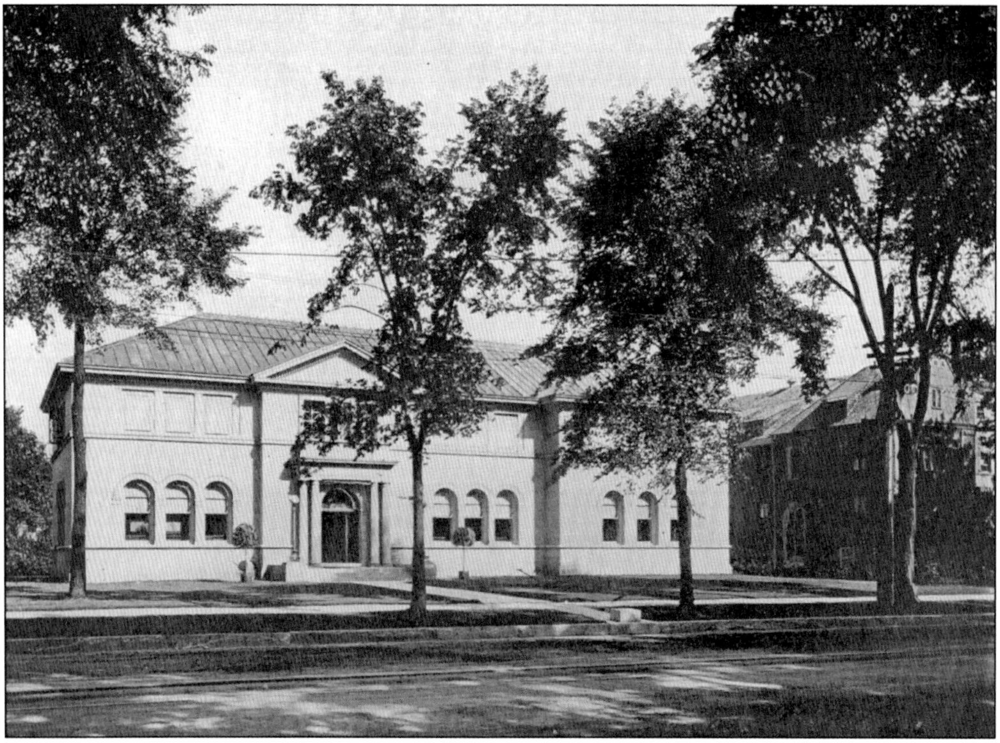

Zenas Crane Jr.'s philanthropy extended beyond the town borders of Dalton and beyond his own workers. While he did own the Government Mill, just over the town line in Pittsfield, Crane's donation in 1903 to create the Berkshire Museum in downtown Pittsfield was intended as a contribution to the entire county. Dedicated to both art and natural history, his new museum freed up space in the adjacent Berkshire Athenaeum that had been built in 1876 as a library and a museum.

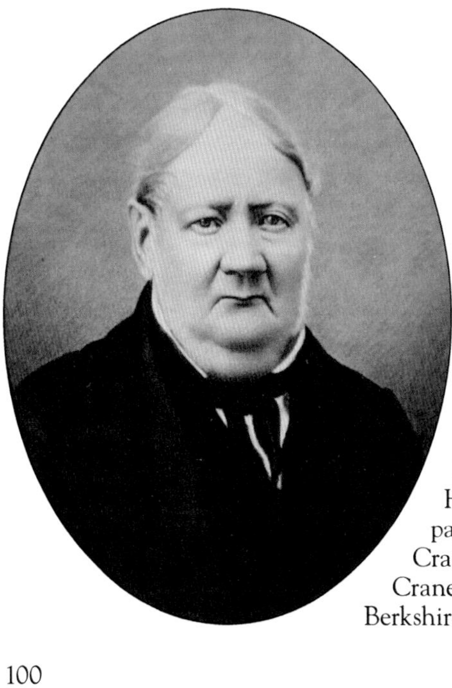

By the time this photograph was taken, David Carson had become one of Berkshire County's leading industrialists, a builder and owner of paper mills, and president of the Pittsfield Bank. Born in Albany in 1783, Carson learned his papermaking skills in Orange County before moving to Worcester, Massachusetts, as a full-time journeyman in the trade. He came to Dalton as one of the early pioneers of the paper business there, securing employment with Zenas Crane. He bought into the Berkshire Mill first set up by Crane and became sole owner by 1816. (Courtesy of the Berkshire Athenaeum.)

Elizur Smith took his small earnings as a clerk in a country store to invest in the Turkey Mill in Tyringham. From there, he and his partner George Platner built a paper empire in Lee that eventually sold more paper than any other company in the nation. He employed hundreds of men, women, and children in his mills that bore patriotic names such as Union, Columbia, and Eagle, as well as local names such as Housatonic, Laurel, and Valley, among others. Smith spent his money and time at his farm High Lawn, breeding trotting horses, and served as a US congressman and state senator. (Courtesy of the Lee Public Library.)

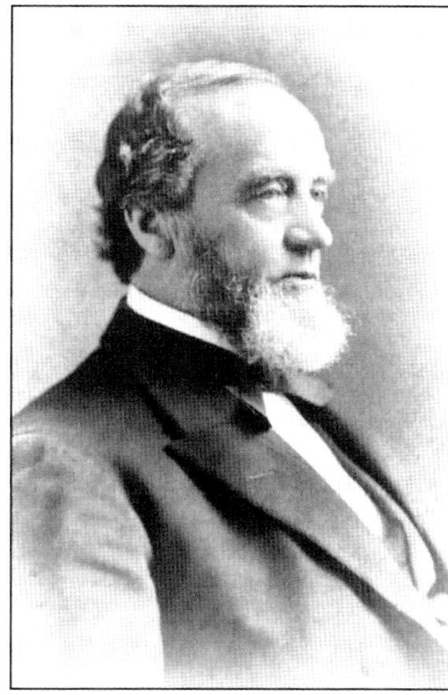

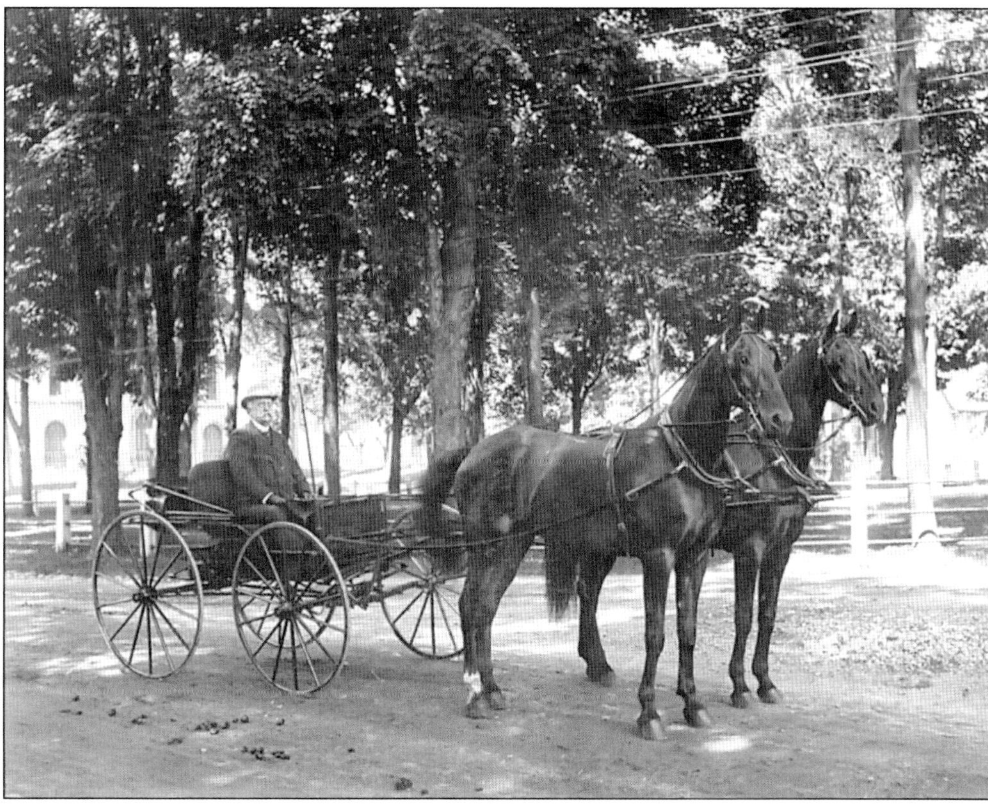

While Elizur Smith retired in 1864, he stayed on as president but turned over daily control to his nephews Wellington and Dewitt. Here, Wellington poses in his carriage parked in the center of Lee, the town that he and his family helped shape into Paper Town. Wellington's fame moved to notoriety when at the age of 75, in New York City, he died in a fluke accident involving the collapse of a folding bed. The woman he was with (scandalously not his wife) barely escaped death herself. (Courtesy of the Lee Public Library.)

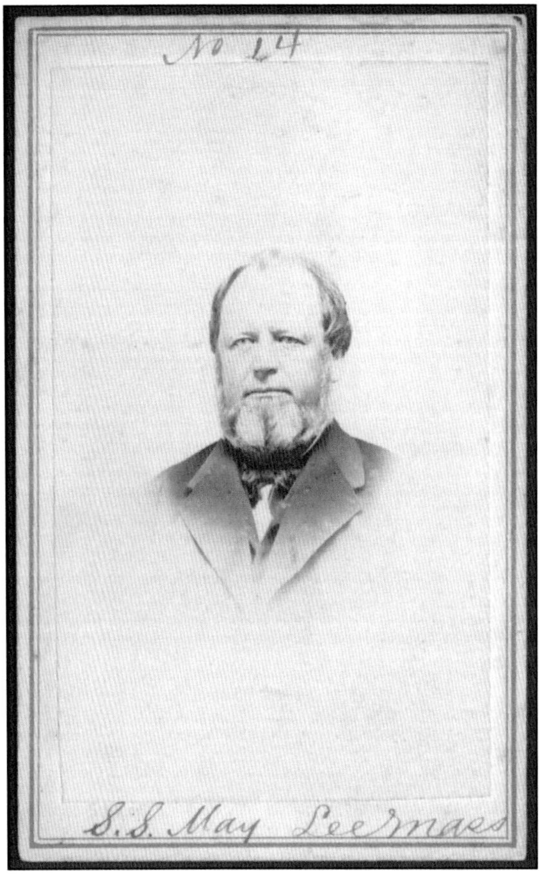

Sylvester May was born in Vermont in 1813 but came to Lee at the age of 21 to work in the Crow Hollow Mill. He quickly bought into the Ingersoll Mill in East Lee. After a fire in 1839, he persuaded his brother to help him buy and rebuild the mill. Over the next 20 years, Sylvester and his brother built two more mills in East Lee, all on Lake May Stream. Their need for more water for their mills drove them to build a dam to enlarge the reservoir. (Courtesy of the Lee Public Library.)

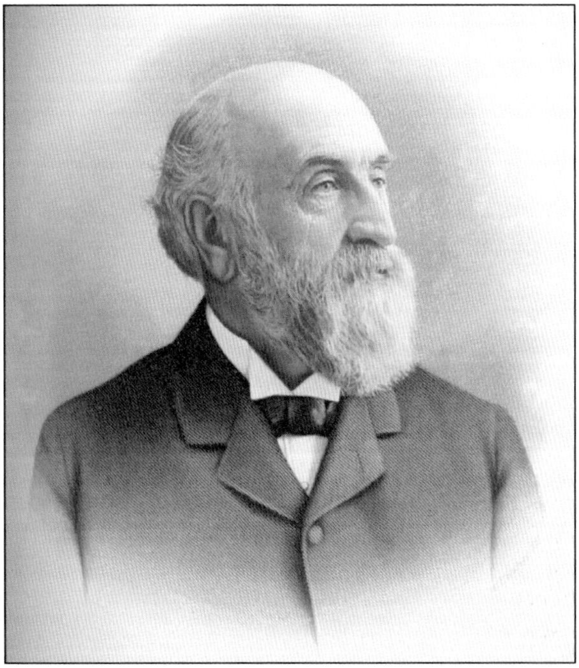

Theodore Ramsdell was a self-made man. Born in 1833, he had little formal schooling, leaving at the age of 13 to work in a cotton mill Greenville, New Hampshire. By 16, he moved up as an overseer of a spinning room. After working in all facets of textile production, he was hired in 1864 to manage Monument Mills in Housatonic. From here, he moved through the ranks, eventually becoming a director and stockholder of the company. (Courtesy of Berkshire Archive.)

Ramsdell served as vice president of Monument Mills until his death in 1903. He accrued tremendous wealth, and like many other mill owners, Ramsdell gave back to his community of roughly 3,000—approximately 10 percent of whom worked in his mill. He helped fund the House of Mercy in Pittsfield and a new church in Housatonic. In his will, he left an endowment for a new library in Housatonic for his workers. The Ramsdell Library was added to the National Register of Historic Places in 2014. (Courtesy of the Berkshire Athenaeum.)

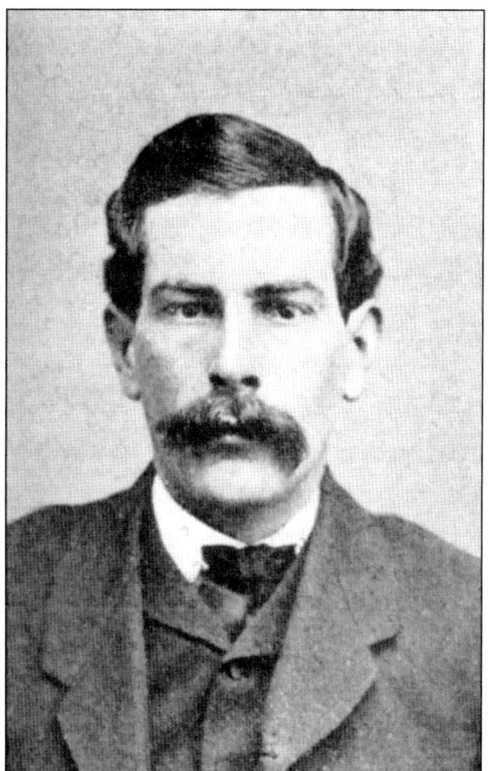

In his history of Pittsfield, Edward Boltwood credits William Tillotson with expanding "the industrial prosperity of the city more effectually than did any other individual textile manufacturer during the quarter-century following 1890." A young Tillotson took over the Osceola Mills in west Pittsfield when his father died. Opening up a new textile mill on Silver Lake helped industrialize that section of the new city, eventually leading the electricity innovator William Stanley to relocate nearby. By the time Tillotson died in 1906, he was beginning to see the advent of a new era of electrical manufacturing. (Courtesy of the Berkshire Athenaeum.)

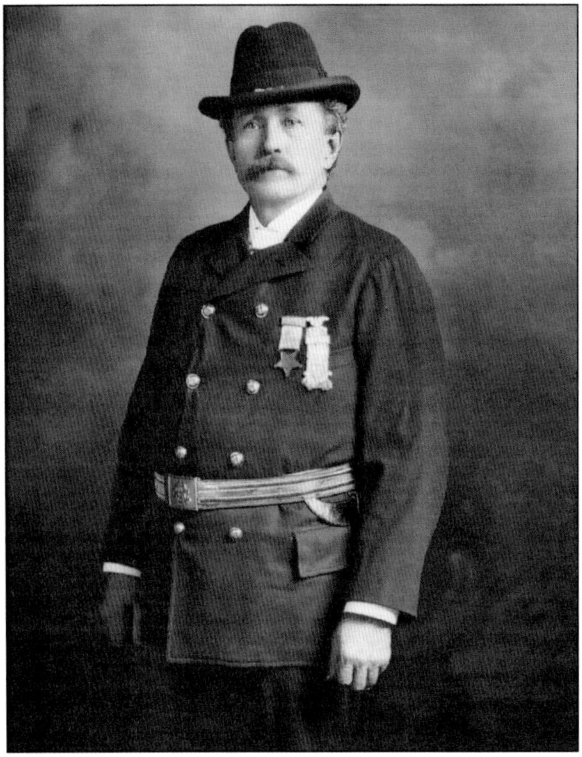

Many of the 19th century industrialists served in the Union army during the Civil War. For many years, the veterans of that conflict participated in parades and other civic gatherings. In full uniform stands John White, co-owner of the brewery that he and Jacob Gimlich, another Civil War veteran, founded. The two were more than business partners, as White married his partner's sister Rachel. They ran the brewery until the 1890s, when they turned over control to their sons. White passed away in 1916, six years before federal officers came to Pittsfield to shut down the brewery, pouring 15,000 gallons of beer down the sewer.

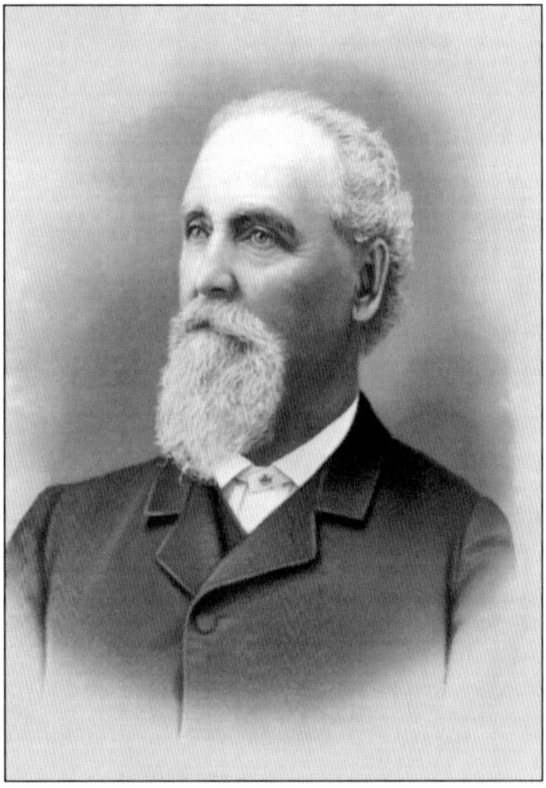

Edward Dorr Jones was born in Otis in 1824, but his family moved to Brooklyn and then to Ohio. After apprenticing with a wheelwright there, he returned to Lee in 1845 and joined a small millwright's shop. He eventually bought out his partner, producing and installing equipment for the mills. Jones moved the company to Pittsfield in 1866 and brought his sons into the business. One son died in a drowning accident, but the other, Edward Archie Jones, took over the company in 1904 when his father stepped down at age 80.

Before E.D. Jones was building the equipment for the mills in Lee, Zalmon Markham had set up shop in Pittsfield and eventually was responsible for waterwheels for over 100 mills in and around Pittsfield. The Shakers owe him a debt of gratitude, as he invented the lathe that turned wood for their chair legs. Markham was a popular figure in the town, known for his philanthropy to the indigent and to children. This photograph was taken shortly before he died at the age of 94 around 1880. (Courtesy of the *Berkshire Eagle*.)

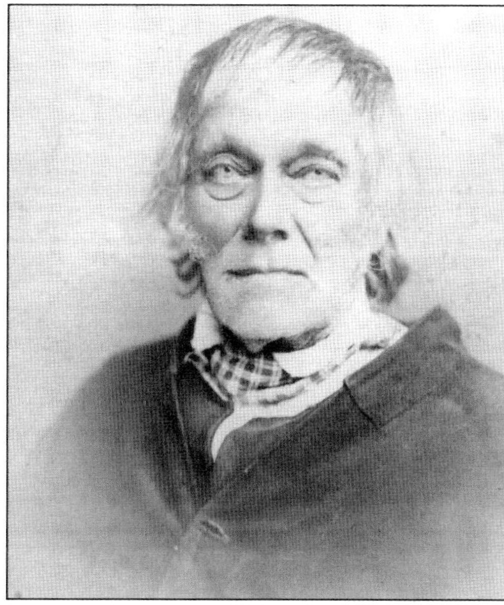

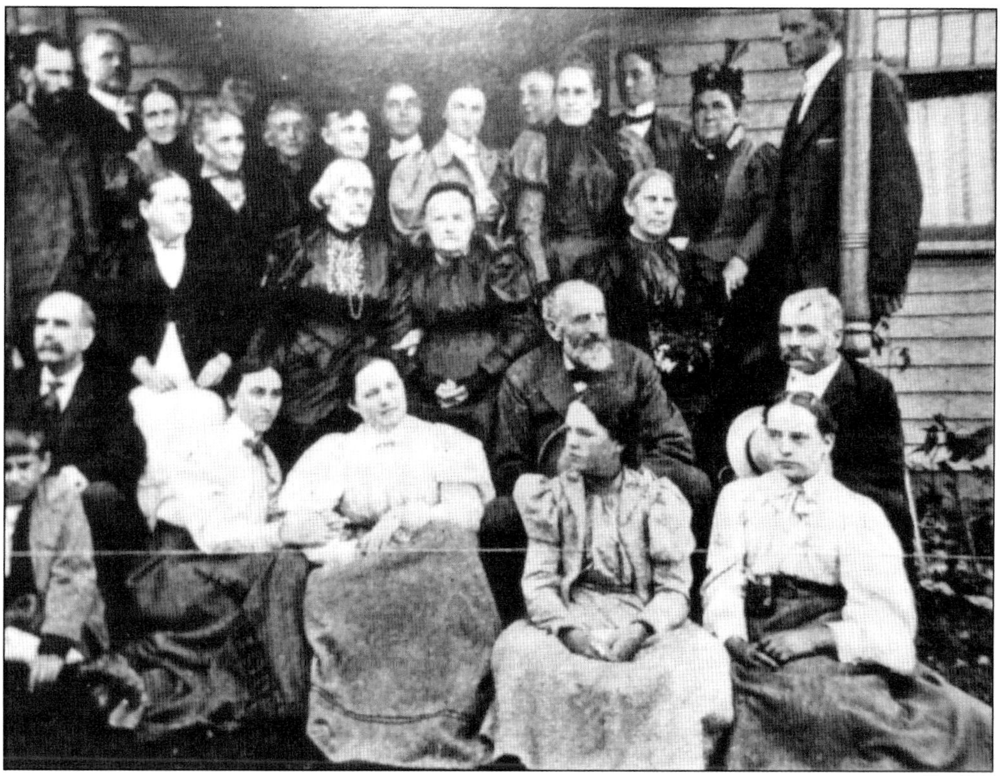

Susan B. Anthony was born in 1820 at Bowens Corners in Adams. When she was just two, her father Daniel and uncle John built the Pump Log Mill on Tophet Brook. They employed 22 girls, whom Susan grew up with, including the 11 who stayed in the Anthony home. At a very young age, Susan helped out at the mill as a spooler when any of the girls fell ill. This photograph is of an Anthony family reunion in Adams in 1897 with Susan (wearing a necklace) and her sisters Hannah and Mary sitting behind their bearded brother, David.

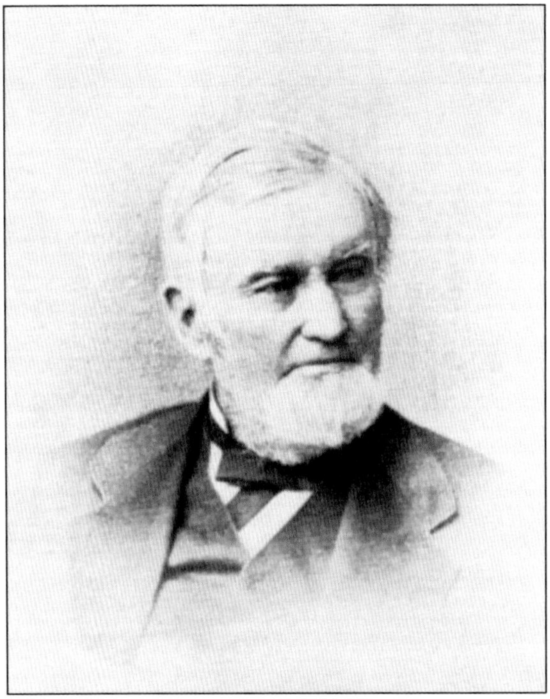

Sanford Blackinton moved to North Adams when he was just two years old. Having worked in a fulling mill as a youth, he built a textile empire that included several mills with over 100 tenement houses. Blackinton helped underwrite a rail line to Pittsfield so his wool could be transferred to the Boston-Albany line for shipment to New York. He brought his son William into the business, but tragedy struck, as young William died of an alleged poisoning. When Sanford died in 1885, he had already turned the company over to his son-in-law William L. Pomeroy. (Courtesy of the North Adams Historical Society.)

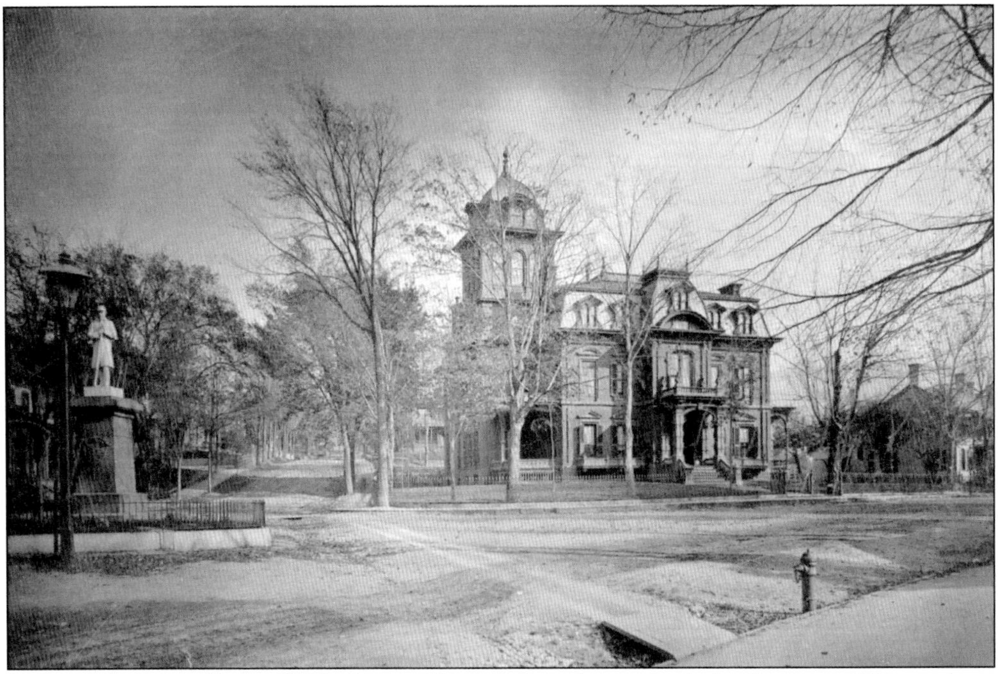

In the early years of his mill, Blackinton chose to live close to both the factory and his workers. Protests from his workers following the Panic of 1857, when he reduced hours, may have spurred him to move into town. When business recovered during the Civil War, he was able to build a grand mansion in the center of the town. After he died in 1885, another textile owner and mayor, Albert Houghton, bought the Blackinton residence and donated it to the town for its library. (Photograph by Frederick Crosier, courtesy of the North Adams Historical Society.)

Born in 1840, James Renfrew left Renfrewshire, Scotland, to settle in Berkshire County. He secured his first employment at Taconic Mills in Pittsfield. Just 27, he joined a new venture started by his uncle with another cousin in Adams. They took over his uncle's Broadley Mill to form Renfrew Manufacturing, and young James used his hands-on knowledge of business to run the day-to-day operations until his death in 1903. By then, the company owned six mills and employed 900 people to operate over 30,000 rug and mule spindles and 1,200 looms.

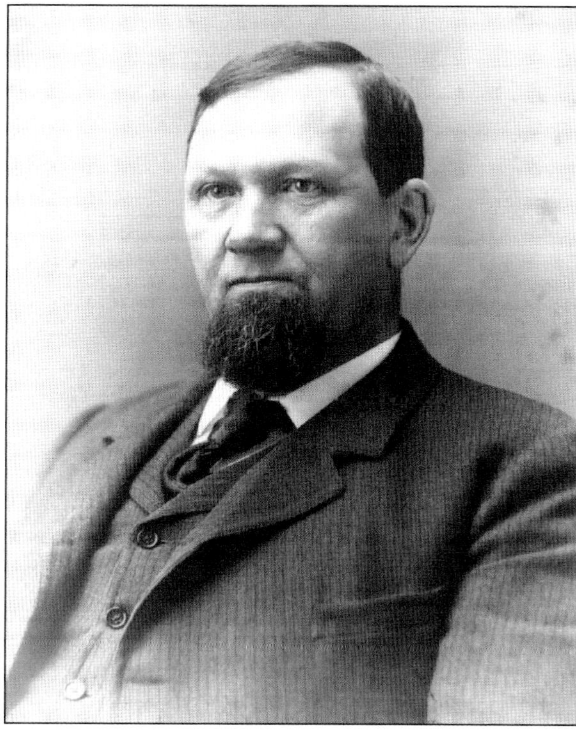

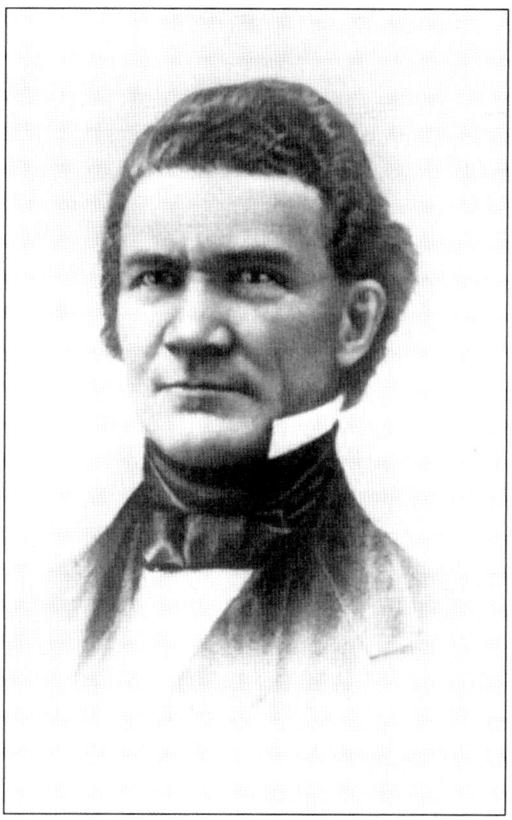

A family reunion of the Plunketts would bring together textile mill owners from North Adams, Adams, Hinsdale, and Pittsfield. Descendants of Patrick and Mary Plunkett, who moved to Lenox in the late 1700s, would dominate Berkshire County industry, banking, transport, and civic life as no other family. Pictured here is William C. Plunkett, Patrick and Mary's eldest son, who resurrected an old mill in South Adams and oversaw his business evolve into multiple complexes in Adams under the name W.C. Plunkett & Sons.

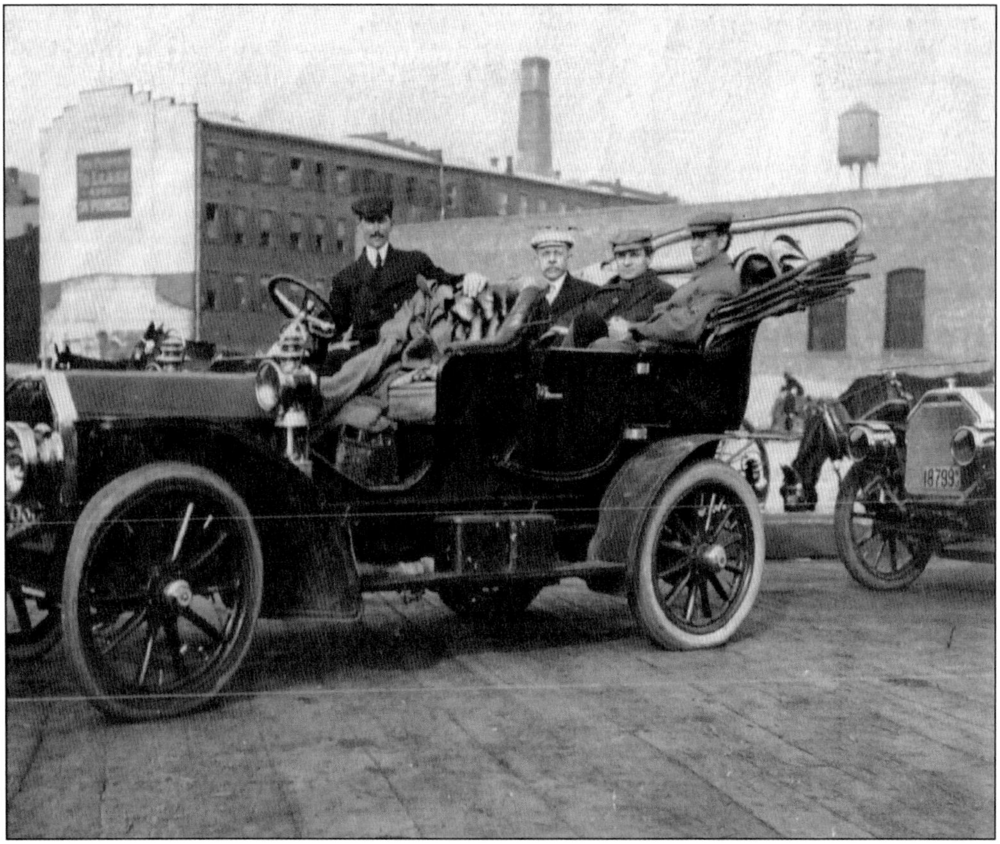

William B. Plunkett sits at the far right in the backseat, in front of a mill whose sign on the side reads "For Lease." By the time this picture was taken, Plunkett had taken over the company following his father's death and ran the original mill as well as the new, large Berkshire Cotton Manufacturing Company. Plunkett became friendly with William McKinley, who visited Adams to lay the cornerstone for Mill No. 4 of Berkshire Cotton. After McKinley was elected president in 1896, Plunkett led the effort to erect a bronze statue of the national leader in Adams.

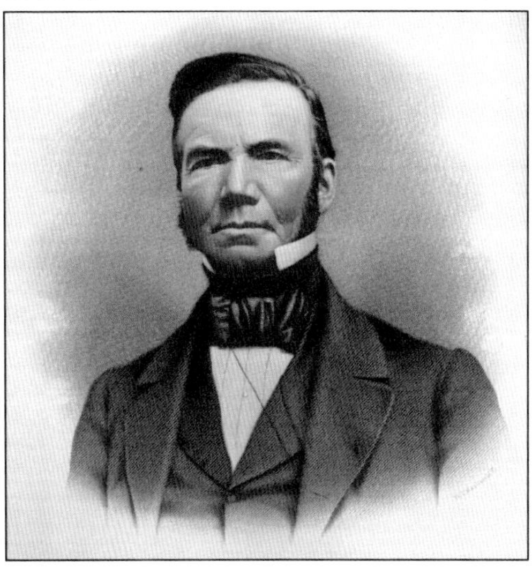

A young Charles H. Plunkett observed the success his older brother had in Adams, so he set out to start his own woolen company in Hinsdale in 1830. Less than a decade later, he had brought his sons Thomas and George into the business; they ended up expanding the mill and buying out a competitor along the same stretch of the Housatonic. The dangers of these mills touched even the owners, as Thomas caught his arm in one of the machines, leaving him with a fractured arm that doctors initially thought would have to be amputated.

The third son of Patrick and Mary Plunkett, Thomas F., moved to Pittsfield and invested in one of the earliest mills there in 1836, eventually selling out to his partner Martin Van Sickler. Thomas's son William R., pictured here, returned to the family interest in textiles, eventually joining and becoming president of Pontoosuc Woolen Company. He also served as president of Berkshire Life Insurance and followed his father on to the board of the First Agricultural Bank.

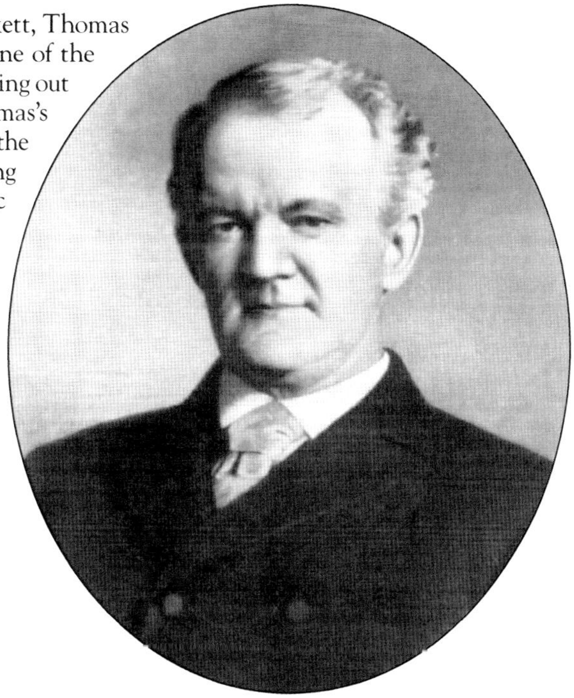

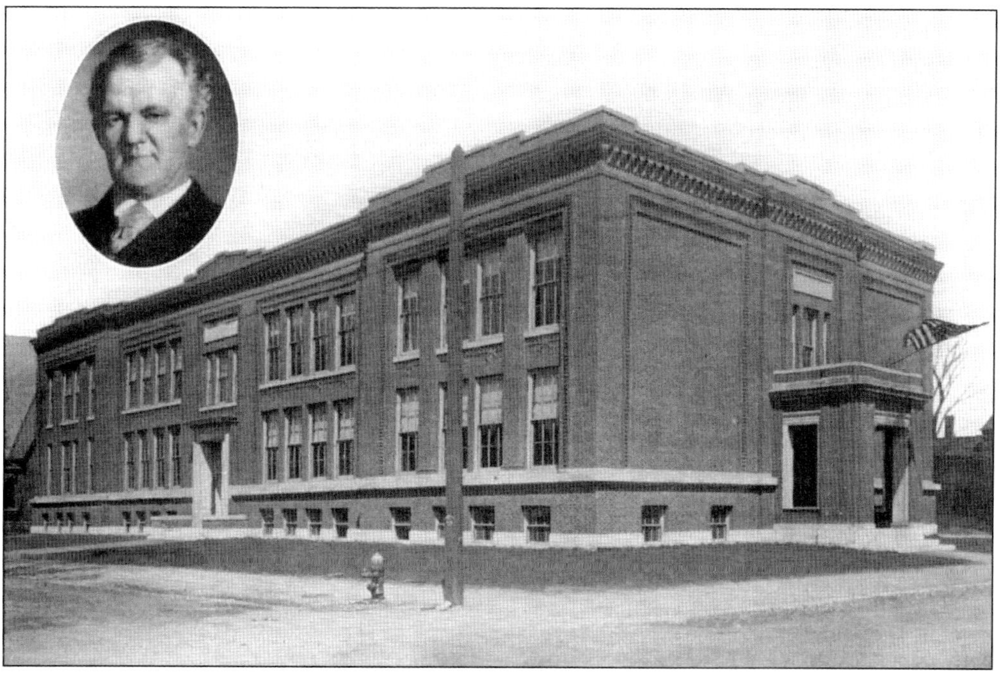

William Plunkett was active in Pittsfield civic and political affairs, serving as head of the trustees of the newly built Berkshire Athenaeum. After his sudden death in 1903, the city bemoaned the loss of a prominent citizen. Within just a few years, the city decided to build a junior high school in his memory. From 1909 until 1977, hundreds of Pittsfield schoolchildren attended the school, a block away from Park Square and within easy walking distance of both the old high school and the new one. The building was torn down in 2016 to make way for a Dunkin' Donuts.

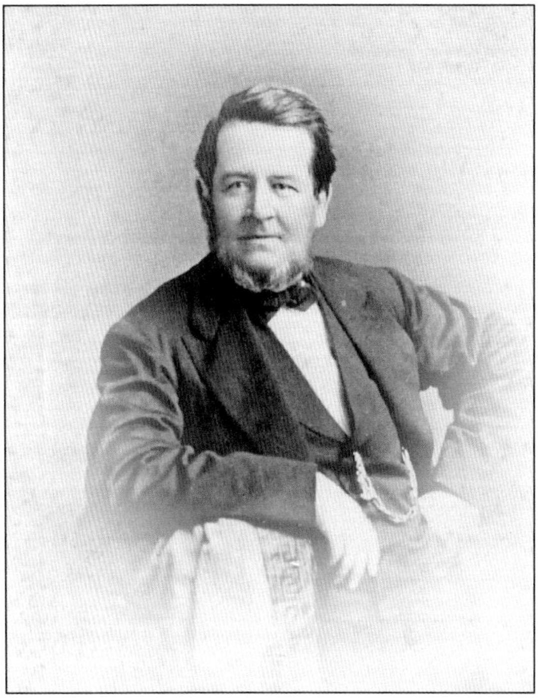

Born in 1823 to a prominent Pittsfield family, Thomas Colt bought into the only paper mill in the town, situated just downstream from the Crane mills. In a search for pure water for his paper, Colt dug through rock and granite to install the first artesian well in western Massachusetts to a depth of 250 feet, tapping into 8,000 gallons of pure water every hour. Eventually, the Crane family bought the mill for its new contract to print paper for US currency. The Coltsville neighborhood of Pittsfield where the factory was located still bears Thomas Colt's name. (Courtesy of the Berkshire Athenaeum.)

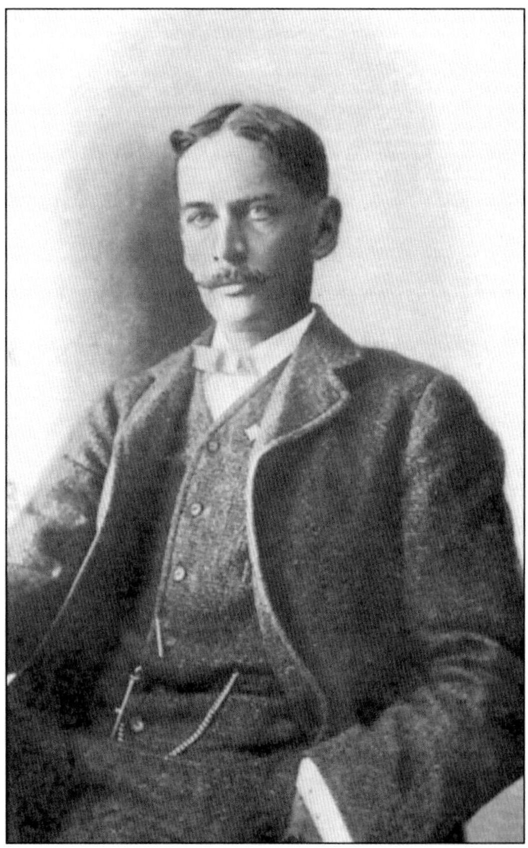

A young innovator named William Stanley arrived in the Berkshires heralding a new era of industrial development. An electrical engineer, Stanley left his partnership with George Westinghouse for health reasons and moved to Great Barrington in 1885. His design for alternating current transformers allowed electricity to be transferred across long distances. In 1887, Stanley founded the Pittsfield Illuminating Company, in which he set up a laboratory and hired 16 men. Demand grew so quickly that in 1895, he built a new factory and founded a new company with 300 employees. General Electric bought the company in 1905, reshaping industry in the Berkshires. (Courtesy of the Berkshire Athenaeum.)

Six

The Work and the Workers

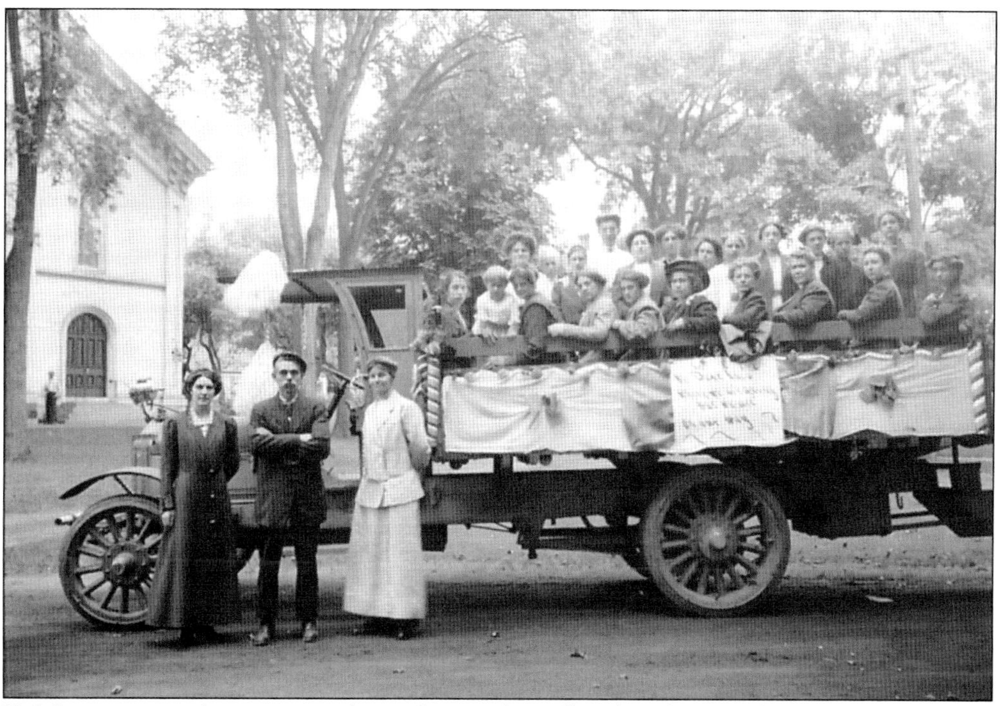

Holidays were a welcome respite for workers at the mills. This photograph from the early 1900s shows a carload of female paperworkers from Mountain Mill in East Lee aboard a delivery truck, prepared to participate in a local parade. The hand-painted sign on the side of the truck reflects perhaps their sense of optimism and confidence: "We don't know where we are going, but we're on our way." (Courtesy of the Lee Public Library.)

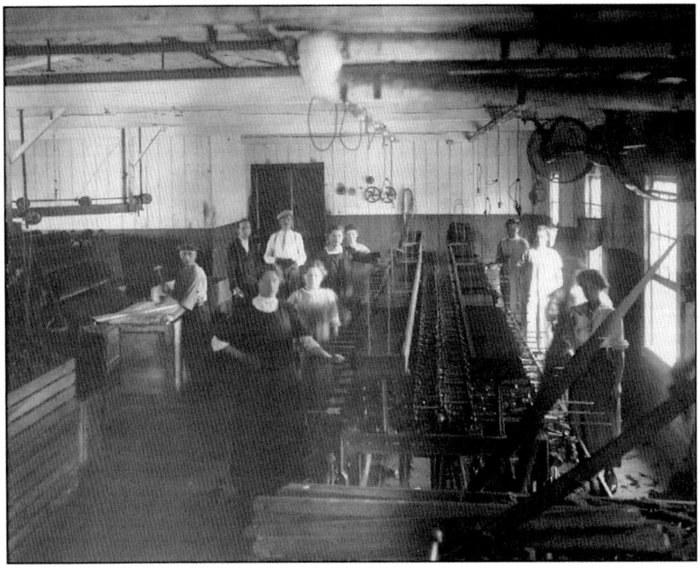

In the early 1900s, the Taconic Mill in Pittsfield allowed a photographer inside the factory to record different operations in producing wool. Here, women in the Taconic Mill in Pittsfield crowd together in a spinning room where they operate machines that spin the wool onto bobbins. A large crate overflowing with bobbins is in the left foreground. Also present is the ever-watchful eye of a manager, dressed in a tie in the background.

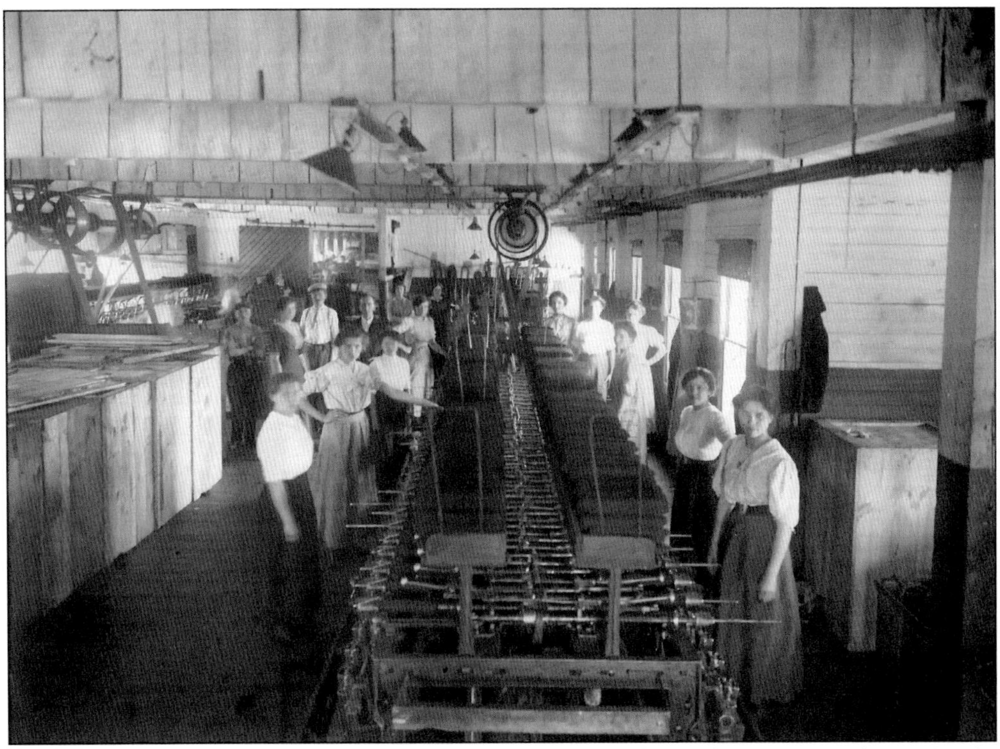

More women workers at the Taconic Mill take their places in front of spinning machines. Stacks of completed bobbins sit in the trays above the machines. Wool production was a labor-intensive industry, with woolen mills generally employing more people than either their cotton or paper counterparts. A survey of women workers in 1880 showed that 85 percent were single and had foreign-born parents. Well over half of the women in the woolen mills were between the ages of 16 and 25, and a surprising 17 percent were under the age of 16.

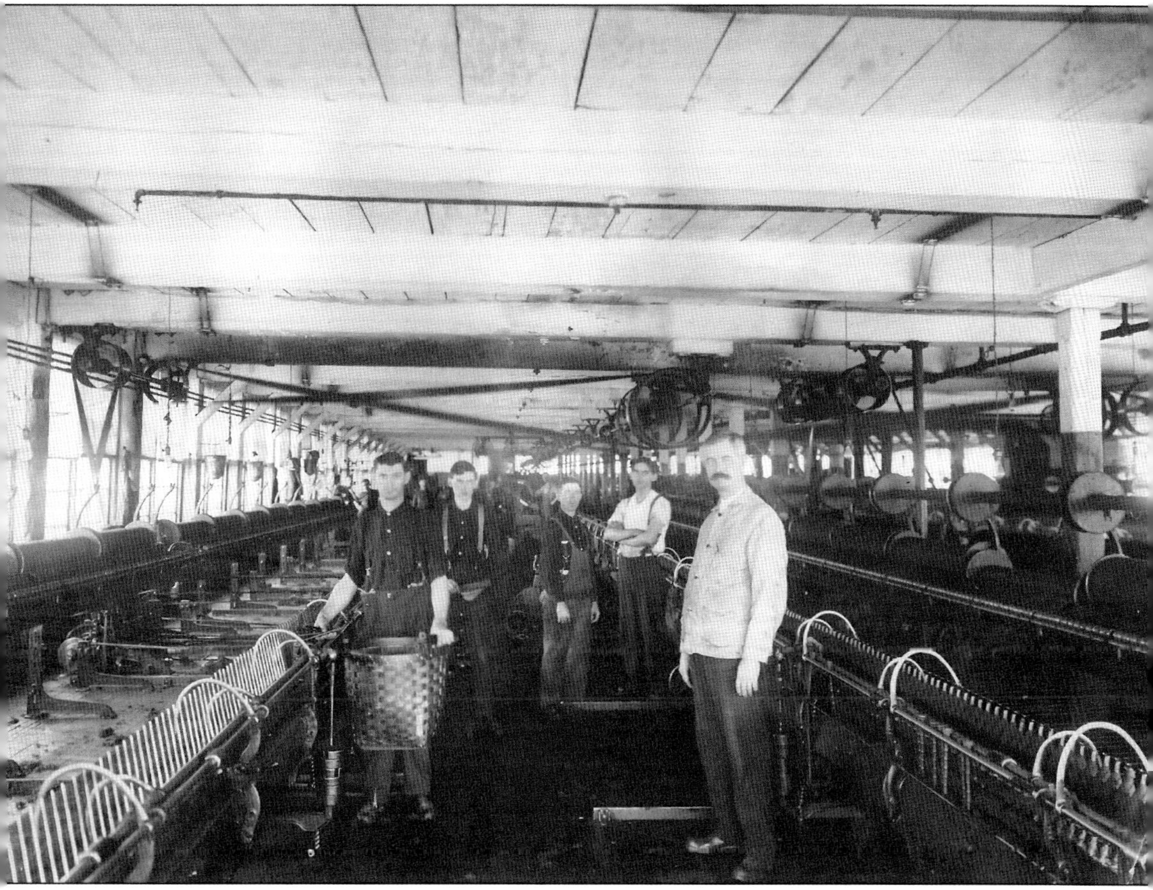

Once the spinning is completed and the tight thread is placed on bobbins, the next step is transferring these threads onto a larger spool that can then be prepared for weaving. At this point, the operation turns over to men. Even though there are single electric bulbs hanging from the ceiling, this narrow room that allowed much natural light indicates that this process was located in one of the original buildings.

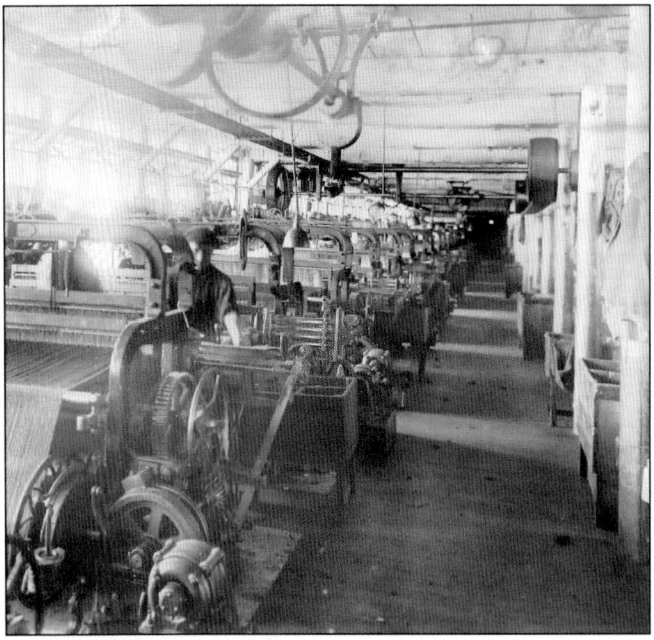

A man peeks out from behind what appears to be a dressing machine, which winds all the threads from two large spools of yarn (probably different colors) to create a pattern on a warp that would be sent to the looms for weaving. In the early mills, laying as many as 2,000 threads could take up to two hours to ensure the proper width and fabric pattern. By the time this photograph was taken, the process has largely been mechanized to allow a small number of men to operate many machines.

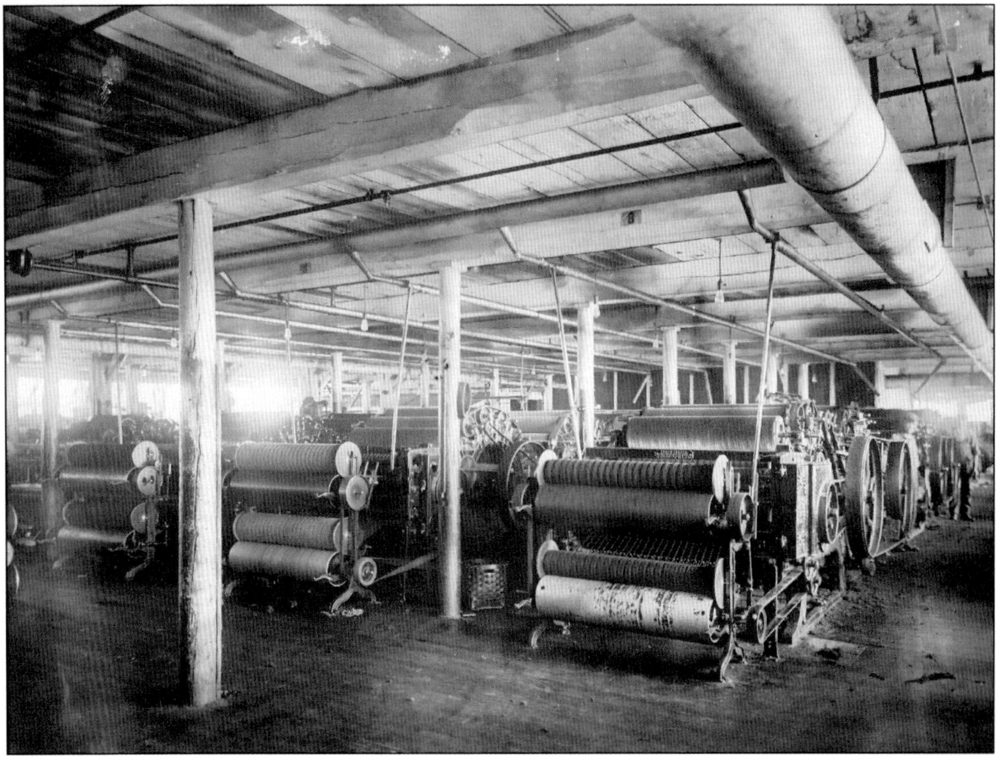

A worker at Taconic Mill operates one of many looms in a weave room. In the early mills, one person would stand over each loom, prepared to replace the shuttles that flew between the threads that produced the tight pattern. Workers faced many dangers in the mills. Machinery was loud, with the moving belts, shafts, frame, shuttles, and other parts combining to produce up to 105 decibels on one machine. Lint particles filled the air, causing brown lung disease.

Here is one of the final stages of cloth production at the Taconic Mill in the early 1900s. By this time, steam- and water-propelled turbines had long since replaced the large waterwheels powering the mechanical looms and spinning frames in the mills. What has remained in place though is the system of overhead shafts, belts, and cams attached to the machines. Electric lights illuminate each of the machines that appear to be a finishing process, softening or fulling the wool.

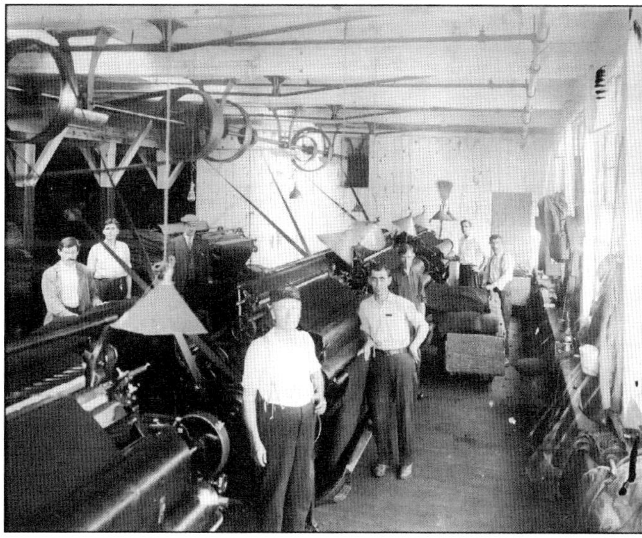

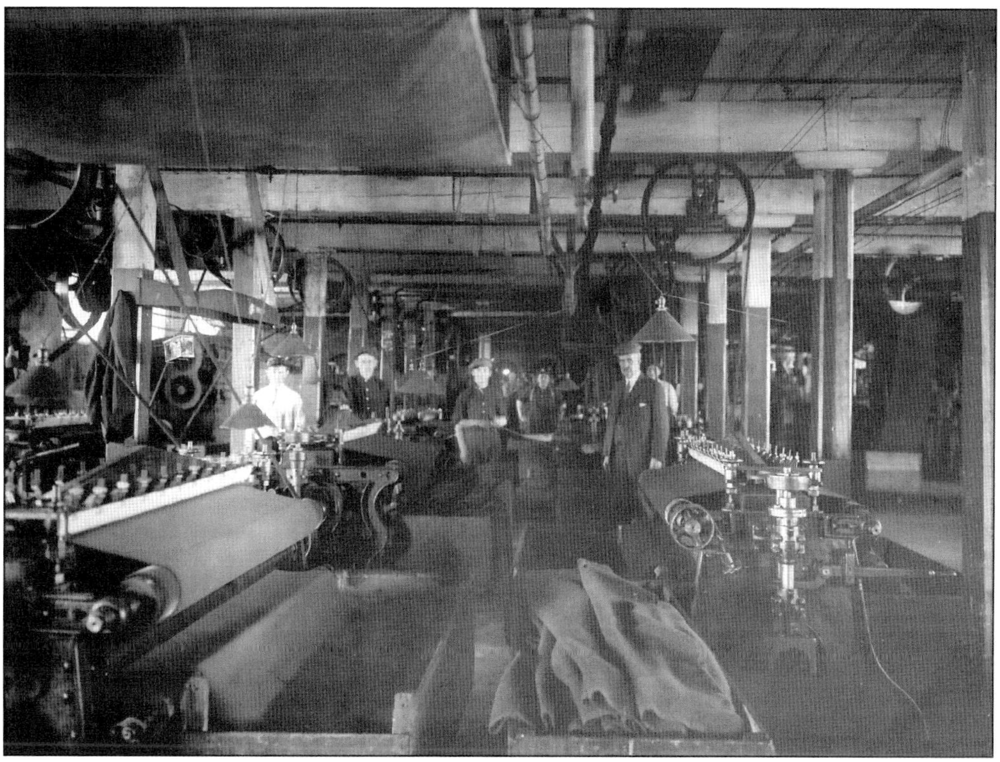

The tight quarters for maneuvering between the machines speak to more dangers in the production of textiles. Occasionally, workers would get caught in the machinery. An article in the *Pittsfield Sun* in 1873 narrates the misfortune of one German immigrant at the Bel-Air Mill who was caught in a machine belt and broke his arm and ribs. Others were even more dangerous as one worker, Michael Murphy, a young Irish immigrant, got caught up in one of the machines and lost his life.

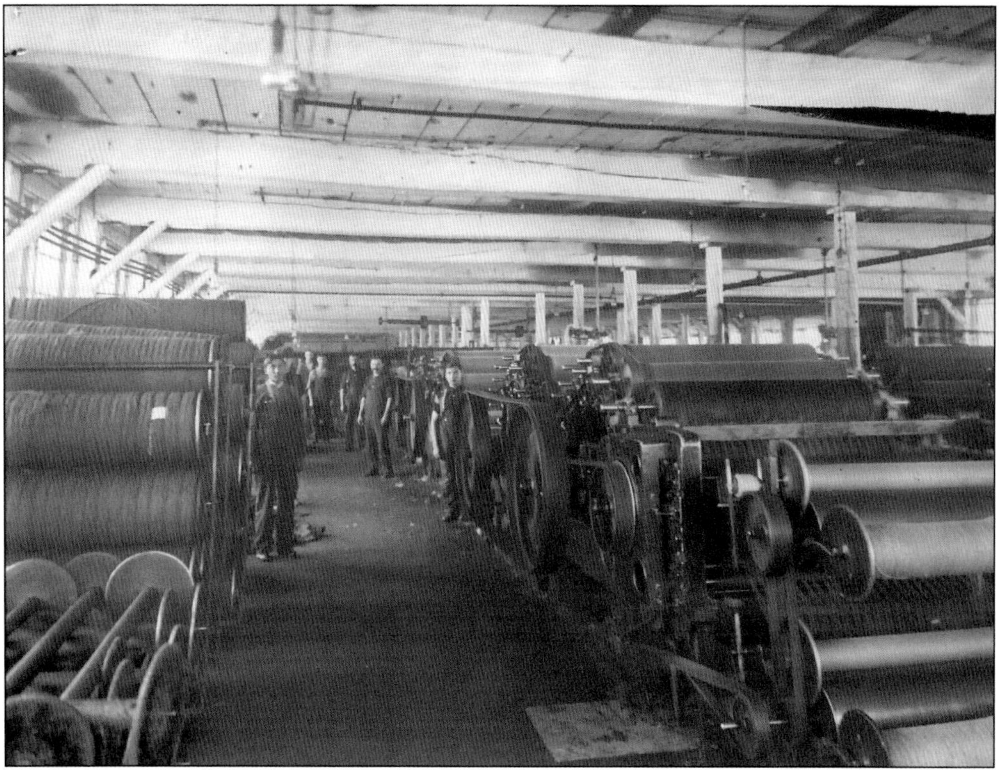

Operators stand in the row between the large spools of yarn and the looms on the right. These looms show the yarn spools close to empty, at which point the workers will place the full ones on the machine. The photograph shows how large these weave rooms are, often the largest in the factory. By the early 1900s, mills had added new large buildings on just to accommodate the large equipment required for weaving.

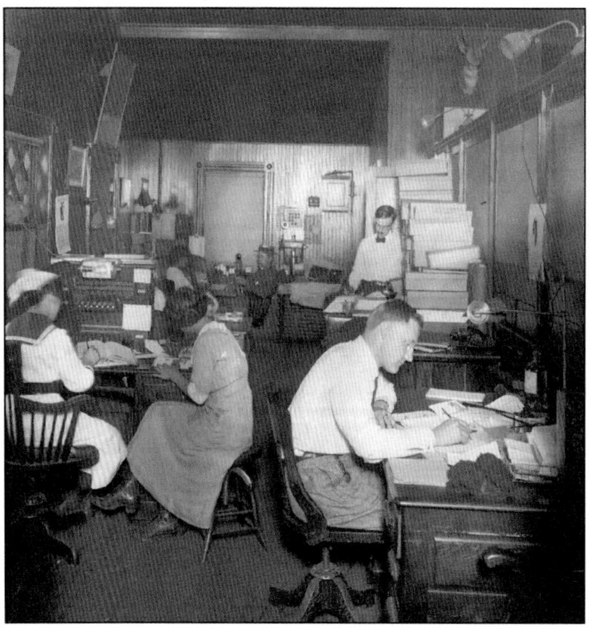

Even the office quarters at Taconic Mill are crowded. The man in the boater hat appears to be the manager, sitting at his rolltop desk in the rear of the photograph. Two men are working separately keeping accounts and preparing correspondence, perhaps filling orders. The women at the switchboard have lines for placing and receiving up to 20 phone calls. In Pittsfield, the first telephone call was placed in 1878 between the Pontoosuc Woolen Mill and Pittsfield National Bank in downtown Pittsfield, just two miles away.

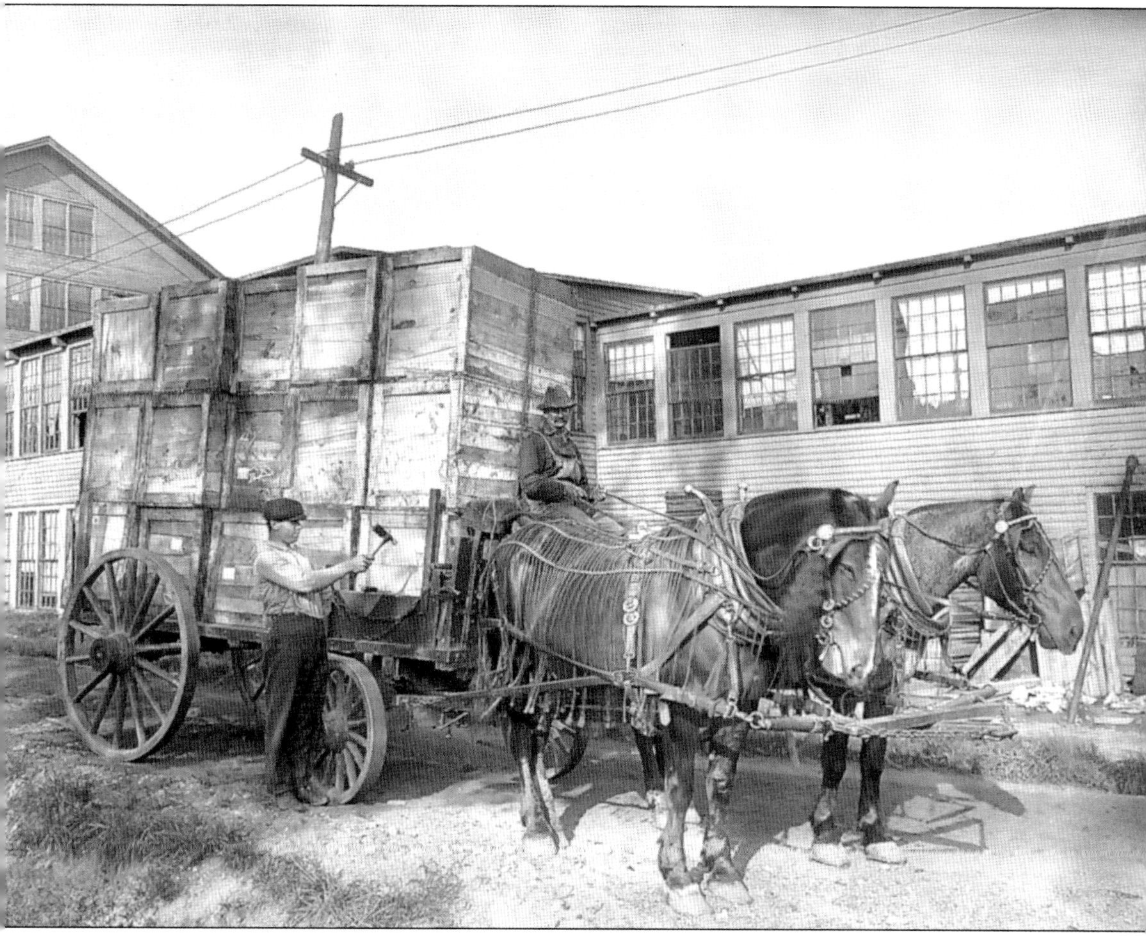

Outside of the Taconic Mill, an overloaded delivery truck carries the crates ready for shipping. Are they carrying wool to the factory or the finished cloth to the railroad depot? The electric lines indicate the photograph was taken after electricity came to the city in the late 1800s but before the use of gas-powered trucks just 20 years later. The clothing of the two men shows the wear expected from the daily grind of loading and unloading the heavy crates.

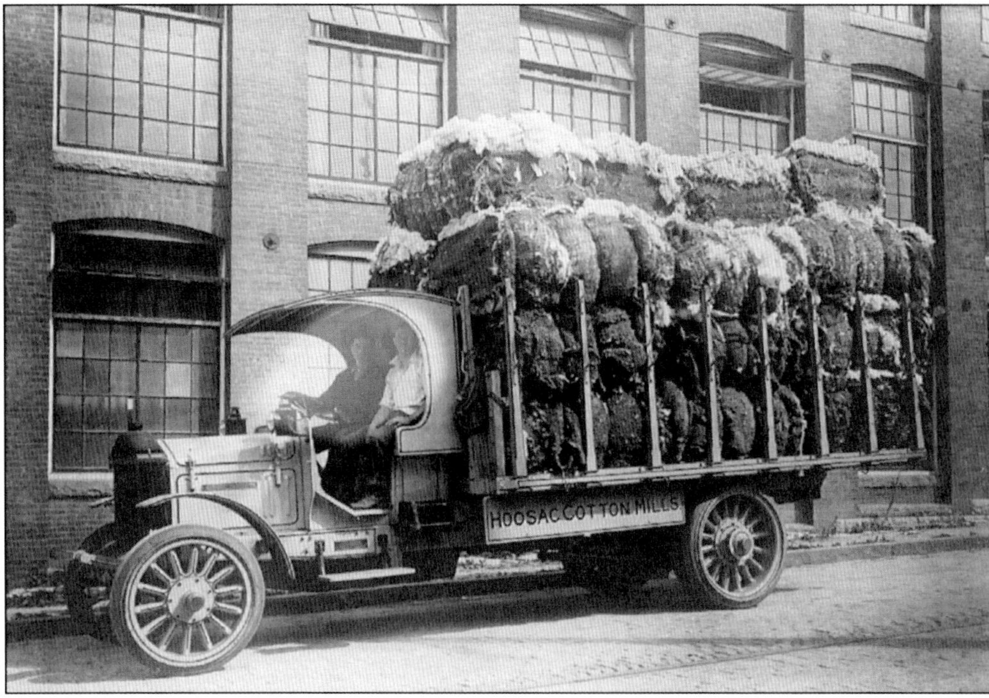

Cotton spills out of bales on this overloaded Pierce-Arrow stake truck on its way to the Hoosac Cotton Mill (formerly the Eclipse Mill) in the early 1900s. Mills initially had their own fleets of horse-drawn wagons and, by the early 1900s, trucks to deliver the raw cotton to the doors of the mills for spinning, weaving, and printing. Unusual on this flatbed truck are the oil lamps used for headlights. (Courtesy of the North Adams Historical Society.)

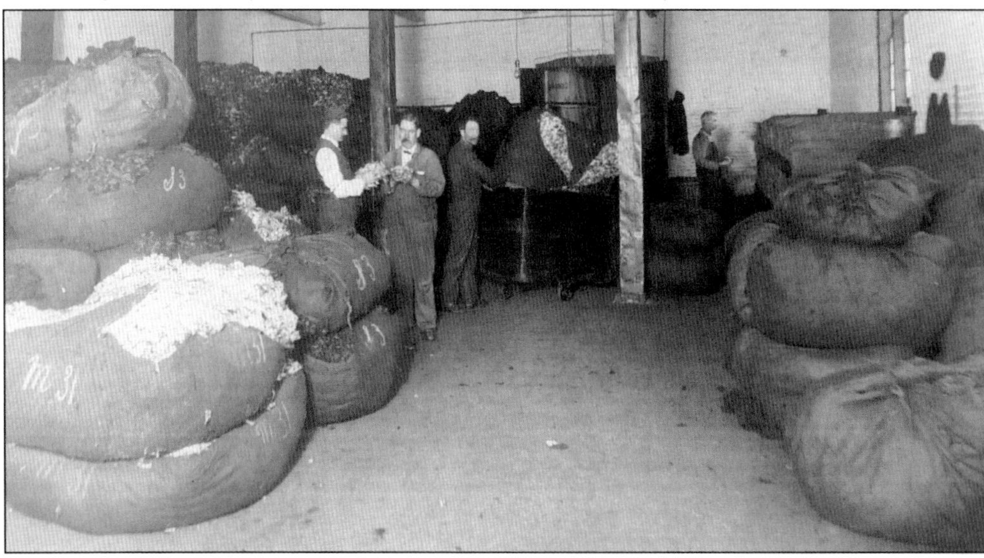

Two workers at Peck's Lower Mill hold raw cotton from bales that have arrived in their warehouse. The markings on the sacks indicate different classes of cotton, as can be seen by the lighter and darker colors of cotton tumbling out of the sacks. Another worker has placed a bale in a wooden cart to be taken to the mill for picking, where it is arranged in sheets and dirt removed to prepare the cotton for carding.

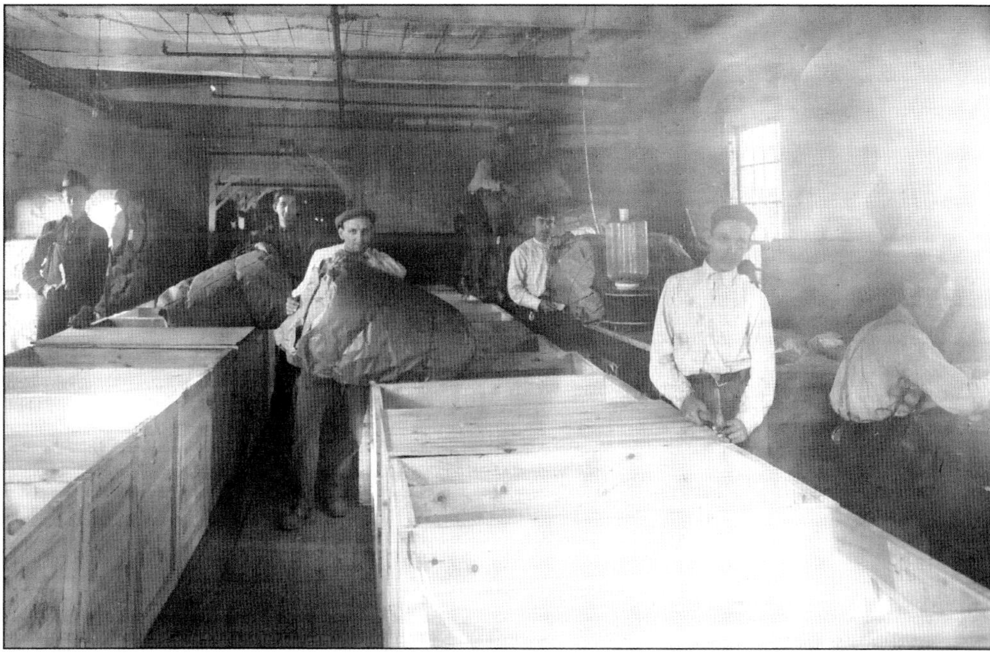

The Taconic Mill, like most mills in Pittsfield, concentrated its production on union cassimere, a cloth of mixed material that is used principally for the manufacture of clothing. In this photograph of the shipping room at Taconic Mill, workers prepare the finished product to transport to customers around the country. They place the rolls of wrapped wool cloth in newly constructed large wooden boxes to withstand the many legs on the long journey to the final customer.

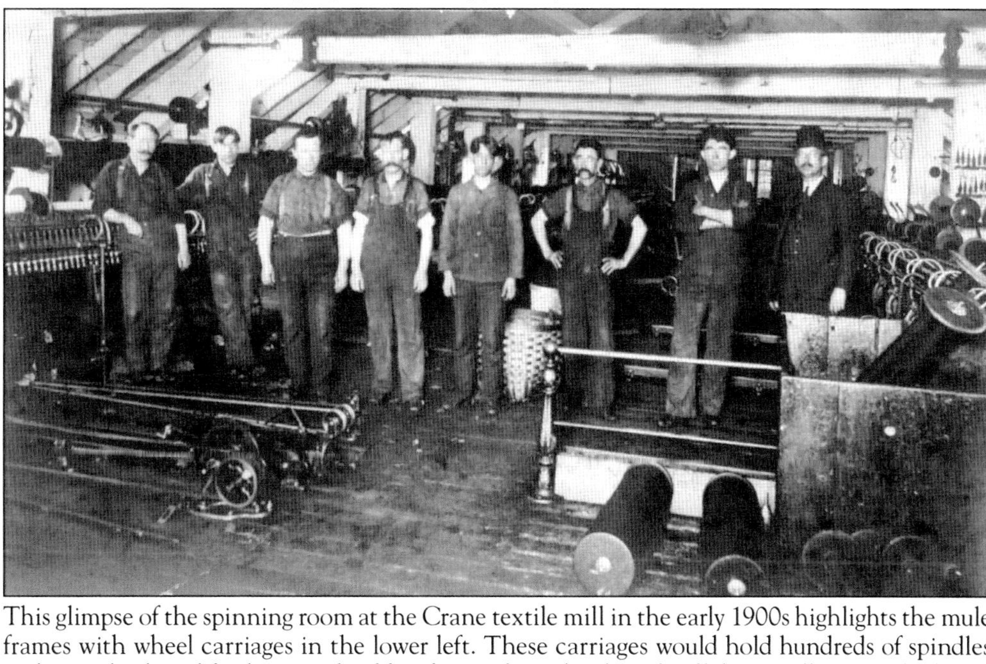

This glimpse of the spinning room at the Crane textile mill in the early 1900s highlights the mule frames with wheel carriages in the lower left. These carriages would hold hundreds of spindles and move back and forth upwards of five feet to draw the threads off the spindles onto the larger spools that can be seen in the foreground. Invented in the late 1700s, this technology was still used 150 years later. Identified in this picture is Patrick Grace at the far left.

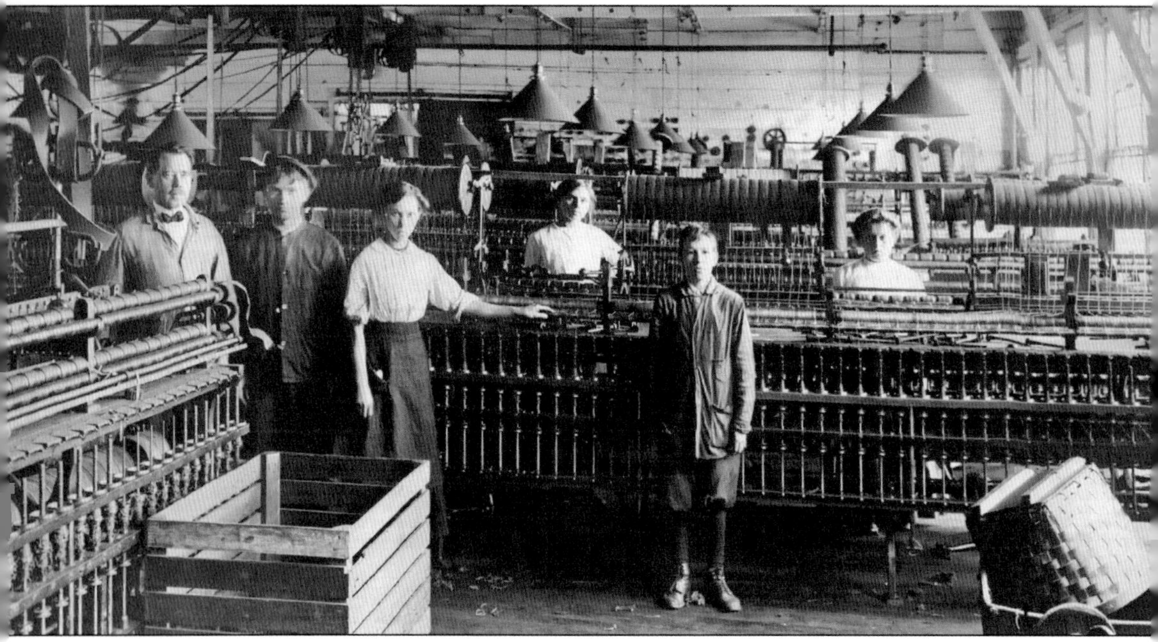

Child workers line up around the spinning machinery in the Taconic Mill in the early 1900s. Under the watchful eyes of adult supervisors, young workers were hired for their agility and speed as bobbin replacers, running from machine to machine as bobbins ran out of thread. In 1832, Massachusetts was the first state to pass a child labor law, but it only limited the number of hours children could work to 10 hours a day. It was only in 1938 that Congress was able to pass and uphold laws to regulate minimum ages and numbers of hours that children could work.

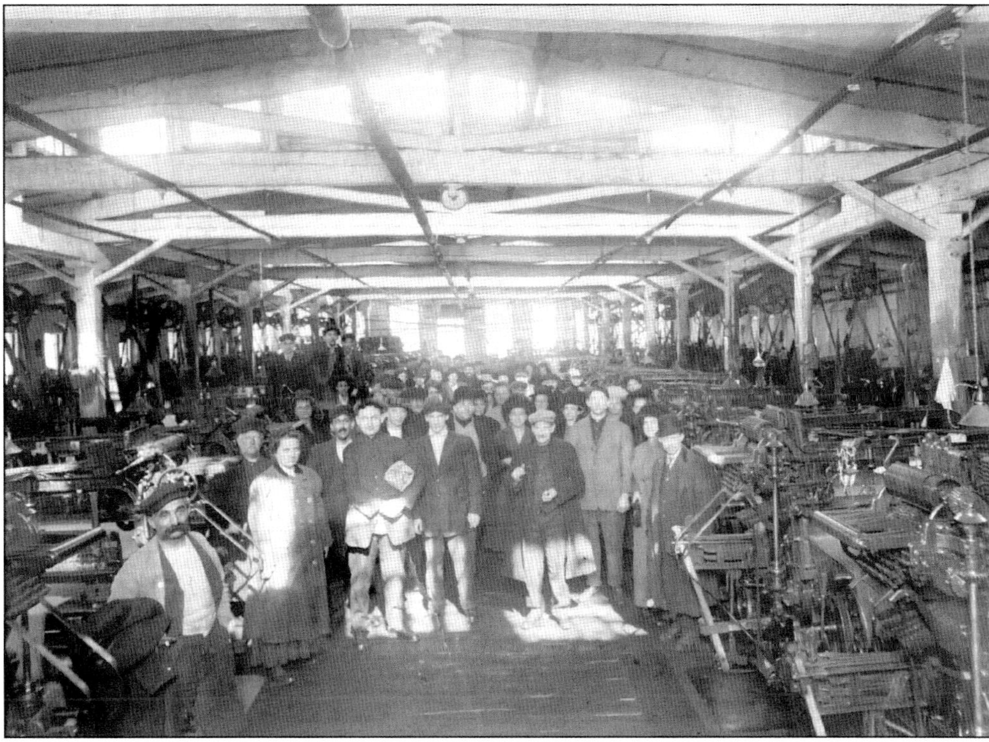

Workers crowd the aisle between carding machines at Pontoosuc Woolen Mill. The variety of hats and clothing reveal these workers were likely recent immigrants. With the first Irish arriving in Pittsfield around 1839, they made up 70 percent of the foreign-born population at the start of the Civil War. French Canadians were also early arrivals, and census figures count over 750 families in 1890. Workers from Italy and Poland began arriving in the 1890s. Pontoosuc Mill timesheets show that job functions were segregated by gender and nationality.

At its height, E.D. Jones & Sons employed hundreds of machinists in its foundry, machine shop, and woodshop. In this 1910 photograph, a group of men and one woman congregates between two of the large machine shop buildings on the expanded site for the company. Railways and steel beams between the structures help move the heavy finished products, but in the background, horse-drawn wagons show how transport overlaps several eras. Sweat and dirt appear on the men's clothing, hinting at the dangers and difficulty of their work.

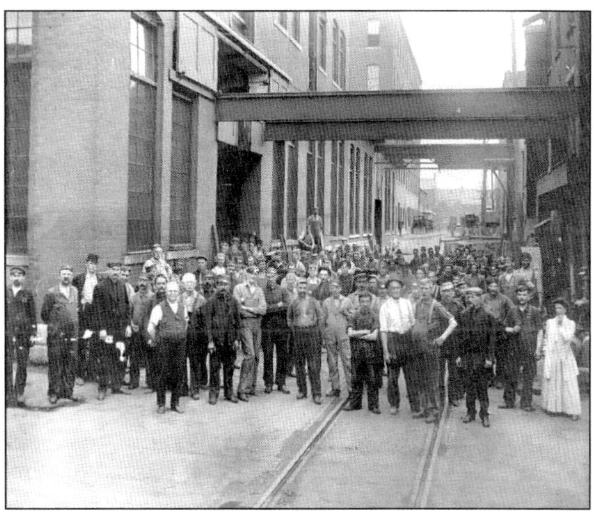

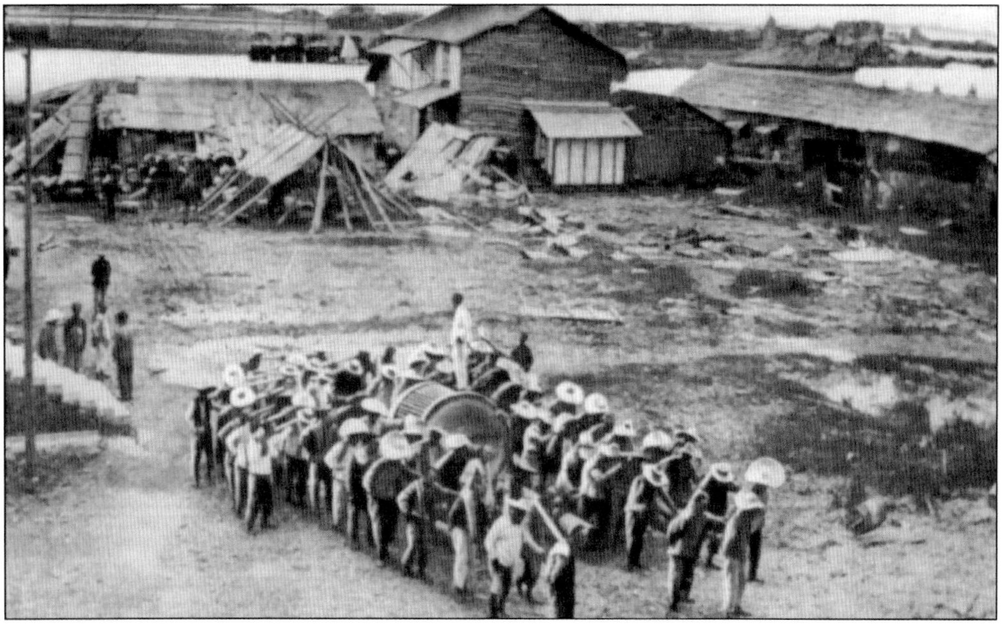

The market for paper-producing machinery extended well beyond Berkshire County, and E.D. Jones had a worldwide reach. In 1910, the Chinese government contracted with E.D. Jones to build a paper factory in Hankou, a port city on the Yangtze River. Employees from Pittsfield traveled to China to supervise the construction. In this photograph, Chinese workers haul a paper beater from the river to the site. The beater weighs six tons; the work is made harder with the weight of an overseer standing on the equipment.

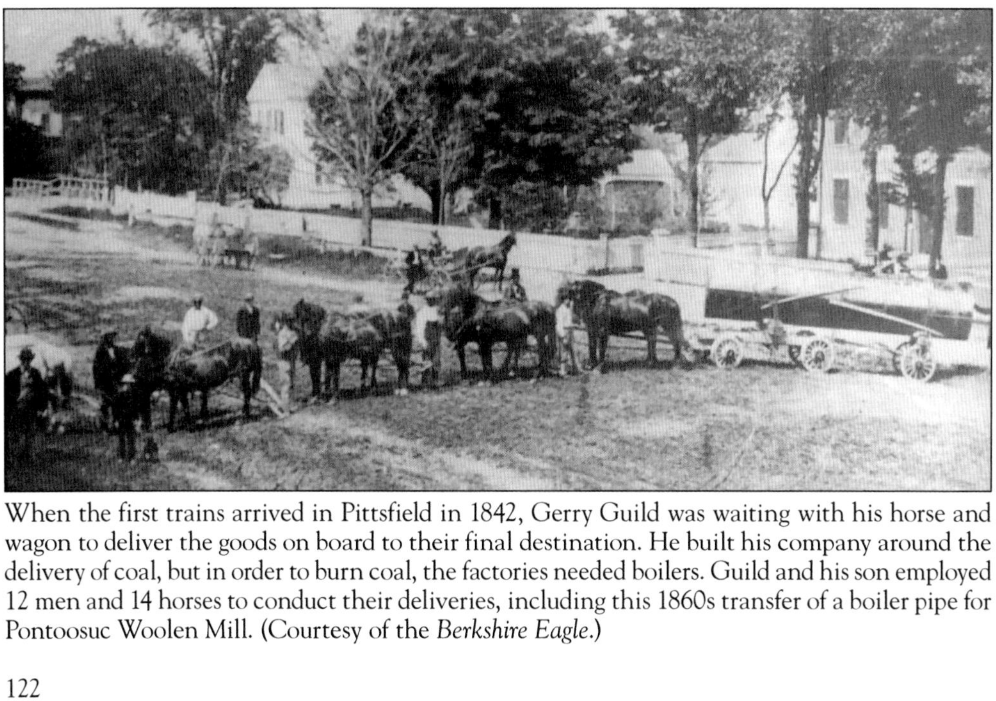

When the first trains arrived in Pittsfield in 1842, Gerry Guild was waiting with his horse and wagon to deliver the goods on board to their final destination. He built his company around the delivery of coal, but in order to burn coal, the factories needed boilers. Guild and his son employed 12 men and 14 horses to conduct their deliveries, including this 1860s transfer of a boiler pipe for Pontoosuc Woolen Mill. (Courtesy of the *Berkshire Eagle*.)

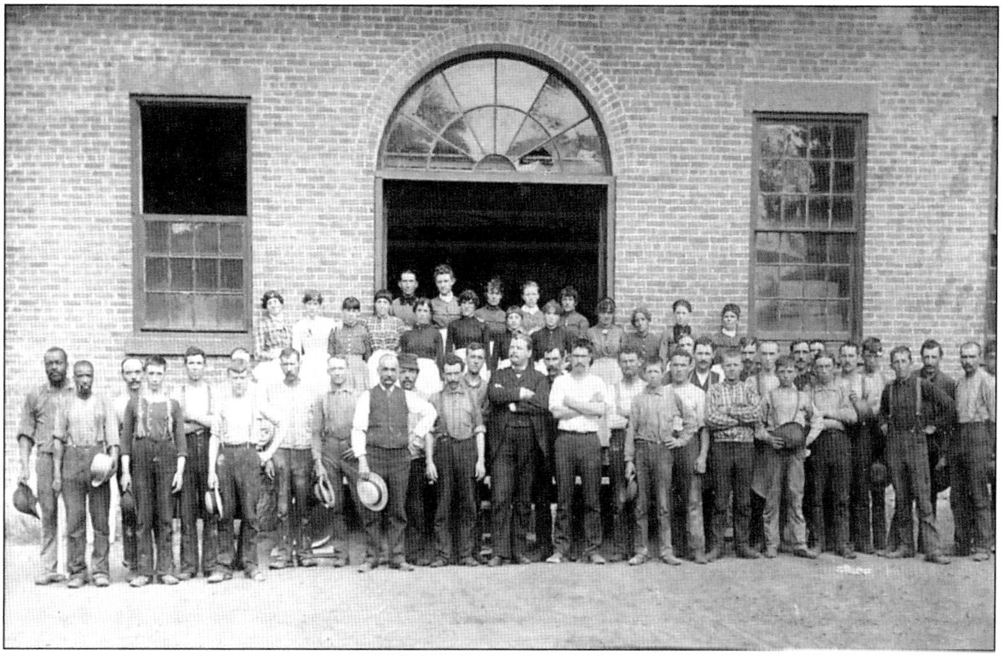

This photograph of workers in front of the Columbia Mill in Lee in the late 1800s is one of the few that show African American workers. The mill's managers stand in the center of the first row. In the early years, women made up two-thirds of the paper mill workforces, employed for rag picking and sorting the finished paper. As more machinery was employed, more men were hired to operate the mechanized processes that used to all be done by hand: breaking down the rags, rolling out the pulp, and drying and cutting the paper. (Courtesy of the Lee Public Library.)

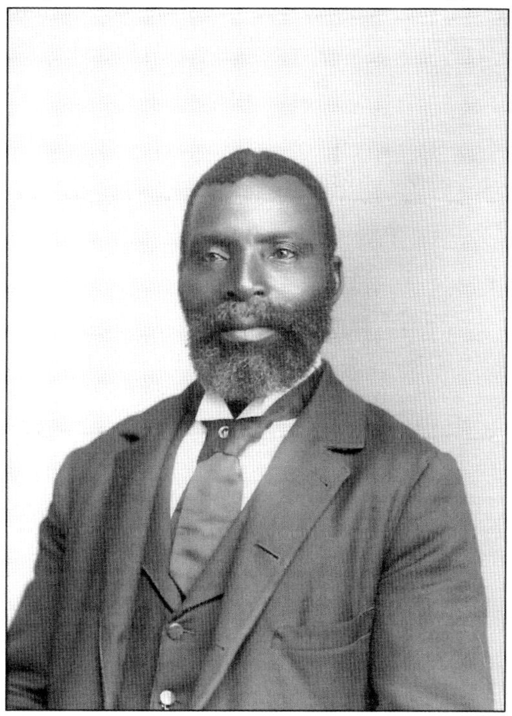

African Americans had a sizeable presence in Berkshire County, judging from census records, church attendance, and registration in the Union army. In the mills, they generally occupied positions in delivery and maintenance functions of industrial operations. Thomas Hawkins (pictured) was the coachman for mill owner James Renfrew and his family. The writing on the back of the image identifies Hawkins as "beloved" by the Renfrews.

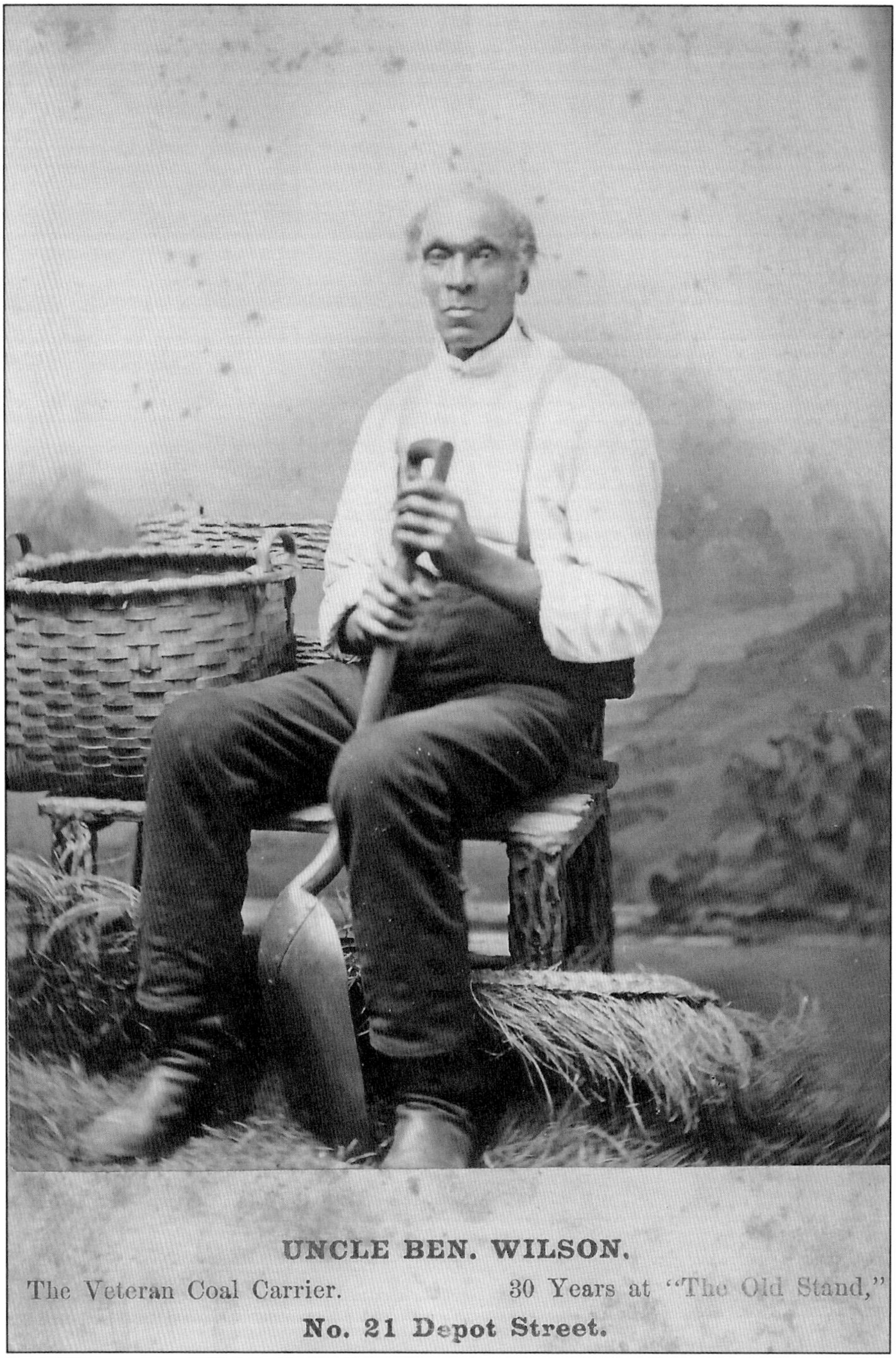

Another coal delivery company in Pittsfield was W.F. Francis Coal, which was established in 1848, on Depot Street adjacent to the rail lines. Pictured here is Ben Wilson, a coal carrier employed by Francis for over 30 years. Too old to fight in the Civil War, Wilson saw his son join an all–African American regiment, the Massachusetts 54th, which was formed in 1863. Wilson mourned his son, who died in South Carolina in July 1865 after the war ended—perhaps from injuries sustained earlier.

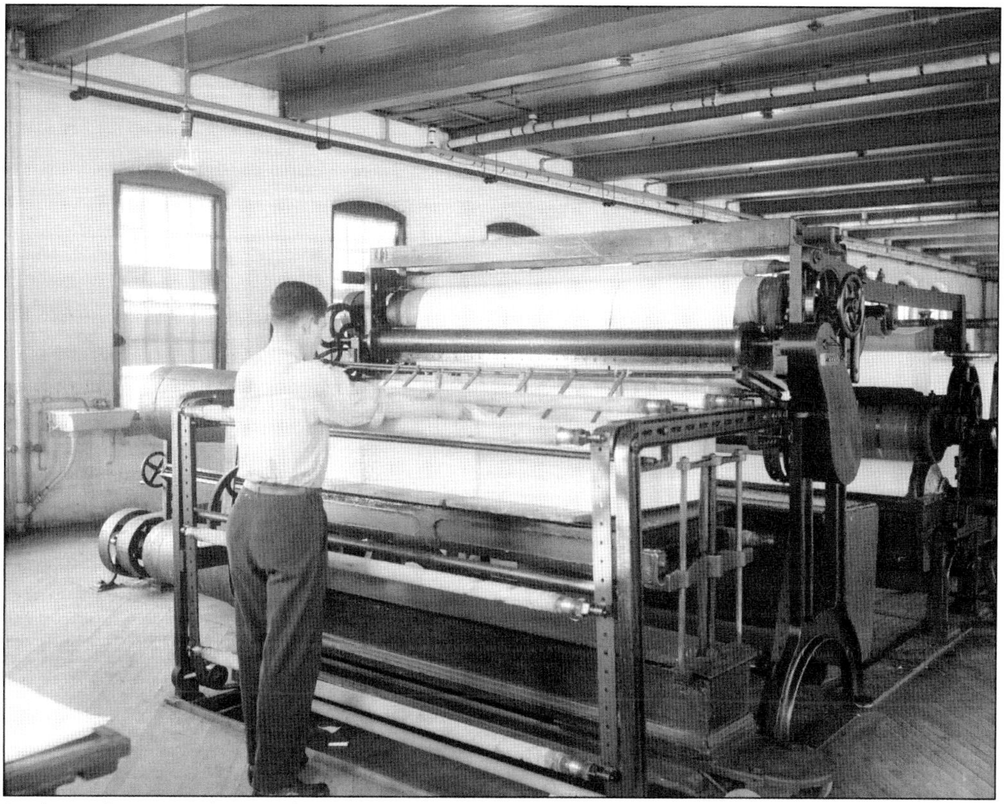

In the early 1900s, the noted naturalist photographer Edwin Hale Lincoln turned his camera on the stationery business at Eaton, Crane, and Pike in Pittsfield. In this photograph, a worker stands at the end of a paper-finishing machine called a "sheeter." At the other end of the sheeter, paper is introduced in three large side-by-side rolls. The paper moves through the machines, and coatings can be applied. Here, the technician pulls off and stacks sheets of the finished, cut product.

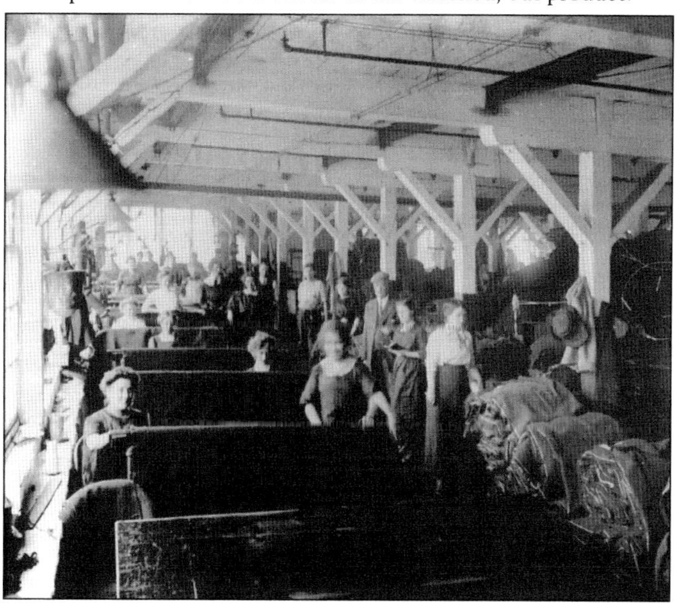

In contrast to paper mills, textile production was both labor- and equipment-intensive. Berkshire's textile mills employed on average almost 140 people, and usually paid better than the paper mills. Paper workforces, though, were split evenly between men and women, while the textile mills had more male operators, so that men made up on average 60 percent of the payrolls there. This photograph of the picking room at Pontoosuc Woolen Mill is notable for its lack of machine equipment.

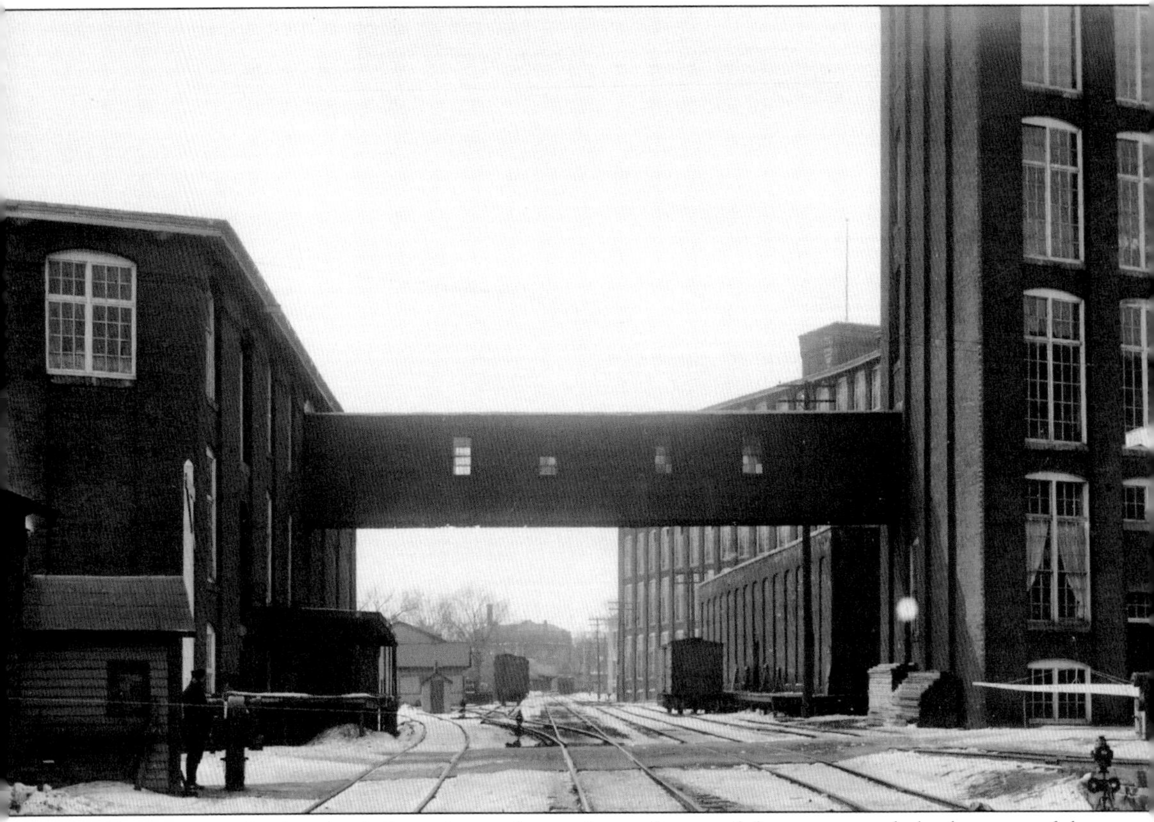

Turnover was high in both factories, as the work was dirty and dangerous and also because of the many opportunities for work in other mills. In Dalton, a paperworker had five different mills to choose from in seeking employment and could move easily to Lee to find work. At the L.L. Brown company in Adams, the average worker lasted only 20 months on the job before moving on to find another position. Here, a lone sentry stands at the rail line switch that runs right through the factory complex, making it easy for loading and unloading finished products and supplies.

Bibliography

Annin, Tharine Huntington. *The Story of a Berkshire Town and Its People*. Richmond, MA: Ledgetop Publishing, 2015.

berkshiremuseum.org/blog/places-of-invention-papermaking-in-the-berkshires.

Drew, Bernard. *18th & 19th Century Waterpowered Industry in the Upper Housatonic River Valley*. Great Barrington, MA: Attic Revivals Press. 2014.

Dunwell, Steve. *The Run of the Mill, A Pictorial Narrative of the Expansion, Dominion, Decline and Enduring Impact of the New England Textile Industry*. Boston: David R. Godine Publisher, Inc., 1978.

housatonicpapertrail.blogspot.com.

Kirby, Ed. *Exploring the Berkshire Hills, A Guide to Geology and Early Industry in the Housatonic Watershed*. Greenfield, MA: Valley Geology Publications, 1995.

McGaw, Judith A., *Most Wonderful Machine, Mechanization and Social Change in Berkshire Papermaking 1801–1885*. Princetown, NJ: Princeton University Press, 1987.

Nash, June, *From Tank Town to High Tech, The Clash of Community and Industrial Cycles*. Albany: State University of New York Press, 1989.

paperindustryweb.com/jones/jonesmain.htm.

"Renfrew Manufacturing Company Mill No. 2 (Arnold Print Works)." Historic American Engineering Record, (National Park Service Northeast Region US Custom House 200 Chestnut Street Philadelphia, PA), 1993.

Sloan, Julie L., and Patriqui, William J. *The Berkshire Glass Works*. Charleston, SC: History Press, 2011.

Susman, Warren. *Culture as History, The Transformation of American Society in the Twentieth Century*. New York: Pantheon Books, 1973.

Tague, William H., Robert B. Kimbal, and Richard V. Happel, eds. *Berkshire, 200 Years in Pictures*. Pittsfield, MA: Eagle Publishing, 1961.

Thornton, John E., ed. "Industrial Edition of the *Evening Eagle*, Illustrating Pittsfield and Dalton, Mass., in the year 1897." Pittsfield, MA: Eagle Publishing, 1897.

Valente, A.J., *Rag Paper Manufacture in the United States, 1801–1900, A History, with Directories of Mills and Owners*. Jefferson, NC: McFarland & Company, 2010.

www.papertownprojects.org/index.html.